"*Worship and the World to Come* is a timely and higl
us how there is a pressing need for careful, theolc
growing contemporary worship scene."
**Pete Ward,** professor at St John's College/Department of '
United Kingdom

"In this book Glenn Packiam offers a deep and insightful perspective on Christian hope as it is
lived out within real Christian communities. While there has been much useful conceptual work
done on the theology of hope from the perspective of systematic theology, relatively little is known
about what it means when it is lived out within worshiping communities. For Packiam, worship
and hope are deeply tied together. Worship is 'the place where we rehearse our hope,' a place where
hope becomes embedded within us. It matters how we worship, and it matters that we look care-
fully at the ways in which we worship if we are to hope faithfully. By gathering rich and deep
empirical data and using it as a locus for theological reflection, Packiam not only helps us to
understand hope more fully, he also moves our understanding on in important ways. This book
is an important contribution to the emerging field of theological ethnography and a worthy
contribution to the church and academy."
**John Swinton,** professor of practical theology and pastoral care, King's College, University of Aberdeen

"Glenn Packiam in this book *Worship and the World to Come* has embarked on a journey less
traveled by a practitioner-scholar in the contemporary praise and worship (CPW) field. Often,
CPW has been accused of valuing emotional experiences at the expense of robust theological
thought. Through this work, Packiam has done much to redress this notion in the investigation
of Christian hope as understood in normative theological thoughts and parsing it within the frame
of CPW worship practices. It is an illuminating work that reflects his keen scholarship while staying true to his spirituality. This book showcases the maturation of CPW practice—or, if we dare,
CPW worship tradition—with its practice undergirded by theological thought."
**Swee Hong Lim,** Deer Park associate professor of sacred music and director of the master of sacred music
program, Emmanuel College of Victoria University in the University of Toronto

"The New Testament is quite clear: Christians are to lean into the future with hope. 'Look forward,'
the Scriptures say time and again. But what is the actual tilt of that leaning found in Christians today?
In his book Glenn Packiam provides a fascinating answer to this question with special reference to
contemporary worship and worshipers. Seeing how he describes how Christians today hope in the
future, I was at times encouraged by what I read and at others deeply alarmed. Scholars, pastors, and
rank-and-file worshipers alike will benefit from Packiam's study. It has immediate pastoral impact
for assessing and promoting a biblical, hopeful leaning into God's future in Christ."
**Lester Ruth,** research professor of Christian worship at Duke Divinity School

"There is now a growing number of theologically trained worship thinkers and practitioners
interested in moving past the old 'worship wars' of style toward a deeper, more thoughtful type
of worship training (or catechism). This book promotes training to produce the fruit the Bible
encourages us to grow—fruit that fills each of us as Christians, that is, as Jesus-followers, with an
irresistible, irrepressible hope for what is to come. Dr. Glenn Packiam is committed to what is
sometimes now out of vogue, the notion of discipleship. His evident dedication to the formation
of the people of God makes this book worth reading. In fact, this is what many of us have long
been hoping for—a book that simplifies complex theological concepts into very useful frames for
worship leaders and worshipers who may not have undertaken any formal study."
**Tanya Riches,** senior lecturer and MTh coordinator at Hillsong College, Australia

"If it is fundamentally impossible to be a Christian without hope, then all Christians at worship are in the business of singing themselves into a new story that beckons from the future—the good future of God in Christ that the Spirit makes palpable here and now in our public worship. That's the basic point that Glenn Packiam makes in this theologically learned, liturgically intelligent, and pastorally sensitive book—a book that deserves careful reading by scholars and pastors, along with every worship leader charged with the holy task of leading the people of God in song. Our calling as church leaders, as Packiam rightly sees it, is not only to announce our new future in Christ; our task is to enact and embody that new future in our songs of praise and proclamation. How and what we sing, then, become a singularly formative means by which the Spirit transforms our lives to be a sign and foretaste of God's new creation. That's the charge! That's the hope!"

**W. David O. Taylor,** associate professor of theology and culture, Fuller Theological Seminary

"Worship songs have a profound influence on the contemporary church both enriching our understanding of the gospel and sometimes corrupting it. In this unique and outstanding book Glenn Packiam, composer, worship leader, and theologian, aids our comprehension of how worship should help us envisage and live in the world that Jesus has already inaugurated."

**David Wilkinson,** principal of St Johns College and professor of theology and religion at Durham University

"Glenn Packiam has taken one of the most elusive ideas in Christian tradition—hope—set it alongside one of the most contested—eschatology—and grappled with how both inform the public worship life of American evangelicals. Set within a rich, multifaceted study of Christian worship in the contemporary United States, the result is a compelling exercise in practical theology that never shies away from uncomfortable truths. Packiam distills a wide range of sources, ideas, and arguments into a discussion of evangelical worship that is both deeply insightful and highly accessible. This is a piece of practical theology that is theologically serious and practically engaged, a consideration of hope and eschatology that is careful in its marshaling of theological scholarship and attentive to the complexities that reflect the life of evangelical churches in the twenty-first century. Scholars of evangelicalism, church leaders, and Christian worship professionals alike will find much wisdom in this timely volume."

**Mathew Guest,** professor of the sociology of religion at Durham University

"Glenn Packiam is a translator, enabling theology to speak to congregational worship ministry and enabling that ministry to communicate to theology. His qualifications? His own biography as both a worship leader and theologian, his sharply observed fieldwork, and his careful sifting of important theological and musical texts. Incisive, measured, and genuinely charitable, this book will provide the help theologians and worship leaders need to glean what they need from each other for their shared work in the kingdom of God."

**Wesley Hill,** associate professor of New Testament at Trinity School for Ministry, Ambridge, PA, and author of *Washed and Waiting*

"In *Worship and the World to Come*, Glenn Packiam delivers an accessible, engaging integration of the eschatological work of leading biblical scholars and theologians N. T. Wright and Jürgen Moltmann within the key and context of the practices of contemporary worship. The result is an inspiring theological vision for worship that situates our present life together as the church within the transformational redemptive purposes of God for all of creation. Packiam's pastoral and theological work in this book will nourish worshipers for the journey of faith by reorienting our gaze toward the goal of salvation—the new creation—as it breaks into the present by the power of the Spirit."

**John Frederick,** lecturer in New Testament at Trinity College in Queensland, Australia, and author of *Worship in the Way of the Cross*

DYNAMICS OF CHRISTIAN WORSHIP

# WORSHIP AND THE WORLD TO COME

## EXPLORING CHRISTIAN HOPE IN CONTEMPORARY WORSHIP

## GLENN PACKIAM

Academic

An imprint of InterVarsity Press
Downers Grove, Illinois

*InterVarsity Press*
*P.O. Box 1400, Downers Grove, IL 60515-1426*
*ivpress.com*
*email@ivpress.com*

*InterVarsity Press® is the book-publishing division of InterVarsity Christian Fellowship/USA®, a movement of students and faculty active on campus at hundreds of universities, colleges, and schools of nursing in the United States of America, and a member movement of the International Fellowship of Evangelical Students. For information about local and regional activities, visit intervarsity.org.*

*Scripture quotations, unless otherwise noted, are from The Holy Bible, English Standard Version, copyright © 2001 by Crossway Bibles, a division of Good News Publishers. Used by permission. All rights reserved.*

*While any stories in this book are true, some names and identifying information may have been changed to protect the privacy of individuals.*

*Published in association with the literary agency of D.C. Jacobson & Associates, an author management company. http://www.dcjacobson.com.*

*Cover design and image composite: David Fassett*
*Interior design: Jeanna Wiggins*
*Images: white wall texture: © Nadine Westveer / EyeEm / Getty Images*
*hands in worship: © Kativ / E+ / Getty Images*

*ISBN 978-0-8308-4931-4 (print)*
*ISBN 978-0-8308-4932-1 (digital)*

*Printed in the United States of America ♾*

*InterVarsity Press is committed to ecological stewardship and to the conservation of natural resources in all our operations. This book was printed using sustainably sourced paper.*

**Library of Congress Cataloging-in-Publication Data**
*A catalog record for this book is available from the Library of Congress.*

| **P** | 25 | 24 | 23 | 22 | 21 | 20 | 19 | 18 | 17 | 16 | 15 | 14 | 13 | 12 | 11 | 10 | 9 | 8 | 7 | 6 | 5 | 4 | 3 | 2 | 1 |
|---|---|---|---|---|---|---|---|---|---|---|---|---|---|---|---|---|---|---|---|---|---|---|---|---|---|
| **Y** | 41 | 40 | 39 | 38 | 37 | 36 | 35 | 34 | 33 | 32 | 31 | 30 | 29 | 28 | 27 | 26 | 25 | 24 | 23 | 22 | 21 | 20 |

TO MY DAD AND MUM

*who taught me to worship with hope.*

# CONTENTS

# ACKNOWLEDGMENTS

THIS BOOK IS THE CULMINATION of my doctoral research, reset and rewritten with church leaders in mind. But I would not have pursued a doctorate if it had not been for my wife, Holly. She encouraged me to reach beyond what I thought possible and to attempt something that had only been a dream. Not only was her prodding the inspiration, her support throughout the process and patience as I worked through late nights and early mornings made the journey possible. Our children—Sophia, Norah, Jonas, and Jane— have also been tremendously long-suffering, particularly in the final months when I would spend many days on end writing. Only a few times in the final days did they ask when my dissertation would be complete. I owe a tremendous debt to my parents for their faithful and sacrificial love. Throughout this process, they were encouraging and always willing to help; my mother even offered to proofread early drafts.

As if the blessing of a loving and supportive family were not already enough, I somehow also had the good fortune of having two exceptional doctoral supervisors, the Reverend Professor David Wilkinson and Dr. Mathew Guest, who were encouraging and insightful at every point. Their enthusiasm from the start and their expert guidance along the way made the process both meaningful and enjoyable. I would also like to express my gratitude to the staff at Cranmer Hall and at the Department of Theology and Religion and to my research colleagues who made the process a joy and who offered their friendship and advice along the way.

Much of the empirical research would not have been possible without the partnership and investment from Integrity Music. My hope is that the connection between practitioners and theoreticians—worship leaders, songwriters, and theologians—is strengthened and that worship songs continue to carry hope to the church. I owe a debt of gratitude for the generosity and hospitality offered to me by the churches who agreed to participate in my fieldwork. They took a big step by agreeing to be part of my research, and have contributed in significant ways to the study of contemporary worship. Their kindness and openness made the time I spent in both churches special experiences.

My pastor, Brady Boyd, and my colleagues at New Life Church gave me the strength of their friendship and support along the way. I am grateful for the time to travel and to write. I experience daily the blessing of their sharing my burdens and multiplying my joys.

I hope this book honors my friends who lead worship and write songs by paying them the "intolerable compliment" of attention. I am grateful for their faithfulness to the Lord and their love for the church. They steward this sacred calling in an inspiring way. May their tribe increase.

Finally, I count it a privilege to have had David McNutt as my editor. His belief in this project and his insights and instincts for what to cut, what to compress, what to add, and how to arrange it all have made this a book better than I imagined. The team at IVP has been a joy to work with. I am grateful for their expertise.

# INTRODUCTION

THE HOUR WAS GETTING LATE, and the wounds on their backs were beginning to burn. The missionaries had ventured beyond their homeland to spread the good news, but maybe they had gone too far. Here on the outskirts of Europe, merchants were threatened by the call to exclusive allegiance to a new king named Jesus because converts had abandoned the worship of the old gods. To make things worse, a girl who could speak with supernatural insight had been loosed of a spirit's control and was no longer of any economic use to her masters. The missionaries were to blame for this. They had been arrested, beaten, and thrown in a prison cell awaiting a verdict.

These men, the first generation of followers of Jesus the Messiah, were convinced that the wandering teacher from Nazareth had been the Son of God. Crucified by the Romans, he had been raised up by the Father and made to be the Lord of the whole world. Chains in a Roman prison in Philippi could not quell the surge of their hope.

And so they began to sing. Paul and Silas, at midnight when the hour was dark and the outlook was bleak, began to sing. Were they singing a psalm, now applied to Jesus? Were they writing a hymn that would be part of Christian worship practice, like the one Paul would quote in his letter to the Philippians a few decades later?

Singing became a signature of the early Christian communities. Several decades after Paul's death, a regional governor named Pliny wrote to the Emperor Trajan that Christians would gather on a particular day of the week and sing hymns to Christ as to a god.

Christians *sing*. In weekly worship and in dark prison cells, when hearts are buoyant and when hope seems lost, Christians *sing*. When Paul and Silas sang, the ground shook and the prison doors flung open. Christians awaken the dawn of the Age to Come with a song. Even when it's midnight in the world.

Christians sing because we are people of hope. In the face of fear, in the shadow of death, in the midst of suffering and pain, the Christian stands tall. We are shaken but not moved, pressed but not crushed, down but never out. Christians are those who believe that because Jesus was raised from the dead, the worst day will not be the last day. Christian hope is resurrection and new creation, and it makes all the difference in the world.

The church, then, is a community formed in hope. The Lord whom we worship is Jesus Christ the crucified and risen. *Christ the crucified* is how we know that *all is not as it should be*. Christ came to bear our sin and the full weight of evil, to rescue us and defeat sin and death. Christ is God suffering with us and alongside us, so that even in suffering and death we are loved and we are not alone. *Christ the risen* is how we know that *it will not always be this way*. At the cross, the Father's love is revealed; at the empty tomb, the Father's faithfulness is on display. The Creator will not abandon his creation; the Redeemer will rescue and renew all things.

To be a Christian is to be grounded on such hope. Our lives in Christ are the first seeds of a new creation. The church is a new community in this new creation. The church pulls together people who otherwise would not belong together except for the saving and redeeming work of Jesus Christ and forms them in one new family, one new humanity. In Christ the crucified and risen Lord, male and female, Jews and Gentiles, slave and free are brought together as one. This new community witnesses to the life of the world to come. The fractured and broken world will one day be put back together again, and the church is a signpost now of what will be then.

This future to which we bear witness is not a future of our own making. Even as we work to make our communities resemble the kind of justice and joy that are hallmarks of the kingdom of God, we are keenly aware that we do not bring the kingdom. Jesus is the kingdom bringer. Yet, Christ has come and the kingdom has begun, even here, even now. We glimpse signs of this new creation as we see transformed lives, most poignantly when the baptized emerge from the waters—restored relationships, reconciliation, reversals of injustice, and more. The Spirit is at work in the world.

So we wait with hope. We work with hope. And we worship with hope.

Christian hope is not optimism. It's not positivity or an upbeat mood. Christian hope is not escapism. It's not the view that the world will get darker but God will get us out of here. Christian hope is not progress. It does not emerge from potential or possibility. Christian hope is uniquely shaped by resurrection—by the resurrection of Jesus Christ, and by the promise of our own future resurrection.

This is a book about worship and hope. It is my conviction that the church's worship is crucial both to the proclamation and to the formation of Christian hope. Our worship together witnesses to the world that there is more than what we can see, more than this moment, more than what we can do on our own. Our worship together is a way of rehearsing our hope in order to embed it deep within us. All day long, we are confronted with news of evil, we are hemmed in on all sides by the word of despair. Yet when the Christian comes to worship, she hears a different word. She enters a community that orients her toward a different future.

This is a study of what Christians sing about when they sing about hope, and about how they experience hope when they worship together. Do Christians experience hope when they gather to sing in worship? If so, what sort of hope is it? Is there any connection between the songs that bring hope and the experience of hope in congregational worship? In short, the question we will set out to explore is this: How does Christian hope relate to Christian worship?

## REFLEXIVITY AND AUTO / THEO-BIOGRAPHY

My introduction to the contemporary worship movement came in the form of a cassette tape. My parents subscribed to the Hosanna! Integrity Music tape-of-the-month club, and deliveries traveled all the way from the United States to Malaysia to reach us. I had some sense that this was a global movement, but at age eight or nine, I was too young to comprehend the market forces involved in distributing worship music from America around the world, let alone the process whereby worship music had been turned into a commodity. Those tapes left an early mark on me; they introduced me to a way of experiencing God and expressing my heart via music. When I was ten, our family moved from Malaysia to America for my parents to attend a Bible college in Portland, Oregon. We attended Bible Temple (later called City Bible Church, and then Mannahouse, as it is called now), a church that played a key role in the spread of the Latter Rain movement particularly through praise and worship. During the years I lived there, one of the leaders in this church created Christian Copyright Licensing Incorporated (CCLI), which not only is responsible for helping churches to be able to sing worship songs with the proper permissions and thus avoid copyright infringement but also is implicated in—intentionally or unintentionally, or better or for worse—the rise of worship songwriting as a viable profession, and a potentially lucrative one at that.

Our family returned to Malaysia after three years in Portland, and I spent my teenage years learning to lead worship and discovering a passion for it. When I returned to the United States to go to college at Oral Roberts University in Tulsa, Oklahoma, I studied systematic theology and church history but also volunteered as a worship leader on the chapel praise and worship team. This team led worship for the mandatory chapel services, which were also televised and broadcast across the nation on Christian cable stations. This was my first regular experience of worship music as a kind of performance and commodity, to put it in terms a sociologist might use.

After graduating from college and working at the university for a year as the main worship leader, I moved to Colorado Springs to be an apprentice to the main worship pastor at New Life Church. New Life Church was founded in 1985 as a nondenominational, evangelical, charismatic church. When I arrived in 2000, the church had four paid, full-time worship pastors and two administrators. Shortly after that, we began producing "live" worship recordings that were purchased and distributed by Integrity Music, one of the largest publishers and distributors of contemporary worship music in the world. I became a contracted worship songwriter, and our youth band—the Desperation Band, named after our youth conference and patterned after the far more influential group Hillsong United—was also releasing albums with Integrity Music. Over the years, I have been part of over a dozen recordings and have published over sixty-five songs that are in the CCLI catalogue, some of which have charted as high as the Top 25. Today, New Life Church has about ten thousand worshipers on a weekend, distributed over seven congregations in four locations and three languages throughout the city.

I say all this to describe my own relationship to the contemporary worship movement. Part of the reason for doing so is in order to engage in reflexivity, which sociologist Charlotte Aull Davies describes as the "turning back on oneself, a process of self-reference."[1] My personal history, or what Pete Ward has described as an auto/theo-biography, is itself data within my research.[2] My relationships, history, or closeness with the context or the people within it is not merely something to disclose but also something to analyze. Further-more, it is my vocational experience as a worship leader and songwriter within the North American context that allowed the churches in my fieldwork to be open to working with me. I am an insider to the contemporary worship movement; contemporary worship music is my native liturgical language.

Yet, at the same time, I am also removed from it. After a decade of worship ministry, I began to transition the focus of my ministry life at the church toward preaching and teaching in 2008. As I stepped away from worship ministry, I became more aware of the lack of theological depth in the songs, in the songwriters, and in worship leaders themselves. A congregant chal-lenged me to visit churches that employ a formal liturgy and historic Christian worship practices such as weekly Eucharist and to ask what they—specifically, an Anglican church, a Presbyterian church, and an Eastern Orthodox church—were doing and why, and to ask what we, as nondenominational evangelicals, had changed and why. The fruits of these visits were manifold, from the dis-covery of the Christian liturgical maxim *lex orandi, lex credendi*—the way we pray and worship becomes the way we believe; worship shapes believing—to the centrality of the Eucharist in Christian practice. As a result of other lead-ers being on a similar journey of discovery, our church has now adopted the Nicene Creed as its statement of faith, and we receive Communion weekly as the high point of each worship service. The desire to increase the depth and widen the breadth of my own theological thinking was the impetus for my journey to seminary and, eventually, to pursue doctoral research.

I have come to understand worship as a theologically catechetical practice. Therefore, worship songs and worship services must be evaluated for their content and for their impact. Yet it would be impossible in the scope of a single research project to interrogate every dimension of Christian theology in contemporary worship. In order to study the operant theology within a

---

[1]Charlotte Aull Davies, *Reflexive Ethnography: A Guide to Researching Selves and Others*, 2nd ed. (New York: Routledge, 2008), 4.

[2]Pete Ward, *Participation and Mediation: A Practical Theology for the Liquid Church* (London: SCM Press, 2008), 29.

worship song or a worship service, a particular aspect of theology must be chosen, which in my case is eschatology. If congregational worship is the context, eschatology is the content.

A personal reason for this choice is that eschatology has become the capstone in my own theological understanding. The early visions of the end times that I received as a young Christian were of a sudden rapture, a tribulation of unspeakably horrific persecution, and a final judgment where salvation may be unexpectedly revoked. Eschatology as it was talked about in the churches I grew up in was theologically marginal, with little to no bearing on Christian life and practice. As I began reading N. T. Wright and Jürgen Moltmann in my twenties, my view of eschatology changed. I have come to see eschatology as teleology, the purposeful completion of creational design. It arises from the doctrine of creation and gives completion to the doctrine of salvation, with Christology at the center.

There you have it. Christians are people of hope. The church is a community of hope. Worship is how we rehearse and embedded that hope deeply within us. Therefore, the encoded hope of contemporary worship songs and the experienced hope of contemporary worship services are worthy of study. I offer my work as an insider, as one who is sympathetic to the movement and who believes in its potential to shape the church for the better. This is not the critical appraisal of an outsider who never liked electric guitars and drums anyway; this is the theological reflection of a practitioner and pastor.

## OVERVIEW

In chapter one, I will lay out what sort of book this is. It is a work of practical theology, but I mean something particular by that term. It is worth taking the time to explain my methodology not only to help the reader know why I have taken the approach that I have in this particular research but also to give a way of doing this kind of practical theology with other questions readers may wish to explore. I will explore models such as the pastoral cycle and find a version of it that is best suited for integrating sociological analysis and theological reflection. I also cover the four voices of theology—formal theology, normative theology, espoused theology, and operant theology—and how they can help delineate the discoveries made along the way.

Chapter two will explore contemporary paradigms for understanding congregational worship, based on a survey of relevant literature and interaction with key voices from each paradigm. Though my goal here is primarily to name these paradigms, I will engage critically with each one along the way.

Chapter three explores hope through a variety of models: a cognitive model, an affective model, a virtue-ethics model, and a phenomenological model. Each one will contribute to our understanding of hope, drawing primarily from the social sciences and from philosophy. Chapter four traces hope as an eschatological vision from the early Christian centuries until the century after the Council of Nicaea. Because the Creed represents apostolic faith and is built on phrases that were passed down through the early centuries and that appear in the New Testament, it represents the authority of both Scripture and tradition. Thus the creed's articulation of eschatology is a normative theology and is what I have termed "creedal Christian hope."[3]

Chapter five turns to two contemporary theologians who have played prominent roles in the promoting and reshaping of eschatology in North American Christian understanding: Jürgen Moltmann and N. T. Wright. Moltmann's theology of hope came to prominence around the time the contemporary worship movement was beginning; Wright's work on hope is widely popular among pastors and leaders in North America today. I outline key features and overlapping aspects of their eschatology in order to allow it serve as a formal theology. Though both offer compelling articulations of creedal Christian hope that are significant for the contemporary context, they do so from different perspectives. Moltmann works within the frame of systematic and philosophical theology, while Wright works as a biblical scholar focused on Paul (and thus Pauline eschatology) and a historian of early Christian origins.

Chapter six begins the turn toward culture, practice, and ethnography through my fieldwork. The chapter begins with a brief description of how popular evangelical eschatology has been distorted and truncated in America over the past few centuries, proposing a four-part taxonomy for popular

---

[3]While neither church in my fieldwork uses the Nicene Creed as its statement of faith, both churches' statements of faith reflect some overlapping language with the Creed; nothing is contradictory. River Valley, the Presbyterian church in my study, does occasionally incorporate a corporate confession of the Creed during its worship, while Pathway, the nondenominational church, does not. Nevertheless, since the Nicene Creed is affirmed in every tradition of Christianity—variations on the *filioque* notwithstanding—it serves as a normative theology, a term defined in chapter one.

evangelical eschatology. From the general North American context, the focus moves to the two fieldwork churches in my research. One is a Presbyterian church, River Valley Church in Denver, and the other is a nondenominational Pentecostal-charismatic church, Pathway Church in Dallas.[4] Both would describe themselves as evangelical because of their belief in the lordship of Jesus, the necessity of personal faith or conversion, the authority of Scripture, and the need to let their faith affect their life in the world.[5]

To discover the espoused theology of hope in each church, my research drew from participant observation in worship services, sermons, semi-structured interviews with pastors and worship leaders at each church, and position papers posted on the church's website. At River Valley I was able to interview the senior pastor and the worship pastor. At Pathway I interviewed the campus pastor and the campus worship pastor. I was also able to participate in preservice gatherings with the worship team and songwriting sessions with its writers. I also designed a survey, which included some demographic questions, some multiple-choice questions related to a theology of hope, and a few open-ended questions on songs and Scripture verses that bring hope. This survey instrument was given to the congregational email list at River Valley for the Saturday evening service. At Pathway, I gave it to my focus group, since the responses were comparable in size to the number of respondents at River Valley. Thus my data gathering involved four data points at the fieldwork churches—participant observation, leader interviews, focus group, and a survey.

Chapter seven seeks to uncover the operant theology of hope by examining how hope is encoded in songs. I surveyed about one thousand worship leaders in North America. Looking at songs specifically named by these worship leaders as songs that bring them and their churches hope, I analyze key words, verbs, and pronouns to study space, time, and agency, three specific aspects of hope identified in chapters four and five. The object of hope

---

[4] The names of both churches, of the suburbs in which they are located, and of all people associated with these churches have been changed to protect the privacy of those who granted me access in my fieldwork.

[5] This follows the National Association of Evangelicals' brief description of evangelicals as people who "take the Bible seriously and believe in Jesus Christ as Savior and Lord," and David Bebbington's quadrangle, which the National Association of Evangelicals also cites, of conversionism, activism, biblicism, and crucicentrism. See National Association of Evangelicals, "What Is an Evangelical?," accessed July 22, 2017, www.nae.net/what-is-an-evangelical.

is compared to that of creedal Christian hope, with specific attention given to the aspects of futurity and materiality. I offer possible explanations for an encoded hope that is focused on the here and now. The patterns from the national survey serve as a backdrop to the patterns in the songs that were named from my fieldwork churches. My fieldwork methodology is shaped by anthropology, phenomenology, and ethnography.

Chapter eight is a study of experienced hope, another dimension of the operant theology of hope. Employing methods of congregational studies such as ethnography and discourse analysis, I invited the people in my focus groups to narrate the meaning they make from congregational worship. I engaged in participant observation with both churches, making at least three site visits to attend services over an eight-month period with Pathway, and an eighteen-month period with River Valley. At both churches, the pastors helped me form a focus group designed to be a representative cross-section of the respective congregations. Drawing from ritual studies, the sociology of "feeling rules," and the psychology of hope, I engage in a description and an appraisal of the kind of hope experienced in each church context and its embedded theology.

In chapter nine, I engage in a situational analysis of theology to allow the fieldwork to raise important theological questions. Despite giving priority to the normative and formal voices by using them to interrogate the espoused and operant voices, listening to the espoused and operant theologies of hope led to an unexpected discovery. Worshipers experienced a high degree of hope despite the low eschatological content of the songs of hope. Three questions emerged from this discovery:

1. How could the experience of hope be consistent when the encoded hope was so theologically weak?

2. Why does the experience of God's presence produce hope?

3. In what ways is the Spirit present and active in congregational worship?

Because the research is being done for theological purposes, it must therefore recognize God as an "actor in the analytical process."[6] It is precisely toward

---

[6]Elizabeth Phillips, "Charting the 'Ethnographic Turn': Theologians and the Study of Christian Congregations," in *Perspectives on Ecclesiology and Ethnography*, ed. Pete Ward (Grand Rapids: Eerdmans, 2012), 106.

that end that responses to these questions were shaped by the inquiry into how the Spirit is an actor in the process of worshipers experiencing hope in congregational worship. The responses to the first two questions draw from Moltmann and Wright's articulation of Christian hope but are placed in conversation with Gordon Fee's work on a Pauline theology of the Spirit. A theology of the Spirit is also the source for addressing the final question as I attempt to address the apparent tension between a social-scientific understanding of congregational worship and a traditionally theological one.

Finally, in chapter ten, the focus turns to praxis. Despite some discouraging findings along the way, there is hope for church leaders today. We can lead our people to see a more robust vision of Christian hope. Toward that end, I make three recommendations to songwriters, worship leaders, and pastors that enable them to address the chief concerns revealed in this research.

With that as our roadmap, let us now begin the journey.

# PART 1

# SETTING
# THE STAGE

# 1

# WHAT IS PRACTICAL THEOLOGY?

**WHAT KIND OF BOOK IS THIS?** Is it a practitioner manual? Is it a textbook? Is it descriptive or prescriptive? The short answer is that it is a work of practical theology.

But the term needs explaining. As a friend once quipped, "Practical theology? That sounds like an oxymoron!" Yes, it often seems like it. Theology can seem like an obsession that bears little fruit in the real world. It is easy to imagine theologians quibbling about esoteric ways of talking about the sublime. But the truth is, nothing could have more bearing on daily life than what one believes about God. This is not to say that academic theology doesn't sometimes get bogged down in debating minutiae; it is only to say that everyone is living with some kind of theology, whether we are aware of it or not. Practical theology tries to bridge the kind of theology that is dealt with in abstract or theoretical terms and the kind of theology that is lived or embodied.

We might say, then, that practical theology, at its most basic level, is the attempt to integrate theory or doctrine and practice.[1] But the term itself can mean different things in different contexts. It is worth outlining four dominant models for placing theory and practice in a dialogical relationship, following the insights of Paul Ballard and John Pritchard and noting the particular shape each takes when integrated in practical theology.

The first is the applied-theory model, which views all practice as a form of applied theory.[2] When the term *practical theology* was initially introduced in

---

[1]Paul Ballard and John Pritchard, *Practical Theology in Action: Christian Thinking in the Service of Church and Society*, 2nd ed. (London: SPCK, 1996), 54.
[2]Ballard and Pritchard, *Practical Theology in Action*, 55.

academic settings, what was primarily meant was applied theology. Practical theology, as Friedrich Schleiermacher and others saw it, was the branch that emerged from the trunk of historical theology and the root system of philosophical theology. The question, in a deductive approach, is which theory to bring to bear on the practice; or, in an inductive approach, which theory is implicit in the practice.[3]

The second model is the critical-correlation model, applied to practical theology most notably by Don Browning. In this model, theology is often paired with the social sciences, where social anthropology can help shed light on human experience or behavior, and theology can help reflect on how this experience or behavior relates to God. James Whyte describes this as a three-fold engagement, rather than a dialogue, between "theological disciplines, the social sciences and the actual situation."[4]

Third is the praxis model, which is primarily concerned with actions and outcomes that aim to be transformative. The praxis model begins with a concrete situation but assumes that no activity is value free and thus critiques every aspect, including the researcher.[5] This analysis is then filtered through a theological imperative in order to develop a new praxis.

Finally, there is the habitus/virtue model, which draws on classical ethical teaching on virtue as a learned habit. The habitus/virtue model moves the paradigms of theory and practice beyond the cognitive and the active and into the communal.

Ballard and Pritchard warn against choosing one model to the exclusion of others. This would distort or restrict theological activity. Rather, they suggest viewing each model as a pathway into the process, a process that is necessarily complex. In fact, for them, these four models are not even to be seen as disparate but rather as "strands which are often woven together and affect each other."[6] Let us turn now to a few methods for integrating these models.

---

[3]Emmanuel Lartey, "Practical Theology as a Theological Form," in *The Blackwell Reader in Pastoral and Practical Theology*, ed. James Woodward and Stephen Pattison (Oxford: Blackwell, 2000), 129; Ballard and Pritchard, *Practical Theology in Action*, 46-47.
[4]Ballard and Pritchard, *Practical Theology in Action*, 55, 62.
[5]Ballard and Pritchard, *Practical Theology in Action*, 55, 66.
[6]Ballard and Pritchard, *Practical Theology in Action*, 55, 57.

## THE PASTORAL CYCLE

The pastoral cycle is a tool that takes into account the contributions and flaws of the four models Ballard and Pritchard list above while also providing a structure that has room for both flexibility and diversity.[7] Though the cycle may have derived from various other models and thus there are other permutations of it, it is given clear definition by Ballard and Pritchard as a series of four phases. The first is *experience*, where a specific situation is chosen and named. The second is *exploration*, where an analysis occurs. Third is *reflection*, where the analysis of the situation is set against the backdrop of beliefs in general and theology in particular. Last is *action*, where initiatives for ministry application are outlined and outcomes of those actions are determined.

Richard Osmer provides a list of the four tasks that practical theology must undertake. Though he does not reference Ballard and Pritchard or the pastoral cycle, the list bears a striking resemblance to the four phases of the cycle. The first task is the *descriptive-empirical task*. This is about gathering data or information in order to "discern patterns and dynamics in particular episodes, situations, or contexts." The second task is the *interpretive task*, which employs theories from nontheological disciplines, specifically the social sciences, in order to understand and explain the occurrence of particular patterns and other dynamics. Third is the *normative task*. Here the goal is to use theological concepts to add another layer of interpretation and to construct an ethical norm. Finally, there is the *pragmatic task*, which involves determining strategies of action to influence or change the situation. Osmer sums up these four tasks as four questions: "What is going on? Why is this going on? What ought to be going on? How might we respond?"[8]

For all of its promise, however, the pastoral cycle has its limitations. Pete Ward points out the irony in the tendency of the cycle to "reinforce the dislocation between reflection and the everyday"; "experience is effectively distanced and distilled through analytical moves."[9] This is largely due to the multistage approach, as though each component—experience, analysis, reflection, and action—could be separated from the others. Furthermore, Elaine Graham

---

[7]Ballard and Pritchard, *Practical Theology in Action*, 74.
[8]Richard R. Osmer, *Practical Theology: An Introduction* (Grand Rapids: Eerdmans, 2008), 4.
[9]Pete Ward, *Participation and Mediation: A Practical Theology for the Liquid Church* (London: SCM Press, 2008), 35.

argues that practical theology in a postmodern context means that theology should function less like disembodied concepts and more like a faith that is enfleshed in practices and community. Where practical theology once moved from theory to practice, Graham's goal is to move from practice to theory. In her words, her proposal is "to reconstitute pastoral theology as the theorization of Christian practices."[10] The pastoral cycle as Ballard and Pritchard and Osmer articulate it allows theory—or theology—to interrogate practice and experience but does not make room for it to flow the other way around.

Emmanuel Lartey, however, adds a fifth stage to the cycle, which addresses the concern to let practice inform theory. His first phase is also called *experience* and deals with the concrete. His second phase is called *situational analysis*, which explicitly calls for "social and psychological analysis" but also makes room for other perspectives. In fact, he is clear that this should be "multi-perspectival rather than inter-disciplinary," since the researcher cannot adequately represent the complexity of different disciplines. The third phase, as in Ballard and Pritchard's model, engages in *theological analysis*. Lartey recommends specific questions for this phase: "What questions and analyses arise from my faith concerning what I have experienced and the other analyses of it?" "How has Christian thought approached the issues raised?" and "Is there a prophetic insight which may be brought to bear on the situation?" Lartey points out that this analysis should engage with both the personal and "with the traditions of Christian faith." The fourth phase is what makes Lartey's version of the cycle different from Ballard and Pritchard's and Osmer's. In what he calls *situational analysis of theology*, Lartey makes "faith perspectives . . . the subject of questioning by the encounter and the situational analysis." This rests on the premise that such experience and situational analysis "may offer more adequate reformulations of Christian doctrine."[11] His final phase, like the final phases in Ballard and Pritchard's model, calls for response.

## LIQUID ECCLESIOLOGY

One of the ways to address the rigidity of the pastoral cycle is to allow the movements between the situation and the theology to be more fluid. This is

---

[10]Elaine Graham, "Practical Theology as Transforming Practice," in Woodward and Pattison, *Blackwell Reader in Pastoral and Practical Theology*, 109.
[11]Lartey, "Practical Theology as a Theological Form," 132-33.

something of what Ward means when he calls for a liquid ecclesiology. Ward writes, "When ministers preach sermons, design liturgies, choose hymns, make pastoral decisions, plan programs of mission, and so on, they are already participating in the expression and circulation of theology." Thus theological reflection is not actually a "distinct moment"; rather, "theology and theologizing of all kinds takes place within and reflects the interests and commitments of individuals and communities." Furthermore, what is needed on the part of the researcher is not an objective perspective—as if that were even possible. Instead, theology that seeks to interact with the "lived reality of the Church," as practical theology seeks to do, "requires a familiarity with the life and expression of the Christian community."[12]

In many books on the contemporary church and its practices, critiques are all too often thinly constructed even while the theological basis for the arguments and prescriptions is rich. Ward sees this as "methodological laziness in ecclesiology." "We base whole arguments on anecdote and the selective treatment of experience. We are prone to a sleight of hand that makes social theory appear to be a description of social reality—which it of course is not."[13]

Ward proposes a liquid ecclesiology, which represents a "shift in the theological imagination from solidity or from 'Solid Church' to fluidity and 'Liquid Church.'" This fluidity is a characteristic of both the divine being and human culture. Thus "Liquid Ecclesiology focuses on the way the divine life passes through the walls and links Church with the wider society." It is a

> cultural theology in the sense that it seeks to interact with patterns of practice and thinking that are operant in the lived expression of the church. Liquid ecclesiology is theological and theoretical, but it develops theology through a deep interaction with cultural expression and the lived. Liquid Ecclesiology is a theology that takes cultural expression seriously as one part of the paradox of the Church.[14]

This proposal is not without objections or cautions. John Webster argues that even in empirical study of the church and its practices, there ought to be a "hierarchy of understanding between the origin of the Church and the phenomena

---

[12]Ward, *Participation and Mediation*, 48-49.

[13]Pete Ward, *Perspectives in Ecclesiology and Ethnography* (Grand Rapids: Eerdmans, 2012), 4.

[14]Pete Ward, *Liquid Ecclesiology: The Gospel and the Church* (Leiden, Netherlands: Brill, 2017), 9-11.

of the Church." More than a specific methodology, Webster wants a hierarchy of knowing: dogmatics over social-scientific inquiry. Yet Ward argues that the "dichotomy between empirical or culturally-generated theological perspective and those developed by scholars working from texts is . . . a false one." Taking the perspective of critical realism, Ward maintains that theologians must acknowledge epistemological relativity even in doctrines, negating the notion of a "fixed reference point for ecclesiology." Even a theologically oriented epistemology, whether applied to texts or to empirical data, requires a "positioning in relationship," which is in essence what is meant by faith. Thus Ward, like Clare Watkins and her colleagues, repeatedly uses Anselm's phrase "faith seeking understanding" to describe an approach to theology that takes the theology encoded in text and preserved in tradition and the theology embodied in practice with equal weight.[15] To Helen Cameron along with Watkins and colleagues we now turn for a methodology that treats practice theologically.

## THEOLOGICAL ACTION RESEARCH

What is needed is a way to delineate what we mean by theology, to distinguish dogmatics from embodied or lived theology. In their book *Talking About God in Practice*, Cameron, Deborah Bhatti, Catherine Duce, James Sweeney, and Watkins propose a method of relating theology and practice that they call theological action research, and an accompanying model for doing practical theology that holds in harmony the four voices of theology.[16] Before describing the four voices, it is helpful to note the five characteristics of Cameron's theological action research method, since the four voices function as a way of delivering on one of these aims in particular.

The first characteristic of theological action research is that it is theological "all the way through." Theology cannot appear only after the data has been gathered, since "the practices participated in and observed are themselves the bearers of theology." This goes along with Ward's criticism of the pastoral cycle as dividing theology from practice artificially. Second, theological action

---

[15]Ward, *Liquid Ecclesiology*, 16-17, 21, 23-26; Clare Watkins, with Deborah Bhatti, Helen Cameron, Catherine Duce, and James Sweeney, "Practical Ecclesiology: What Counts as Theology in Studying the Church?," in Ward, *Perspectives on Ecclesiology and Ethnography*, 180.

[16]Helen Cameron, Deborah Bhatti, Catherin Duce, James Sweeney, and Clare Watkins, *Talking About God in Practice: Theological Action Research and Practical Theology* (London: SCM Press, 2010), 2.

research is to be located in the heart of the four "distinct, but interrelated and overlapping 'voices'" of theology because of a conviction that within the diversity there is coherence. This leads to the third characteristic of theological action research, that theology must be disclosed through a conversational method where the voices are placed in conversation with one another so that they can be heard together. Fourth, theological action research is meant to be a "formative transformation of practice." Like all practical theology, there must be a change that results. Cameron and colleagues see one of the key places of change as being the "change of learning and changed attitudes" of the researcher, who in the case of practical theology is a reflective practitioner. Finally, theological action research is a method that allows practice to "contribute to the transformation of theology."[17] Like Ward and Graham, Cameron moves practical theology out of the paradigm of modern theology, where the tradition is largely fixed and unchanging, and into the context of postmodern theology, where theology is seen as dynamic and fluid. I am cautious about theological action research because of this final characteristic. The theology of the church must have certain fixed aspects.

## THEOLOGY IN FOUR VOICES

The model of theological action research Cameron and colleagues propose is helpful because of its view of theology in four voices. These voices are not independent of one another, though they are distinct. The first is what Cameron and colleagues call normative theology. This refers to that which the group that is being studied names as its theological authority, an authority that informs and corrects operant and espoused theologies. Some examples of a normative theology would be the Scriptures, the creeds, official church teaching, and in some cases even the liturgy. The second voice is espoused theology. This is the theology that is "embedded in a group's articulated beliefs."[18] There is some similarity here with what Jeff Astley has called ordinary theology, the way people talk about theology ordinarily and in the course of life.[19] Third, there is the voice of operant theology. This is the theology that

---

[17]Cameron et al., *Talking About God*, 51, 58-59.
[18]Cameron et al., *Talking About God*, 54.
[19]Jeff Astley, *Ordinary Theology: Looking, Listening, and Learning in Theology* (Surrey, UK: Ashgate, 2003).

is "embedded within the actual practices of a group."[20] Naming it this way helps us take seriously Ward's claim that every decision, program, practice, and more within the life of the church is a participation in "the expression and circulation of theology."[21] The fourth and final voice is formal theology. This is the theology of the academy, of the so-called professional theologian. It is possible, and in fact likely, that this voice may resonate with the voice of normative theology. Yet Cameron and colleagues make clear that the voice of academic theology has the distinct role of offering an articulation of the faith and of the tradition.[22]

Watkins, writing with Bhatti, Cameron, Duce, and Sweeney in a later work, describes the need for an "'authentic ecclesiology'—one that is able to speak truthfully about concrete realities, and faithfully about the historical and present promise of the work of the Spirit, enlivening what we understand to be 'the body of Christ,' the church." Their proposed four-voices method was developed in answer to the question of how to give practices their "proper place within the theological discourse of the church" in order to develop an "authentic ecclesiology."[23]

The four-voices method is shaped by a desire to "listen" to practices as "embodied works of theology." Watkins and colleagues see the temptation in traditional systematic-theology work to only study practice as a way of unearthing a question or a challenge and then to employ the resources of theological tradition to supply the answers. But if practices are themselves "bearers of theology," then these voices must be held in conversation with each other. Even what they call formal and normative voices of theology must function as "one voice in an ongoing conversation, in which all voices, in their distinct and proper ways, are understood as theological." They ground this approach in the doctrine of the Spirit as both the promised guide for the church and the God who is radically free to act through many means. Thus for the church to be charismatic for Watkins and colleagues, its theology must be "multivoiced." Practical ecclesiology "requires ongoing conversation as the appropriate pattern of theology," where the maxim "faith seeking

---

[20]Cameron et al., *Talking About God*, 54.
[21]Ward, *Participation and Mediation*, 48.
[22]Cameron et al., *Talking About God*, 55.
[23]Watkins et al., "Practical Ecclesiology," 168-69.

understanding" results in the "recognition of an ecclesial faith as something necessarily communal, discursive."[24]

Yet there is a danger here. The Creed leads us to say of the Spirit that he *has spoken* through the prophets. There is a certain fixedness to the faith. So, even as I find the four voices a helpful way of naming the theology found in a practice, I don't hold to the view that voices are equally interpretative of one another. As will become clear by the end of the chapter, formal and normative theologies ought to ask the final questions of espoused and operant theologies.

## ETHNOGRAPHY AND THEOLOGY

Since practical theology involves theological reflection on a particular experience or practice, different tools from the ones theologians are used to using are required to analyze the experience or practice adequately. "Genuine attentiveness to people and genuine engagement with the complexities of their lives are only possible through research methods that take theologians beyond the desk and the library and into those lives," Elizabeth Phillips argues, and therefore practical theologians must be "serious apprentices of sociologists, anthropologists, philosophers, and historians."[25] Because of its communal, physical, and repetitive nature, contemporary Christian congregational worship can be studied as a ritual. Ritual studies, traditionally the domain of sociologists and anthropologists, is one way for the practical theologian to gain an illuminating perspective on congregational worship. Phenomenology and ethnography are also methods from philosophy and social anthropology that may guide the study of congregational worship.

The turn toward ethnography in theology gained prominence with James McClendon's 1974 work, *Biography as Theology*, in which McClendon, according to Phillips, suggests that the "task of theology is 'investigation of the convictions of a convictional community.'" This was followed by George Lindbeck's argument in *The Nature of Doctrine*, which proposed a cultural-linguistic model of theology as a way of understanding religion as a culture with a language. Stanley Hauerwas, influenced by McClendon, has "advocated the narrative description of specific congregations as an important task for

---

[24]Watkins et al., "Practical Ecclesiology," 170, 178, 180.
[25]Elizabeth Phillips, "Charting the 'Ethnographic Turn': Theologians and the Study of Christian Congregations," in Ward, *Perspectives on Ecclesiology and Ethnography*, 105.

both theologians and congregations themselves," as Phillips writes.[26] Max van Manen writes about a "phenomenology of practice" as "research and writing that reflects *on* and *in* practice, and prepares for practice" in his own book, which he views as itself a "phenomenology of phenomenology." Phenomenology begins with a sense of wonder, an awed curiosity, which turns into a question about the nature or meaning of a particular experience. To do phenomenology is to "start with lived experience, with how something appears or gives itself to us."[27]

Van Manen, however, makes a point to distinguish ethnography from others "forms of meaning in social inquiry." In his view, psychological, sociological, ethnographic, biographic, and other forms of the social sciences or human sciences have explanation as their aim, while phenomenology seeks to provide description and interpretation.[28] He concedes that ethnography does share some overlapping features with phenomenology but maintains that their purposes are different. Even so, it is difficult to imagine doing phenomenology without the aid of ethnography.

Ethnography is the description of a particular people, culture, or subculture with the goal of discovering "cultural meanings."[29] The archetypal form of research within ethnography is participant observation. Charlotte Aull Davies writes that the "hallmark of participant observation is long-term personal involvement with those being studied, including participation in their lives to the extent that the researcher comes to understand the culture as an insider." Even so, ethnography relies on more than participant observation; it requires a "cluster of techniques" that grant the researcher access into the culture and meaning-making narratives. Thus "key informants" are needed who can translate, interpret, narrate, or relate their experiences. This can occur through structured, semistructured, or unstructured interviews. It is important to select people who would be somewhat representative of the larger group. Davies also finds it better to choose not leaders but rather "outsiders" who have become "more aware

---

[26]Phillips, "Charting the 'Ethnographic Turn,'" 97-98.
[27]Max van Manen, *Phenomenology of Practice: Meaning-Giving Methods in Phenomenological Research and Writing*, 879, Kindle. ed. Janice Morse (Walnut Creek, CA: Left Coast, 2014), locs. 508, 726, 850, 879.
[28]Van Manen, *Phenomenology of Practice*, loc. 1142.
[29]Van Manen, *Phenomenology of Practice*, loc. 1145.

of the assumptions and expectations of their own society, often because they flaunt them or fail to fulfill them."[30]

One question that arises in the use of ethnographic methods it about the role of the theological tradition—the normative and formal voices—in evaluating the espoused and operant theologies that ethnographic work helps to uncover. While ethnography is a valuable way to study the complexities of Christian practice and to name the theology that is embedded in practice, it provides no framework for evaluating those constructions of meaning. Hauerwas, as Phillips writes, has argued that social-scientific methods are "unhelpful to . . . theologians" when they "methodologically preclude the theological claims necessary for the church's intelligibility." Thus Phillips sees the challenge of practical theology being now not a question of whether theologians can use the social sciences but rather "how theologians can deeply engage with and thickly describe social groups and realities—as social scientists have done—while not accepting the premise of social sciences, but allowing research to be shaped by theological traditions and normative concerns."[31]

Because of this rejection of the premise of the social sciences and because theologians do not engage in ethnography with the kind of comprehensive approach that anthropologists employ, Phillips suggests that the term *theological ethnography* be used to denote "theological practices of thick description." Theological ethnography belongs to the wider field of study often referred to as congregational studies, where practitioners have theological interests as primary and are thus often referred to as practical theologians.[32] Theological ethnography requires taking social-scientific methods seriously while retaining theological priorities.

## PUTTING THEORY AND PRACTICE TOGETHER

What are to make of all this, then? The kind of practical theology I'm trying to do here looks like putting theory and practice in a mutually interrogative relationship with each other. I aim to uncover the theology of hope that is encoded in contemporary worship songs and is experienced in contemporary

---

[30]Charlotte Aull Davies, *Reflexive Ethnography: A Guide to Researching Selves and Others*, 2nd ed. (New York: Routledge, 2008), 77, 81, 90.
[31]Phillips, "Charting the 'Ethnographic Turn,'" 99.
[32]Phillips, "Charting the 'Ethnographic Turn,'" 102-3.

worship services by engaging in theological ethnography. Though this work does not follow the same sequence, I approached my research with Lartey's version of the pastoral cycle in mind, choosing an experience and moving from situational analysis to theological analysis of the situation to situational analysis of the theology and concluding with a response. Cameron's theology in four voices serves as the method for naming the kinds of theological content I encounter, from the normative and formal to the espoused and operant. Though the theology is multivoiced, I am not treating each voice with equal weight; to borrow a metaphor from music recording, some voices are louder in the mix than others. I am allowing the normative and formal voices to interrogate the espoused and operant voices. Perhaps another way to think of this is that some of these voices are the melody; the others will either be in harmony or in dissonance.

Having outlined the kind of practical theology we are endeavoring to do here, I will now offer a brief overview of the history of contemporary worship and propose three paradigms for congregational worship today.

# 2

# CONTEMPORARY PARADIGMS FOR CONGREGATIONAL WORSHIP

## DEFINITION AND ORIGINS OF THE CONTEMPORARY WORSHIP MOVEMENT

CONTEMPORARY WORSHIP is nearly ubiquitous within global Christianity. Songs from Hillsong, Bethel, the Passion movement, and more are sung around the world. These songs come from and often carry with them a particular understanding of what corporate worship is for. This chapter will explore three different paradigms for understanding the purpose of congregational worship. These paradigms emerge from a brief survey of literature on church services in general and worship in particular over the past few decades.

But before we explore these contemporary paradigms for understanding the purpose of congregational worship, it is worth briefly surveying the contemporary worship movement itself. Though the movement is pluriform, there are defining features and traceable roots for it. The term *contemporary worship* in North America has become an identifiable genre of Christian congregational music. The term has surfaced in density of usage in three clear time periods: the 1920s–1930s, the 1960s–1970s, and the 1990s. In the first decade of its widespread use, it was not a technical term; it simply referred to the worship of its own day. But the rise in usage of the phrase in the 1960s and 1970s corresponded with an innovation and experimentation in worship during those years, particularly as the Jesus movement spread. After several decades of use, its surge in usage in the 1990s marks the phrase as a "clear technical name."[1] But the

---

[1]Swee Hong Lim and Lester Ruth, *Lovin' On Jesus: A Concise History of Contemporary Worship* (Nashville: Abingdon, 2017), 2.

widespread use of the term was not always in a positive light.[2] Worship historians Lester Ruth and Swee Hong Lim note, "Almost as soon as the term *contemporary worship* had begun to appear in publications so too writers began to note the 'worship wars' being waged in congregations."[3]

Nevertheless, as a movement that now has a history, "contemporary worship has become an identifiable phenomenon." Lim and Ruth identify nine qualities that they cluster into four groups. The first group is a set of fundamental presuppositions, which are composed of the following: the use of "contemporary, nonarchaic English"; a "dedication to relevance regarding contemporary concerns and issues in the lives of the worshippers"; and a "commitment to adapt worship to match contemporary people," which includes using the right instruments, a "popular sound," and familiar song lyrics and lyrical structure. The second cluster of attributes are musical. These involve "using musical styles from current types of popular music, engaging in 'extended times of uninterrupted congregational singing,' and making musicians the visual center of 'the liturgical space' as well as central to the 'leadership of the service.'" The third group is what Lim and Ruth call behavioral. Here they cluster the identifying marks of a high level of "physical expressiveness" with a "predilection for informality." In Lim and Ruth's final grouping of key attributes of contemporary worship, they name a "reliance upon electronic technology" as a "key dependency."[4]

In their survey of the literature of these decades, along with dozens of interviews with key leaders and teachers within the movement, Lim and Ruth discovered several shared points of emphases in these various accounts. There is "the importance of congregational singing," "the focus in the singing on the heart-felt love for God (or Jesus)," "the criticalness of singing *to* God (or Jesus) and not just *about* God," the necessity of "full, sincere engagement of the worshipper," and finally the need for "an experience of God during this kind of worship."[5]

---

[2]Because the alternate name "modern worship" is used in some circles today, it is worth noting here that in Ruth's appraisal the term *modern worship* was coined by music executives as a way of "promoting worship music that was an edgier style of rock, much of it originating from outside the United States"—mainly Australia and the UK (Lim and Ruth, *Lovin' On Jesus*, 15).

[3]Lim and Ruth, *Lovin' On Jesus*, 11.

[4]Lim and Ruth, *Lovin' On Jesus*, 2-3.

[5]Lim and Ruth, *Lovin' On Jesus*, 13.

Lim and Ruth's work also names four key sources of the contemporary worship movement. One source was the development taking place in youth ministry. It became a truism in the 1960s that churches need to reach the next generation. Appeals were made with urgency, warning that the church was in danger of losing the youth. The youth movement was so influential in effecting widespread changes to church programming, sermon content, and worship design that some scholars have considered this youth movement the cause of a "'juvenilization' of American Christianity."[6]

A second source that contributed to the rise of the contemporary worship movement is Pentecostalism. Pentecostalism shaped contemporary worship in four important ways. The first was the way Pentecostalism shaped the expectation that praise and worship should be "physical and expressive." Second, Lim and Ruth note the role of Pentecostalism in highlighting "intensity as a liturgical virtue." Third, Pentecostalism brought the "expectation of experience" to contemporary worship. I will say more about this later, but for now it is important to note that it was Pentecostal teaching that moved the encounter with God from being a possibility to being an expectation. Finally, Pentecostalism effected a "sacramentalization of music," which will also be explored further below and which led to the fourth aspect of Pentecostal influence, the centrality of musicians to the service.[7] Congregational music scholar Monique Ingalls adds another layer to Pentecostalism's influence, citing its impact on style, songs, and structure in noncharismatic evangelical churches in the United States starting in the early 1980s. This "blending of evangelical and pentecostal practice" has been referred to as "the 'pentecostalization of evangelicalism.'"[8]

A third source, according to Lim and Ruth, for the rise of contemporary worship was the priorities of the baby boomer generation. Boomers are known for the questioning of tradition and for treating authenticity as a virtue in itself. Thus, contemporary worship was shaped by the freedom to depart from tradition in order to worship in a way that was true to oneself.[9]

---

[6]Bergler's term, quoted in Lim and Ruth, *Lovin' On Jesus*, 17.

[7]Lim and Ruth, *Lovin' On Jesus*, 18.

[8]Monique Ingalls, *The Spirit of Praise: Music and Worship in Global Pentecostal-Charismatic Christianity*, ed. Monique M. Ingalls and Amos Yong (University Park: Pennsylvania State University Press, 2015), loc. 209, Kindle.

[9]Lim and Ruth, *Lovin' On Jesus*, 19.

The fourth source from which the contemporary worship movement is said to have arisen is church-growth missiology. Traced back to Fuller Theological Seminary professor Donald McGavran, the church-growth movement made prominent a homogenous unit principle, which taught that people are most effective at reaching people who are just like them.[10] (This has had disastrous effects in terms of furthering segregation in what was already the most divided hour in America, but that critique cannot be adequately offered here.) Using music as a stylistic brand that unified a particular group and provided a sense of belonging was a way of growing the church. It was vital that the unsaved came to church and heard musical styles they recognized and sermons on topics to which they could relate. This approach was not actually revolutionary; it was merely the next iteration of a technique developed to great success by Charles Finney and others during the Second Great Awakening, which I will say more about below. In this paradigm, "creativity and innovation became self-evident virtues."[11]

In summary, contemporary worship is recognizable by its use of contemporary English, relevant themes, popular instrumentation and musical style, extended times of congregational singing, the centrality of a band or worship team, physical expressiveness, and a preference for informality. It resulted from the rise of youth ministry, the spread of Pentecostalism, the priorities and preferences of baby boomers, and the influence of church-growth missiology.

## THREE PARADIGMS FOR CONGREGATIONAL WORSHIP

What is congregational worship for? From my own survey of the literature on contemporary worship, from my experiences leading worship and preaching in various churches in North America, and from my experiences leading worship and teaching workshops at regional and national worship conferences, I propose that there are three paradigms for understanding the purpose of congregational worship. My focus, once again, will be on the North American context, though I suspect that readers may discern these paradigms at work in other contexts as well.

The three paradigms for understanding the purpose of congregational worship are worship as *mission*, worship as *formation*, and worship as

---

[10]Donald A. McGavran, *Understanding Church Growth*, 3rd ed., ed. C. Peter Wagner (Grand Rapids: Eerdmans, 1990), x.

[11]Lim and Ruth, *Lovin' On Jesus*, 21.

*encounter*. Each paradigm is a kind of theological frame that shapes choices within the churches that adopt them—choices such as the order of the service, the songs that are sung, and the place of sung worship within the service. These paradigms are not mutually exclusive. Though a church may prioritize one paradigm over the other two, often all three paradigms are at work in any given church context. These paradigms also informed the ethnographic research that follows in chapters six, seven, and eight. As evangelical churches, both of the churches in my fieldwork study have been influenced by the worship-as-mission paradigm, either in partial conformity to it or by consciously constructing a response to it. Additionally, my fieldwork examined one church that embraces the worship-as-formation paradigm of worship and is grounded within the Reformed tradition, and one Pentecostal-charismatic church that operates within the worship-as-encounter paradigm.

## WORSHIP AS MISSION: THE EVANGELICAL PARADIGM

***Frontier roots.*** Lim and Ruth observe that white mainline congregations in the 1990s adopted contemporary worship for "tactical reasons." They were driven by missional goals of reaching more people: "Whereas the Pentecostal approach had been to adopt the new music as a way of encountering God, these congregations tended to implement contemporary worship as a strategic way of attracting new people." This impulse to adopt new techniques in order to reach new people is endemic to American evangelicalism, with its roots in the Second Great Awakening. Liturgical scholar Melanie Ross writes that while Jonathan Edwards during the First Great Awakening described "revival as 'a marvelous work of God,' Charles Finney about a hundred years later argued that revival was the result of employing 'appropriate means.'"[12]

Though Finney is famous for his new methods, his legacy is not actually about innovation; it is the relativization of form. Finney's premise was that the end justified the means; so long as souls were "getting saved," it did not matter what the methods were.[13] In the face of harsh criticism, Finney defended his philosophy by comparing his approach with the one he perceived Jesus and the apostles using:

---

[12]Lim and Ruth, *Lovin' On Jesus*, 131; Melanie C. Ross, *Evangelical Versus Liturgical? Defying a Dichotomy* (Grand Rapids: Eerdmans, 2014), 14.

[13]Ross makes a similar point in *Evangelical Versus Liturgical?*, 15.

When Jesus Christ was on earth . . . he had nothing to do with forms or measures. . . . The Jews accused him of disregarding their forms. His object was to preach and teach mankind the true religion. . . . No person can pretend to get a set of forms or particular direction as to measures out of [the Great Commission]. Their [the apostles'] goal was to make known the gospel in the *most effectual way*.[14]

Finney's innovation of methods and relativization of form were not the only marks he left on American evangelicalism. Ross credits Finney with creating a threefold *ordo* that is still followed in many evangelical churches. This order of service, created in reaction to liturgical traditions, has become, in an irony of church history, a new tradition and a new liturgy adhered to by modern American evangelicals even without their realization. The pattern is roughly as follows: songs, readings, or dramatic elements to warm up the crowd; a sermon, employing theatrical speech and communication techniques; and an opportunity to make a decision, such as an altar call.

The frontier tradition succeeded in the prioritization of mission and the personalization of salvation. Both of these have developed into traits that Bebbington has enshrined in the evangelical genetic code: activism and conversionism.[15] Yet it also laid the groundwork for a wholesale departure from tradition and with it the theological depth of the past. Pastors not only lacked theological education; they boasted about it. Kevin Vanhoozer and Owen Strachan note how Billy Sunday, famous evangelist of the early twentieth century, famously bragged "that he knew as much about theology as a jackrabbit knows about Ping-Pong." It is not unfair to say that the "church's evangelistic apparatus was strong, but its theological muscles had atrophied due to disuse."[16]

***Relativized forms and relating to culture.*** Perhaps the greatest negative legacy of the frontier tradition is the aforementioned unashamed relativization

---

[14]Quoted in Ross, *Evangelical Versus Liturgical?*, 15.

[15]Bebbington lists conversionism, activism, biblicism, and crucicentrism as the four primary traits. See David W. Bebbington, *Evangelicalism in Modern Britain: A History from the 1730s to the 1980s* (Abingdon, UK: Taylor & Francis Group, 1989), 2-3. To demonstrate that this is not simply a description of British evangelicalism, the National Association of Evangelicals in the United States cites Bebbington to describe what an evangelical is. See National Association of Evangelicals, "What Is an Evangelical?," accessed July 22, 2017, www.nae.net/what-is-an-evangelical/.

[16]Kevin J. Vanhoozer and Owen Strachan, *The Pastor as Public Theologian* (Grand Rapids: Baker Academic, 2015), 90-91.

of forms; any method can be used if it proves to be effective in winning someone to Christ. Thus James White sees the "seeker-sensitive" services of the 1980s and 1990s as the natural fruit of Finney and the frontier tradition. This philosophy has been articulated more recently by megachurch pastor Craig Groeschel, who publicly and regularly claims that he would "do anything short of sin" to win someone to Jesus.[17] At the rise of the seeker-sensitive movement in the mid-1990s, two landmark books written by megachurch pastors sought to define a new approach to church ministry and practice. One is Rick Warren's *The Purpose Driven Church* and the other is Bill and Lynne Hybels's *Rediscovering Church*, both of which were published in 1995.[18] While Warren's book may have been less direct about catering worship services to nonbelievers, Hybels is seen as the founder of the seeker-sensitive movement, and his book functioned as a de facto manifesto for the movement. Each book devotes a portion of its content to a discussion about congregational worship. That same year, Sally Morgenthaler provided worship leaders their own charter on why and how worship could be evangelistic precisely by being worshipful—designed to engage the congregation in glorifying God rather than functioning as warm-up music. Her book, *Worship Evangelism*, in part affirmed the core desire of both Warren's and the Hybels's approaches but also redirected its practice with regard to sung worship. All this focus on worship design with the seeker or unbeliever in mind may have also prompted the writing of a text frequently quoted by worship professors or liturgical scholars to validate their criticisms of contemporary worship: the provocatively titled *Reaching Out Without Dumbing Down*.[19]

The struggle to determine how evangelicalism relates to culture in its effort to "win the lost" has resulted in three approaches, articulated by Mathew Guest as resistance, cultural accommodation, and engaged orthodoxy. Guest shows how each approach emerged in response to Peter Berger's foundational

---

[17]Craig Groeschel, *How Churches and Leaders Can Get It and Keep It* (Grand Rapids: Zondervan, 2008), 93.

[18]Rick Warren, *The Purpose-Driven Church* (Grand Rapids: Zondervan, 1995); Lynne Hybels and Bill Hybels, *Rediscovering Church* (Grand Rapids: Zondervan, 1995).

[19]Sally Morgenthaler, *Worship Evangelism* (Grand Rapids: Zondervan, 1995); Marva Dawn, *Reaching Out Without Dumbing Down: A Theology of Worship for This Urgent Time* (Grand Rapids: Eerdmans, 1995).

work on modernity and religion.[20] Those who understand evangelicalism's
relationship with culture to be shaped by resistance tend to be less enthusi-
astic about contemporary worship because of its adopting of "secular" musical styles. Those who favor more cultural accommodation embrace it. Yet
Guest highlights Christian Smith's work on evangelicalism as "engaged orthodoxy," where there are "clear symbolic boundaries" and also an "orientation
characterized by active engagement with the world," seen in mission projects
and in the daily lives of individual evangelicals. Guest notes that this "process
of accommodation involves a revitalization of evangelical identity."[21] But this
can only be if the core of evangelical identity remains intact. In my view,
contemporary worship is a kind of engaged orthodoxy because of the way it
demonstrates resistance in its lyrical content and accommodation in its musical form. Yet this approach is predicated on the assumed neutrality of forms,
and it is this assumption of the neutrality of forms that the next paradigm
challenges directly.

## WORSHIP AS FORMATION: THE REFORMED PARADIGM

*Formative practices: Human reenactment and divine action.* One of the
strongest critiques of the evangelical paradigm of worship as a form of mission has arisen from contemporary writers in the Reformed tradition. Within
the Reformed paradigm, worship is not simply what the gathered people of
God do; it is what God does by the Spirit through the proclamation of the
gospel. The heart of worship's formative power is its rootedness in and faithfulness to the gospel; thus worship must be "gospel-centered."

A key component of the Reformed understanding of congregational worship is that it is a reenactment of the gospel. Presbyterian pastor Tim Keller
writes that the built-in order of Reformed liturgy in its "foundational rhythm
and flow" is "gospel re-enactment."[22] Moreover, at the center of this gospel

---

[20]For examples of Berger's work, see Peter Berger, *A Rumour of Angels: Modern Society and the Rediscovery of the Supernatural* (London: Penguin, 1969), and Peter Berger, 'The Desecularization of the World. A Global Overview', in *The Desecularization of the World. Essays on the Resurgence of Religion in World Politics*, ed. Peter Berger (Washington, DC: Ethics and Public Policy Centre; Grand Rapids, MA: Eerdmans, 1999), 1-18.

[21]Mathew Guest, *Evangelical Identity and Contemporary Culture: A Congregational Study in Innovation* (Milton Keynes, UK: Paternoster, 2007), 7, 16.

[22]Alan Rathe, *Evangelicals, Worship, and Participation: Taking a Twenty-First Century Reading* (Burlington, VT: Ashgate, 2014), 79.

reenactment is the proclamation of Scripture and the response of the congregation. It is through the Word that God acts in corporate worship.

The lack of gospel reenactment in contemporary worship is a major criticism of the movement. As noted above, Marva Dawn's landmark work, *Reaching Out Without Dumbing Down*, appeared in the same year as books by the Hybels and Warren, who championed versions of a seeker-sensitive approach. Dawn's book was clearly a challenge to their movements. Yet Alan Rathe's appraisal of Dawn's central contributions consists of the twin themes that "God is both subject and object of worship, and a respect for the deeply formative power of corporate worship." Because God is the subject—the active agent—in worship, worshipers can expect to be transformed. But for Dawn, neither God's action nor the worshiper's transformation is a given. A church's worship practices must provide the "proper place and scope" for God's work.[23] Rathe writes:

> Dawn especially stresses this deeply formative power of corporate worship. She understands that power to be, on the one hand, wholly God's. She also recognizes that the practices of the gathered community, especially in connection with worship, are powerfully formative in and of themselves. The structures and elements of worship "subtly influence the kind of people we are becoming." Insofar as God is subject, liturgical practices may either make space for or impede God's work. Insofar as God is the object of worship, liturgical practices may either shape or misshape human spirituality with respect to God.[24]

***You are what you love: James K. A. Smith on worship.*** While many within the Reformed tradition advocate the view of worship as formation, one of the primary proponents of such a view is Christian philosopher James K. A. Smith. As a professor at the Reformed Calvin College, Smith captures the key components of the worship-as-formation perspective by drawing from both the Reformed tradition and the sacramental traditions to show the importance of mystery, story, and beauty in Christian worship as a means of formation.

Smith's argument is threefold: we are what we love; we may not love what we think; and our loves have to be shaped by intentionally God-centered, counterformative practices in Christian worship. Smith's first claim, that we

---

[23]Rathe, *Evangelicals, Worship, and Participation*, 129-30.
[24]Rathe, *Evangelicals, Worship, and Participation*, 130.

are what we love, is rooted in a philosophical anthropology. Smith begins with Edmund Husserl's phenomenology that "consciousness is always consciousness *of*" as opposed to René Descartes's view that a person might just "think." A human is aimed toward something, "*intending* something as an object." As Smith puts it elsewhere, humans are "existential sharks," perpetually moving in order to stay alive.[25] To explain *how* we aim at a particular end, Smith traces Martin Heidegger's debate with Husserl, in which Heidegger argued that humans do not primarily "*think* about a world of objects" but that humans are "*involved* with the world." To push the shark metaphor further, the world is not a picture that we observe from a distance; it is the very sea in which we swim. But the critical move Heidegger makes, the move that shifts the "center of gravity of the human person from the cognitive to the noncognitive," is his argument that "*care* is the most primordial way that we "intend" the world." Summing up the anthropology that emerges from the phenomenology of Husserl and Heidegger, Smith writes, "The point is . . . that the way we inhabit the world is not primarily as thinkers, or even believers, but as more affective, embodied creatures who make our way in the world more by feeling our way around it."[26]

Smith's final piece in forming his first and foundational claim that we are what we love is to bring Husserl and Heidegger in conversation with Augustine, to whom Smith argues Heidegger already owed a large debt. Augustine would refine Heidegger's notion of care or concern by arguing that the "most fundamental way we intend the world is *love*." Thus, Smith writes, "We are essentially and ultimately desiring animals, which is to say that we are essentially and ultimately lovers. To be human is to love, and it is what we love that defines who we are."[27] What we love can be identified as love in this "thick" sense—as opposed to a preference or inclination or weaker desire—by identifying its telos. Drawing from the Greek notion of virtue as being shaped by a particular vision of flourishing, Smith writes that "what we love is a specific vision of the good life, an implicit picture of what we think human flourishing looks like. Love has a *telos*."[28]

---

[25]James K. A. Smith, *You Are What You Love: The Spiritual Power of Habit* (Grand Rapids: Brazos, 2016), 8.

[26]James K. A. Smith, *Desiring the Kingdom: Worship, Worldview, and Cultural Formation* (Grand Rapids: Baker Academic, 2009), 47, 49.

[27]Smith, *Desiring the Kingdom*, 50-51.

[28]Smith, *Desiring the Kingdom*, 52.

This leads us now to Smith's second claim: we may not love what we think. This is true because our loves work below the level of our consciousness, and because our love is being shaped by habits and practices that we do not always recognize as formative. Smith calls these powerful, physical, and habitual practices "liturgies" because they function like a communal ritual that aims our worship at a particular telos. Here Smith relies on Charles Taylor's notion of a social imaginary, which is a way of referring to the "way ordinary people 'imagine' their social surroundings," which is "not expressed in theoretical terms, but is carried in images, stories, and legends." Smith then cross-references Taylor's social imaginary, which creates a dynamic relationship between understanding and practice, with Pierre Bourdieu's "logic of practice."[29] Both Taylor and Bourdieu assert that there is a kind of understanding that is implicit in practice even when that understanding cannot be spelled out. In a fascinating section, Smith outlines the cultural liturgy of the shopping mall, which aims our love at the telos of consumerism, through its architecture and decor, its chapels (stores) with various icons (mannequins) of the life we want, the acolytes (salespeople) who welcome us in, the racks full of tokens and relics (clothes), and the altar (cashier) where our transaction of sacrifice is complete.

Finally, Smith's third claim is that Christian worship is critical because of its potency as a kind of counterformation, recalibrating our heart toward love for God and love for neighbor. Smith argues that the "practices of Christian worship are the analogue of biking around the neighborhood, absorbing an understanding of our environment that is precognitive and becomes inscribed in our adaptive unconscious." Thus the "rhythms and rituals of Christian worship are not the 'expression of' a Christian worldview, but are themselves an 'understanding' simplicity in practice."[30] This forms the basis of Smith's critique of what he calls elsewhere the "expressive" paradigm of Christian worship.[31] Christian worship is not simply an expressive practice; it is fundamentally a formative practice.

Smith rightly asserts in *You Are What You Love* that worship, though entirely embodied, is not "*only* material," and though wholly natural is "never *only* natural." He expounds on this by invoking trinitarian theology, describing

---

[29]Smith, *Desiring the Kingdom*, 65-67.
[30]Smith, *Desiring the Kingdom*, 68-69.
[31]Smith, *You Are What You Love*, 75.

worship as an invitation to "participate in the life of the Triune God." Smith also clarifies what he means by the "'form' of worship" as twofold: the "overall narrative arc of a service of Christian worship," and the "concrete, received practices that constitute elements of that enacted narrative." Smith is in good company by advocating for a particular narrative shape to Christian worship—gathering, Word, Table, sending—which Smith names as "gathering, listening, communing, and sending." The value of both the narrative and the practices for Smith is that they form character and recover beauty. As the worshiper enters the story of God's redemption reenacted in worship, she realizes which character she is to be in the drama and thus is able to develop the character necessary to participate. "Worship that restores our loves will be worship that restor(i)es our imagination," Smith asserts.[32]

***Evaluating Smith's model.*** Though Smith's thesis on the formative nature of what he calls liturgies is more comprehensive than previous models that privilege rationality, his specific conclusions for Christian worship are untested by ethnographic work and therefore lack nuance or differentiation. For example, Smith pays little attention to the particular ways Pentecostal-charismatic worship operates. Smith goes to great lengths to say that contemporary worship, operating out of an expression paradigm, focuses on human activity rather than God's activity. Yet, Pentecostal-charismatic worshipers, as will be evident in my fieldwork on experienced hope, routinely arrive to a worship service with the expectation of God "showing up." Smith casts aspersions on the focus on the presence of God in contemporary worship, suggesting that it is simply a modern iteration of the medieval mistake of gathering to be near the mystical presence. Rather, Smith argues, Christians should come expecting an interaction with God, placing primacy on God's activity over his mere presence. Yet this is precisely the thing Pentecostal-charismatic worshipers expect: God is going to speak, to move, to do something. Mostly, they expect this will take the form of various spiritual gifts—understood as the manifestations of the Holy Spirit.

Another example of Smith's lack of differentiation comes in the way he discusses megachurches. Offering a reflection on the disappearance of confession in contemporary worship, he takes aim at megachurches, stating that

---

[32]Smith, *You Are What You Love*, 70, 78, 94, 96.

the "philosophy of ministry and evangelism behind the mega-church movement was often described as 'seeker sensitive.'"[33] This is certainly an echo of the critique espoused by Marva Dawn and others, but this is only half the story. Many megachurches are far from seeker-sensitive, as I will show in chapter eight.

Smith also misses the sociological data that demonstrates that church movements with "low forms" have high social engagement. If biblical, Christ-centered, Spirit-breathed forms plus faith equals rightly formed loves, and rightly formed loves result in working toward the shalom of the world, then one might expect the highest levels of social engagement to emanate from denominations with forms that most resemble historic Christian worship practices. Conversely, one might expect that worship traditions with "low church" forms, such as Pentecostalism, would be less likely to produce worshipers who are socially engaged.

However, sociologists Donald Miller and Tetsunao Yamamori discovered that "some of the most innovative social programs in the world are being initiated by fast-growing Pentecostal churches." Miller and Yamamori sent four hundred letters to "mission experts, denominational executives, and other informed people" requesting nominations of churches around the world that fit the following criteria: are quickly growing, are located in the developing world, run active social programs that address needs in their communities, and are indigenous movements that are self-supporting and not dependent on outside contributions. Nearly 85 percent of the churches that were nominated were Pentecostal or charismatic. As Miller and Yamamori discovered on their global tour, the relationship between an approach to worship and an engagement in society is not simply a correlation; it is causal. Miller and Yamamori conclude that the "single most important element that empowers Progressive Pentecostals" is "unequivocally" the "energizing experience of worship."[34] They argue that social ministry work, because

---

[33]Smith, *You Are What You Love*, 103.

[34]Donald E. Miller and Tetsunao Yamamori, *Global Pentecostalism: The New Face of Christian Social Engagement* (Berkeley: University of California Press, 2007), 5-6, 221. They define progressive Pentecostals as "Christians who claim to be inspired by the Holy Spirit and the life of Jesus and seek to holistically address the spiritual, physical, and social needs of people in their community. Typically, they are distinguished by their warm and expressive worship, their focus on lay-oriented ministry, their compassionate service to others, and their attention, both as individuals and as a

of its difficulty and potential to drain an individual's energy, requires hope and a spirit of joy, both of which are found in worship for Pentecostals.

> For Pentecostals, worship provides the opportunity to experience an alternative realty. It is a moment when mind and body can potentially connect; it is a space in which worshippers imagine impossible possibilities; it is a time when they are filled with new hope and desire for a better world. The challenge is to channel these emotions, these feelings, these desires. And that is where teaching and preaching enter, they say. But it is also where potentially mysterious encounters happen. It is where, according to Pentecostals, the Holy Spirit speaks to them about their duties as Christians. . . . The key, however, as our respondents have told us, is to have daily periods of renewal in personal prayer. It is in these moments of meditation and prayerful reflection over scripture that they realize that if the work is going to go forward, it will not be on the basis of their personal strength alone.[35]

Smith's work would do well to interact with such sociological research.

Nevertheless, the contribution of this paradigm of worship as formation is that it reminds us that worship practices are not merely expressive. It invites us to reflect on the kind of person we are becoming as a result of these practices. More specifically, it asks what kind of Christian we are becoming. By examining what sort of view of God and the gospel we are embracing, implicitly or explicitly, in our worship practices, we can become more attentive to our spiritual formation or de-formation, as the case may be.

## WORSHIP AS ENCOUNTER: THE PENTECOSTAL-CHARISMATIC PARADIGM

*Tracking a global phenomenon.* The third paradigm is of worship as encounter. This paradigm seems to be at work in Pentecostal and charismatic Christians in worship. It is estimated that there are about five hundred million Pentecostal Christians in the world today, which accounts for roughly 25

---

worshipping community, to what they perceive to be the leading of the Holy Spirit" (*Global Pentecostalism*, 2-3). Miller and Yamamori notably exclude from their definition Pentecostals who are aligned with "right-wing repressive governments," who focus exclusively on faith healing or "health and wealth" without connecting their Christian faith to socially beneficial programs for their community," and who "emphasize conversion as their only mission to the community" (*Global Pentecostalism*, 2).

[35]Miller and Yamamori, *Global Pentecostalism*, 221-22.

percent of the world's Christians.[36] Pew Foundation's 2006 report marked Pentecostals and charismatic "renewalists" as 28 percent of US Protestants and 23 percent of the total US populations. One of the most prominent features of Pentecostal spirituality is its music. Yet, as noted in an earlier chapter, Pentecostalism is responsible for exporting its particular approach to music beyond the boundaries of its own theology. These songs and practices may be Pentecostalism's most successful global export; they have been "adopted, adapted, or resisted by Christians in a variety of local communities within and outside pentecostalism." Congregational music scholar Monique Ingalls notes, "Moving along pathways formed by mass mediation, migration, and missionization, pentecostal music and worship evidence and spur on religious globalization, as songs from influential pentecostal churches—and the record companies and media industry to which they are often intimately connected—make their way into in churches across denominational lines."[37]

It has become common practice to mark the history of Pentecostalism in three waves: classical Pentecostals, charismatics, and neo-charismatics (or "Third Wave"). Classical Pentecostalism is generally thought to have begun in 1901 in Topeka, Kansas, through the ministry of Charles P. Parham.[38] But the spark was fanned into flame in the Azusa Street revival in Los Angeles from 1906 to 1909, led by William Seymour. The charismatic movement began as a renewal movement among mainline denominations in the 1960s. It draws its name from the Greek work for "gift," *charism*, and was evidenced by various spiritual gifts, such as healings, miracles, and even the one most associated with Pentecostalism—speaking in tongues. The renewal movement began first with Episcopalians and caught on among other Protestant denominations. Renewal movements with similar phenomena also occurred in Catholic and Orthodox churches. While classical Pentecostals sought to differentiate from culture, charismatics tended to focus more on the supernatural while being affirming of culture in general.[39] This may have contributed to the ease of charismatics adopting musical forms from the culture of their day, since, as noted above, the praise and worship movement began in the 1960s, the same decade as the charismatic renewal.

---

[36]Ingalls, *Spirit of Praise*, loc. 77.
[37]Rathe, *Evangelicals, Worship, and Participation*, 9.
[38]Rathe, *Evangelicals, Worship, and Participation*, 246.
[39]Rathe, *Evangelicals, Worship, and Participation*, 246.

The Third Wave is sometimes called the neo-charismatic movement and is the hardest to place boundary markers on. Rather than a unified movement, it is a general category for the "18,810 independent, indigenous, post denominational denominations and groups that cannot be classified as either pentecostal or charismatic but share a common emphasis on the Holy Spirit, spiritual gifts, pentecostal-like experiences . . . signs and wonders, and power encounters."[40] Ingalls uses the term "'pentecostal-charismatic' to invoke the constellation of twentieth- and twenty-first-century Christian renewal movements that are related to one another as part of a transnational social network connected by shared beliefs and practices—of which music is, of course, key." While recognizing their contingence, the music and worship practices described as Pentecostal-charismatic share an emphasis for Ingalls on "the presence, work, and gifts of the Holy Spirit as manifest in glossolalia, healing, ecstatic worship practices, and prophecy."[41] This emphasis on the presence and activity of the Spirit portrays a God who is different from humans without being distant from them; it maintains transcendence while adding a "vital role for personal experience and spirituality."[42]

Music is such a key element of the Third Wave or Pentecostal-charismatic movements that Ingalls argues that "pentecostal-charismatic Christianity in the early twenty-first century is inseparable from its unique practices of music and worship." In the introduction to the landmark volume *Spirit of Praise*, on "music and worship in global pentecostal-charismatic Christianity," Ingalls writes:

> Corporate worship and music making are important ways in which this broad religious network constitutes itself, represents and replicates its values, and transforms the sociocultural, religious, and economic spheres that its members inhabit. As such, music is an essential lens through which to view pentecostal-charismatic movement's growth, ethos, and identity, and a full understanding of this important Christian modality requires close attention to its songs and patterns of worship.[43]

As crucial as music is in Pentecostal-charismatic contexts, it did not remain in those settings. The exporting of charismatic worship began from a group

---

[40]Rathe, *Evangelicals, Worship, and Participation*, 247.
[41]Ingalls, *Spirit of Praise*, loc. 124.
[42]Alan Aldrige, *Religion in the Contemporary World* (Cambridge, UK: Polity, 2007), 130.
[43]Ingalls, *Spirit of Praise*, locs. 476–77.

of affiliated churches within the Third Wave: the Vineyard movement, which began in California with John Wimber and has since spread around the world. Known as much for its music as for its message, the Vineyard movement was the frontrunner in spreading its renewal through charismatic-styled worship beyond its own movement. Thus, churches that do not share the history or confessional theology of the Pentecostal or charismatic movements have nevertheless imported a paradigm for worship that was shaped by these movements. Contemporary worship—whether the churches who employ it realize it or not—has a "Pentecostal genetic code."[44] This export of charismatic worship has only accelerated with changes in recording, production, and distribution technology. Combine these technological advances with global migration patterns and Pentecostalism's knack for connecting with "people on the move," and the charismatic worship paradigm becomes something of a global brand.[45] Ingalls writes:

> Migration and mobility ensure that worshipping bodies remain a powerful medium of transport for music and worship practices; likewise, through a "secondary orality" (Ong [1982] 1988) brought about by new electronic media technologies, audiovisual media networks increasingly comprise the main conduits along which pentecostal music, songs, and worship practices travel. Internet-based digital media players, stores, and platforms have enabled musical materials and practices to travel not only between pentecostal-charismatic communities but also increasingly among international and interdenominational networks.[46]

*The sacramentality of Pentecostal praise and worship.* Since the Pentecostal-charismatic paradigm of congregational worship has been adopted beyond those contexts, we must examine this paradigm more closely. Because the Eucharist has historically been the central focus of God's presence in Christian worship, and because the Pentecostal approach to praise

---

[44]Lim and Ruth, *Lovin' On Jesus*, 123.

[45]An essay in *The Economist* explores how "charismatic Christianity thrives among people on the move" and concludes that "wherever people are on the move, and are culturally receptive to Christianity in some form, charismatic religion will surely follow." See "Ecstasy and Exodus: Charismatic Christianity Thrives Among People on the Move," *The Economist*, January 23, 2016, www.economist.com/international/2016/01/23/ecstasy-and-exodus/.

[46]Ingalls, *Spirit of Praise*, loc. 158.

and worship places the presence of God as the goal and center of its practice, Lim and Ruth explore what other dimensions of the Eucharist as a sacrament may be found in a Pentecostal paradigm of worship.[47] They find at least five corresponding elements.

First, Pentecostal paradigms of praise and worship emphasize the notion of sacrifice in the act of praising God. This theme can be further parsed out in four particular strands. The Latter Rain revival, which was influential in making praise an emphasis among Pentecostals and charismatics in the late twentieth century, portrayed the sacrifice of praise as "the focused, intense, and extensive periods of corporate praising, spoken and sung." Other teachers emphasized the obedience involved in the act of praise—making praise an act of the will rather than the fruit of one's feelings. Another strand of the sacrificial dimension of praise underscored the costliness of a sacrifice, which in praise and worship meant that the worshiper was to offer God praise even in the face of "distress, grief, or great trouble."[48] One final subtheme in the sacrificial dimension is the effort to associate praise and worship with the tabernacle of David—rather than any temple—because of its lack of animal sacrifices. The link is often then further made to worshipers offering themselves as living sacrifices before God (see Rom 12:1-2).

Second, Pentecostal paradigms of praise and worship share the notion of "confidence in its instrumental effectiveness." Lim and Ruth use this phrase simply to mean that just as the Eucharist is believed to "achieve what it symbolizes," so "praise and worship thinkers" have a similar sort of confidence that when "God's people praise, God will be present." They compare the confidence of the instrumental effectiveness of the Eucharist as manifest in the scholastics of the late Middle Ages with the Pentecostal confidence in praise and worship's instrumentality as manifest in the book titles and statements in the 1980s and 1990s. They give a few samples: "*God's Presence through Music*, 'praise and worship is one of the simplest forms of entrance into the presence of God,' and a job search that stated that the church was looking for someone who could 'make God present through music.'"[49] This paradigm derives most often from a reading of Psalm 22:3 as a divine promise and thus an implicit pattern for congregational worship.

---

[47]Lim and Ruth, *Lovin' On Jesus*, 132.

[48]Lim and Ruth, *Lovin' On Jesus*, 132.

[49]Lim and Ruth, *Lovin' On Jesus*, 134.

Third, Pentecostal paradigms of praise and worship have an "anamnetic" quality, which is one the sacramental dimensions of the Eucharist. The Eucharist is done "in remembrance" of Christ, the biblical phrase in which the Greek word *anamnēsis* appears. In the 1970s, many Pentecostal preachers and teachers began to distinguish praise from worship. While worship was the "direct adoration of the person of God," praise "was about remembering God's nature and activity, past and present, honoring him on that basis."[50]

Fourth, Pentecostal paradigms of praise and worship also had an epicletic dimension. Here Lim and Ruth are referring to the invitation of the Spirit over the elements of bread and wine in the Eucharist, known as the epiclesis. Ruth draws on his expertise as a historian as he demonstrates the prominence of an invitation for God to come in contemporary praise and worship:

> Throughout contemporary worship's history there has been a strong desire (and expectation) that God would come, both in terms of Christ's return and, especially, of God's arrival in corporate worship. The name of one of the original music companies (Maranatha! Music, which means "Come, Lord" in first-century Aramaic) verbalized this dimension.
>
> But the real evidence of the epicletic, sacramental quality of contemporary worship is how common the petitioning in song of God (or Jesus or the Spirit) to come in worship. *Come* is one of the most used verbs in the lyrics of contemporary worship songs. Among the most popular songs, it stands equal with *save* as the most common divine actions.[51]

Finally, Lim and Ruth note that music—beyond just the Pentecostal paradigm of music—shares a sacramental dimension with not only the Eucharist but also with baptism: its ability to create a sense of unity. This is particularly evident in the way one discerns whether one belongs in a particular church based on its style of worship. "The style gathers, joins together, and excludes those who have not accepted the style." This is also seen in how churches that employ a multisite model typically choose to stream only the sermon and not the music.[52]

These various dimensions of sacramentality are not always present in every church that embraces and employs contemporary worship. Even where

---

[50]Lim and Ruth, *Lovin' On Jesus*, 136.
[51]Lim and Ruth, *Lovin' On Jesus*, 137.
[52]Lim and Ruth, *Lovin' On Jesus*, 138.

churches incorporate songs that were written in Pentecostal or charismatic contexts—such as Hillsong or Bethel—they may not import the underlying paradigms or encoded theology of those contexts. These sacramental dimensions are much more likely to be the animating theology in Pentecostal-charismatic contexts of praise and worship.[53]

***Personhood and presence.*** Lim and Ruth's delineation of various sacramental dimensions in the Pentecostal paradigm of praise and worship is helpful. Yet the use of a sacramental paradigm to explain a Pentecostal one is questionable because *sacrament* is a term alien to Pentecostalism. It is being imported and superimposed over Pentecostal practice to make sense of it. This raises the question of whether it is being imported because liturgical theology is the dominant frame of liturgical scholars or because liturgical theology is perceived to be the "correct" paradigm and because Pentecostalism needs legitimating.

Second, if one were to listen to Pentecostals or charismatics themselves explain their own paradigm, the language is deeply personal. "Encounter" is not framed sacramentally; it is framed personally. Even the notion of the presence of God is not used with all the conscious context of Eucharistic theology or the sacramental concept of real presence. It is used as a way of referring to a person being present with another person.

I suggest that to understand this paradigm of encounter we turn not to a theology of the Eucharist but to theories of personhood. Alistair McFayden, in his foundational work on personhood, argues that a person is "formed through social interaction, through address and response." In fact, a "dialogical understanding of personhood" is based on the premise "that we are what we are in ourselves only through relation to others."[54] To be a person is to be in relation to another—specifically, to another who sees you as a person. Jewish philosopher Martin Buber famously used the phrase "I-You" in contrast with "I-It" to show a sacred relation. For Buber, to fail to treat another human as a Thou is to do that person a great injustice; it is to treat a person as an object. A person only "becomes an I through a You."[55]

---

[53]Lim and Ruth, *Lovin' On Jesus*, 138-39.

[54]Alistair McFayden, *The Call to Personhood: A Christian Theory of the Individual in Social Relationships* (Cambridge, UK: Cambridge University Press, 1990), 9.

[55]Martin Buber, *I And Thou: A New Translation with a Prologue "I and You" and Notes*, trans. Walter Kaufmann (New York: Simon & Schuster, 1996), 63, 80.

Praise and worship, for the Pentecostal-charismatic, is an I-You encounter; the human, the collective I, meets the divine You in song and prayer. Though the notion of a "personal relationship with God" is tainted by American individualism and frontier-revival conversionism, Pentecostal-charismatics do not see the need to legitimate this approach via comparisons with what they might see as human traditions such as formal eucharistic theology. Thus, to expound on a paradigm of personal encounter, Pentecostal-charismatic teachers do not go to the Reformers or the Scholastics or even to the patristics; they go to Scripture. In Genesis, they find God walking in the garden in the cool of the day with Adam, and God speaking with Abraham as one speaks with a friend; in the Psalms they find deeply personal, guttural prayers; in John's Gospel, they find a Jesus who has many personal conversations that become life-changing encounters—including one with a Samaritan woman in which Jesus talks about worship and worshipers; and they find in the book of Acts an outpouring of the Holy Spirit that allows people to hear the gospel in their own tongue—a profoundly intimate experience. In Paul's letters to the Corinthians and the Ephesians, they find the Spirit's work in expressing *charismata*, gifts for the edification of the gathered church (1 Cor 12; 14). A reading of Ephesians 5:18-19 would even suggest that one of the ways that believers are renewed in their experience of the Spirit is through "songs, hymns, and spiritual songs."[56]

In Pentecostal-charismatic practice, the worship set list is designed to facilitate a journey to an encounter, not simply a musical flow. Vineyard leader John Wimber, along with one of the worship leaders, Eddie Espinoza, developed a five-stage pattern of forming set lists. It began with an invitation, then led to engagement, then intimacy, then visitation, and concluded with the "giving of substance."[57] For Pentecostal-charismatics, the presence of God means the activity of God; one knows or senses God's presence in a service by God's activity within it. Thus, I suggest that the paradigm of encounter—which arises from an understanding of personhood and relationships—is endemic to Pentecostalism, while the notion of sacramentality is alien.

---

[56]The CEB renders these verses with its imperative verb and accompanying participles this way: "Don't get drunk on wine, which produces depravity. Instead, be filled with the Spirit in the following ways: speak to each other with psalms, hymns, and spiritual songs; sing and make music to the Lord in your hearts." Gordon Fee argues that the experience of the Spirit has a "renewable" dimension. See *Paul, the Spirit, and the People of God* (Grand Rapids: Baker Academic, 1996), 202.

[57]Lim and Ruth, *Lovin' On Jesus*, 130.

Worship as encounter will feature most notably in my fieldwork with the charismatic church, seen in chapter eight. But it will also resurface as we explore why the experience of hope in both churches might have been different than one might expect given the lyrical content of the songs. Without giving too much away here, *something happens* when Christians gather in worship—and it is more than what words can say, even if those words are sung.

## CONCLUSION

Contemporary worship has emerged from two impulses: one evangelistic and the other charismatic. One root system is the motivation to reach the unchurched or unsaved; the other is the belief that God is present when the people of God gather in Jesus' name. The history of the movement—or movements—reveals three ways of understanding the purpose for the gathered church. The paradigms of mission, formation, and encounter each tilt the gathering in different ways. To focus on mission tips the focus of corporate worship *outward* toward the seeker or the lost. To focus on formation is to prioritize the *inward* power of words and practices to shape us as disciples. To focus on encounter is to orient *upward* toward a meeting with the living God.

Each paradigm can be defended from Scripture; each could find antecedents from church history. Yet each paradigm is also incomplete. As demonstrated in particular with the mission and formation paradigms above, when a particular way of approaching congregational worship is emphasized to the exclusion of the others, distortions occur and dangers abound. This is not the place to adequately grapple with how to hold the best contributions of each paradigm in a kind of generative tension with one another. For now it is sufficient to name these paradigms and their key proponents, along with weaknesses in their outlook, as a backdrop for the two congregations featured in the fieldwork found in chapters six, seven, and eight. Both are evangelical and thus have been influenced by the mission paradigm; one is Presbyterian and therefore leans toward the formation paradigm; and one is Pentecostal-charismatic and operates from an encounter paradigm.

But before turning to these congregations, we must spend some time clarifying what I mean by *hope*. We will employ several models to help: some nontheological, some theological; some historic, some contemporary.

# PART 2

# HOPE AND ESCHATOLOGY

# 3

# WHAT IS HOPE?

## EXPLORING VARIOUS MODELS OF HOPE

WHAT IS HOPE? How are we to define it or measure it? This chapter will focus on psychological, sociological, and philosophical perspectives on hope. Because of the scope of perspectives, I am limiting my exploration of each to one or two voices. These voices are not meant to be fully representative of their discipline's contribution to the study of hope but rather of the contributions that are relevant to my study. It must also be noted that these models are not analyses of different components of hope, as though hope could be disassembled or dissected. I take as a premise that these models are simply perspectives of an idea, not compartments of a machine. As such, there is sure to be overlap between these perspectives. For example, emotions—specifically, hopeful feelings—are a point of reflection from both the psychological and philosophical perspectives, to say nothing about their more obvious role in a phenomenological perspective. The first perspective we will explore is a *cognitive* model, which helps us to explore hope as a "positive motivational state."[1] The second is an *affective* model, which allows us to examine hope as an emotional experience. Third, the model of *virtue ethics* shows what it takes to develop the character of hope. Finally, a *phenomenological* model identifies the structural elements of the act of hoping.

## THE COGNITIVE MODEL: HOPE AS A STATE

A cognitive model of hope views hope as a state of mind based on a positive appraisal of one's own power and plan in a given situation. Psychologist

---

[1]Quoted in Andrew J. Stobbart, "Towards a Model of Christian Hope: Developing Snyder's Hope Theory for Christian Ministry," *Theology and Ministry*, 1, no. 7 (2012): 3.

Charles Snyder constructed a cognitive model of hope as the result of agency and pathway: "Hope is defined as the perceived capability to derive pathways to desired goals, and motivate oneself via agency thinking to use those pathways."[2] Snyder has alternatively described agency and pathway as willpower and "way power," respectively. In those terms, hope is "the sum of the mental willpower and way power that you have for your goals."[3]

Snyder and a team of other researchers used this cognitive model of hope to construct the Adult Hope Scale. The scale employs a twelve-part questionnaire, with each question answered on an eight-point scale, from definitely false to definitely true. Four of the questions are related to agency ("goal-directed energy"), four of the questions are related to pathway ("planning to accomplish the goals"), and four of the questions are fillers.[4] This is an attempt to quantify hope along two axes to be able to measure how much hope one possesses. While the scale itself may be questionable, the identification of hope as the confluence of agency and pathway is a significant contribution.

One critique of Snyder's model is that "laypeople do not usually include pathways thinking in their understanding of hope." For example, in research conducted by Eddie Tong and colleagues involving four empirical studies, laypeople connected hope only with agency. Snyder agrees that agency has primacy in producing hope. Yet, pathway as a dimension of hope shifts hope from being seen only as affective to also being cognitive. Hope as way power is the "mental capacity we can call on to find one or more effective ways to reach our goals," or "the perception that one can engage in planful thought."[5]

The challenge with Snyder's model is that it has little to say about the grounds or basis for hope. Whether one has any basis for one's confidence in one's own agency seems to be inconsequential. One's appraisal of agency may be inaccurate, and one's plan or pathway may be flawed, but if one believes agency and pathway are present, hope may abound. Consider, for example the four questions on Snyder's Adult Hope Scale related to agency:

---

[2]C. R. Snyder, "Hope Theory: Rainbows in the Mind," *Psychological Inquiry* 13, no. 4 (2001): 249.
[3]Stobbart, "Towards a Model of Christian Hope," 3.
[4]C. R. Snyder, "Adult Hope Scale," 2017, https://ppc.sas.upenn.edu/resources/questionnaires-researchers /adult-hope-scale.
[5]Stobbart, "Towards a Model of Christian Hope," 3, 5.

+ I energetically pursue my goals.
+ My past experiences have prepared me well for my future.
+ I've been pretty successful in life.
+ I meet the goals that I set for myself.

The last two contain some element of objectivity, or a measurable reference, but they still rely on one's own appraisal of things. The four questions on the Adult Hope Scale related to pathway seem to require an even more subjective self-appraisal:

+ I can think of many ways to get out of a jam.
+ There are lots of ways around any problem.
+ I can think of many ways to get the things in life that are important to me.
+ Even when others get discouraged, I know I can find a way to solve the problem.

From a Christian perspective, the reliance on self-appraisal with relatively little attention to the grounds or basis for hope makes Snyder's model of hope indistinguishable from optimism. Snyder may argue that optimism is merely a wish for something over which one has no control. But there are certainly other forms of optimism that result in a positive appraisal of one's own agency and "planful thought" that does not correspond to reality. A Christian would also want to ask *whose* agency and *whose* pathway—God's or ours—matters in an appraisal of a given situation.

## THE AFFECTIVE MODEL: HOPE AS AN EMOTIONAL EXPERIENCE

The affective model views hope as an experience of a positive emotion. Hope is not, strictly speaking, an emotion, but it does have an emotional dimension; it can be experienced as a feeling. Because my research will explore this experiential dimension of hope within congregational worship, it is helpful to note a few things about emotions in general before looking at hopeful feelings.

Philosopher Bob Roberts writes that emotions are a "concern-based construal," a way of perceiving the world rooted in the concerns one has.[6] Roberts

---

[6]Robert C. Roberts, *Spiritual Emotions: A Psychology of Christian Virtues* (Grand Rapids: Eerdmans, 2007), 11.

adds that emotions have "perceptual immediacy"—they arise prereflectively. Psychologist Paul Ekman attributes this to brain functions that he calls autoappraisers. It must be noted, however, that emotions do not only arise prereflectively. After more than four decades of study on emotions, Ekman lists nine paths for accessing or turning on our emotions, eight which are additional to autoappraisers: a reflective appraisal, a memory of a past emotional experience, imagination, talking about a past emotional event, empathy, being instructed by others about what to be emotional about, social norms being violated, and assuming the experience of emotion.[7] Many of these complex triggers of emotion will be part of the discourse analysis in my fieldwork focus groups, which I will explore in chapter eight. As a construal or perception, emotions also represent a particular interpretation of a scenario. As interpretative perceptions, emotions help make sense of a situation. Finally, because emotions arise from a concern (in Roberts's language) or "something important to our welfare" (in Ekman's phrase) emotions contain a motivational power.

Optimism, though not strictly an emotion, is related to emotions in a specific way. Christopher Peterson, an expert on optimism, posits that optimism is "an attitude about the likelihood of experiencing enjoyable emotions." In a description that is resonant with Snyder's cognitive model of hope as agency and pathway, Ekman notes that optimism is "found in people who have more enjoyment in their lives, greater perseverance, and higher achievements." This seems to confirm my suspicion that what Snyder calls hope relies quite heavily on what may be properly named as optimism— a positive appraisal of one's own power and plan. Peterson suggests that optimism results in desired outcomes because it "produces a general state of vigor and resilience."[8]

A Christian view of hope would press further questions: Where does optimism come from? Why do some people have more of it than others? Peterson's hypothesis is that optimism "may be a biologically given tendency, filled in by culture with a socially acceptable content," but that would be inadequate for a Christian.[9]

---

[7]Paul Ekman, *Emotions Revealed*, 2nd ed. (New York: St. Martin's, 2003), 37, 74.
[8]Ekman, *Emotions Revealed*, 37.
[9]Ekman, *Emotions Revealed*, 37.

## THE VIRTUE-ETHICS MODEL: HOPE AS A VIRTUE

The virtue-ethics model of hope constructs hope neither as a state, nor as an emotion, nor the anticipation of an emotion; instead, hope is a virtue to be cultivated. Unlike Snyder, Roberts, operating from a Christian theological framework, makes a point to distinguish hope from optimism. Optimism may lead to a propensity to hope, but it does not in itself rest on any reason for hope. "A pre-reflective optimism built into us, and deeply confirmed by a happy childhood, gives us resiliency in the midst of suffering and a tendency to hope in the face of dismal prospects. It is not built on any actual calculation of prospects or even the most cursory reckoning with actual possibilities." For Roberts, a goal of Christian formation is to transform a base optimism into "the solid emotion-virtue of an eternal hope."[10]

How does the transformation from the experience of optimism to the virtue of hope occur? If emotions are episodic states, lasting at times for seconds, and at other times for much longer, passion is "an orienting, integrating kind of concern." Passion gives a person's life a center and can "integrate and focus the personality and give a person 'character,'" and therefore is "a concern that defines one's psychological identity." If emotions are rooted in concerns, some concerns are deep enough to be named passions. And if passions are "master concerns that deeply characterize a person," then some emotional experiences may be the expression of character.[11] To put it another way, the feeling of *optimism* may arise as an experience of emotion, but the feeling of *hopefulness* has to emerge from a deeper passion.

In order for emotion to develop into a passion, in order for hope to be not just an experience but a character trait, "it has to be characterized by 'endurance' . . . by the ability to feel the emotion even in situations that don't seem very propitious for it." As a Christian philosopher, Roberts believes that hope moves from an optimistic emotion to a virtue or character trait through the endurance of suffering. Roberts grounds his view in Romans 5: "suffering produces endurance, and endurance produces character, and character produces hope" (Rom 5:3-4). For Roberts, it is not so much a particular kind of suffering that does this, but rather what we do with the suffering that allows

---

[10]Roberts, *Spiritual Emotions*, 159.
[11]Roberts, *Spiritual Emotions*, 17, 20.

it to teach us hope. Though we are tempted to either wallow in suffering or to flee it, we can welcome suffering as an ally, allowing it to remind us that the world as it stands is not our home. Suffering ought not make us despise the prospects of hope in this life; and yet, it can teach us not to put our deepest heart into prospects that are bound only to this life. The advantages of this kind of Christian hope for Roberts are threefold: one is "capable of an honest joy in life," since one has a real hope that transcends all finite hopes; one has a better prospect of detaching oneself from finite hopes; and one is able to be less wary of one's finite hopes and can instead gratefully receive the happy prospects that come from this earthly life from the hand of God.[12]

Yet while the object of Christian hope is eternal and fixed, the experience of hope often fluctuates, "shifting with circumstances and our moods," or, as Roberts quips, "with the company we keep and the books we happen to be reading." It is helpful to note briefly here that moods, like bodily sensations, cannot be justified or unjustified; they not subject to rational adjudications. Moods may have causes, but they do not have reasons. This is because moods do not have objects. Thus, when it comes to hope, "being in an optimistic mood is not the same as hoping."[13] Hope, then, for the Christian must be fixed on a particular object. The virtue-ethics model, particularly as employed by a Christian philosopher, gets us closer to the mark. But on its own, it still leaves several questions about the object and grounds of hope unanswered.

## THE PHENOMENOLOGICAL MODEL: HOPE AS AN ACT

A phenomenological model of hope focuses on the act of hoping itself. Christian philosopher James K. A. Smith examines hope as a way of "'intending' the future." Since "consciousness is intentional," "the object intended is constituted by the ego," by which he means that the ego makes sense or gives meaning to experience. Moreover, the "process of constitution can only happen within the horizons of constitution, which provide the context within which I 'make sense' of what is before me."[14]

Within this perspective, there are five key structural elements of hope. There is a *hoper*, a subject who hopes. There is an *object*, that which is hoped

---

[12]Roberts, *Spiritual Emotions*, 19, 152.
[13]Roberts, *Spiritual Emotions*, 155, 159.
[14]James K. A. Smith, "Determined Hope: A Phenomenology of Christian Expectation," in *The Future of Hope*, ed. Miroslav Volf and William Katerberg (Grand Rapids: Eerdmans, 2004), 206.

for. Here Smith clarifies that it is only hope if the object is good, for that which is in the future and bad is feared. Third, there is the actual *act* of hope—not an act from hope or out of hope or in hope, but the very act of consciousness that is hope. This flows from Husserl's description of a cogitation as an intentional act. Fourth, there is a *ground* of hope, a basis for hoping. Finally, there is the *fulfillment* of hope. For Smith, if any of the above elements of hope are missing, it is not really hope, though it would still be a way of intending the future such as wishful thinking, fear, or even anxiety.[15]

***Critiquing hope in modernity.*** This structural framework becomes the premise for a critique of modernity and postmodernity. Smith, working with Charles Taylor's sweeping analysis of how the "secular age" emerged, hypothesizes that in modernity, the *object* of hope has not changed—or at least has not radically changed—but the *ground* of hope has. Yet, the *object* of hope did change in a few key ways, most notably with regard to space and time. Smith includes the *when* (time) of hope as a sort of subset of the *what* (object) of hope. But this may downplay the change of the "locus of [hope's] arrival" in the eighteenth and nineteenth centuries in Europe and North America from "eternity to future time." This change in timing has necessarily included a change in focus. The shift away from eternity has meant an accompanying shift away from divine favor. Human action is no longer concerned with gaining favor from "God" but rather with planning for the "happiness of future generations." Only God can secure a desired eternity; but human agency and pathway (Snyder) can secure a desired future. Modernity also modified the space in which this hope will occur. Smith includes the *where* (space) in his structural nomenclature of the *object* of hope. While it has conceptual coherence, such a move risks obscuring the significance of this shift. "What modernity hopes for carries on the tradition of Christian expectation, but it diverges from that tradition of Christian expectation . . . with respect to where those hopes will be realized or fulfilled." Modernity has the same general "what," but not the same "where" and "when" of Christian expectation. Smith, employing Charles Taylor's language about our secular age, describes this as an "'immanentization' of the locus/object of hope' to a 'this-worlds utopia.'"[16]

---

[15]Smith, "Determined Hope," 207-10.
[16]Smith, "Determined Hope," 211-12.

Nevertheless, Smith sees the most notable difference between modern, secular eschatology and Christian hope as the immanentization of the ground of hope. The ground of modern hope is not transcendent. Modern hope arises from human self-sufficiency to fulfill one's own hopes. This is demonstrated in Snyder's psychological perspective of hope as way power and willpower.

**Critiquing hope in postmodernity.** If postmodernism represents at least in part the crumbling of modernity and with it its sense of optimism, then hope seems to be going out of fashion. Out of the wasteland emerge Richard Rorty and Jacques Derrida in order to help humanity not to lose hope. Yet both are critical of Christian hope. Rorty sees the New Testament as promoting an otherworldly hope that leads one to acquiesce to social conditions in the present. Derrida views Christian hope as politically violent because of its determination of a particular vision of justice.[17]

Smith finds both Rorty's and Derrida's attempts to rescue hope inadequate. In his critique of Rorty, Smith contends that hope, as opposed to wishful thinking, must have some ground, and that ground must bear some proportionality to the object of hope. Rorty's hope is often without ground, even admitting that there are valid reasons for "historical pessimism."[18] Smith then argues that Derrida's object of hope is ill-defined and thus the very act of hoping is uncertain. Derrida wants a hope that is "undetermined," since, in his view, determination is a form of violence because to define what it is must by default define what it is not, and therefore enact the violence of exclusion. What is hoped for is a sort of existential eschatology that is messianic without religion or messianism. But Smith rejects Derrida's premise that determination is a form of violence. For Smith, a completely indeterminate hope is not hope. Though hope need not have absolute determinacy, it must have a degree of determinacy in order to be hope. In fact, even Derrida's hope contains too much determinacy by his own theoretical standards. Thus, for Smith, Derrida's horizon-less hope is a philosophical impossibility. Even the wholly other must appear within the horizon of our experience or it cannot be awaited or hoped for.

**The structural elements of Christian expectation.** What would it look like to plot out the shape of Christian expectation along the five structural elements

---

[17]Smith, "Determined Hope," 204.
[18]Smith, "Determined Hope," 216.

in Smith's paradigm of hope? Smith offers a sketch. First, the hoper in Christian hope is the Christian community, not merely the individual. Thus the gathered church hopes together. Second, the act of hope is done by waiting expectantly, impatiently, anxiously, and eagerly.[19] Here Smith notes that it is hope that is a virtue, not merely the act of waiting. This is consonant with Roberts's arguments above that, for the Christian, hope is not simply a feeling, or, in this case, even a one-time act.

Third, for Smith the object of Christian hope is a kind of justice that is "continuous with the present order" (God will redeem creation) and discontinuous (current structures will be revolutionized). In order to fill out the content of the object of hope, Smith directs readers to Jürgen Moltmann's *Coming of God*, to which we shall turn shortly. For now, we note that Smith counts it important that while there is a "degree of determinacy," there is also a necessary "*lack* of specificity." A blend of vision and mystery is needed to help Christians "reject the myth of progress in favor of the narrative of grace."[20] To believe in grace is to be open to new possibilities of what God will do. It must embrace both transcendence and immanence while being opposed to immanentization as seen in modern eschatologies.

Fourth, the ground of hope is the revelation of God in Christ, which reveals the "faithfulness of God to his creation, his identification with the struggles of creation, and his power and providence to bring about its restoration." Smith contends that all hope, even that of modernity, rests on faith—a belief in something. Christian eschatology argues that God is the only hope. This represents both a "scandal and good news."[21] Smith adds little to the fifth element, as it is simply the fulfillment of that for which one hoped.

## CONCLUSION AND CONNECTIONS

This chapter has outlined four models that provide a textured understanding to hope. The cognitive model identifies hope as a positive motivational state based on a favorable appraisal of both agency and pathway. The affective model demonstrates how hopeful feelings arise. The virtue-ethics model forms connections between emotion and character, allowing hope to become

---

[19]Smith, "Determined Hope," 224.
[20]Smith, "Determined Hope," 225-26.
[21]Smith, "Determined Hope," 226-27.

a habit. Finally, the phenomenological model provides a structural analysis of hope in terms of its subject, object, grounds, and act.

Each of these models offers a fruitful framework for my research. Snyder's description of hope as agency and pathway shaped my focus group interviews and the survey I developed. As will become evident in later chapters, the sense of divine versus human agency, and therefore a divine versus human pathway or plan, was a key element in the experience of hope in worship. The emotional dimension of hope provided a way to explore the experience of congregational worship. From my own participant observation and in my focus groups, I note the aesthetic elements of services in chapter eight, specifically the musical elements.[22] Conformity to and deviation from "feeling rules" (Arlie Hochschild) are also a key part of the discourse analysis in chapter eight. The perspective of hope as a virtue to be cultivated through communal practice means that congregational worship is an important context for this act to occur. Moreover, if hope is a virtue that must be cultivated by a lifelong habit of practice, and if virtue is shaped by practices that are both habitual and communal, then congregational worship becomes a key practice for the cultivation of hope.

Yet these models on their own are insufficient for understanding hope in a Christian sense. Though Smith's use of phenomenology to outline the structural elements of hope is helpful, there are several places where it is inadequate for my research. First, as referenced earlier, space and time ought not be collapsed into the *object* of hope, even though it may make conceptual sense to do so. Because space and time are foundational to experience, a phenomenology cannot ignore it. Furthermore, in Christian eschatology, space and time are the key ways of understanding where and when God will bring about his promise, as I will demonstrate in the next chapter.

Second, Smith notes that in Christian hope, "the object and ground are identical," though they operate in different modes.[23] God is both the ground

---

[22]Jeremy Begbie names at least four ways music and emotion are related. Music can embody emotion by mimicking the vocal features and bodily gestures that accompany emotions; music can concentrate and clarify our emotions by the way that it embodies it; music can evoke emotion by mimicking our vocal and bodily gestures of emotion, provoking the brain to trigger the same sorts of responses through proprioceptive feedback; and music has the power to educate emotion by adding to the repertoire of expression. See "Faithful Feelings: Music and Emotion in Worship," in *Resonant Witness: Conversations Between Music and Theology*, ed. Jeremy S. Begbie and Steven R. Guthrie (Grand Rapids: Eerdmans, 2011), 343.

[23]Smith, "Determined Hope," 209.

of hope and the object of hope. But the Nicene Creed confesses, "We look for the resurrection of the dead and the life of the world to come." This is not the same as the ground for hope. Furthermore, Smith does not say why Christ is the ground of hope or how the faithfulness of God is revealed in the life, death, and resurrection of Christ. In a chapter to come, I will draw from N. T. Wright's work to demonstrate how the faithfulness of God is revealed in the life, death, and resurrection of Christ, making the resurrection itself the ground of Christian hope.

Third, the agency of hope is not clearly outlined. Smith may view agency as included in the *ground*, but one can have a basis for hope—past experience, requisite elements of success or desired outcome—without knowing who will bring it about. From a psychological perspective, agency is one of two critical dimensions of hope. Fourth, to use Snyder's terms again, the pathway of hope is missing from Smith's elements.

When the elements of hope are listed as a set of pronouns, a clear picture of what is missing from Smith's list emerges. What the list includes are *why* (ground), *who* (a community of hope), *what* (object), and *that* (act). What is missing is a crucial set of interrogative pronouns: *where* (space), *when* (time), *who* (agency), and *how* (pathway). These specific pronouns are precisely the ones addressed in the next chapter as we take a closer look at the theology of hope. There we will begin to fill in the "answers" to these questions.

# 4

# WHAT IS CHRISTIAN HOPE?

## EARLY VISIONS OF ESCHATOLOGY

THE CHAIRS SQUEAK LOUDLY as the five hundred or so people stand to recite together the words that appear on the screen. We are in the oldest high school in Colorado Springs, but this is the American West, so that is not saying too much. The building is about one hundred years old, but the words the people are saying are much older. They have nourished and sustained followers of Jesus for over sixteen hundred years; they have served as a safeguard from error and as a unifying force. For the hundreds gathered on this Sunday in Eastertide, they serve as an anchor. They tether a congregation composed heavily of twenty-somethings and thirty-somethings to a faith that has been tested and tried. Even more than that, they connect nondenominational, charismatic evangelicals to a wider church—a global and historic church.

The scene I have described is one of the services at one of our congregations at the church where I serve. The truth is, the creed is regularly said at all of our congregations—from micro to mega, with the backdrop of shining new technology or amid the noise of old wooden chairs. Saying the creed regularly in worship has been a powerful way of reminding our church that this faith is a *received* faith. It did not begin with us, and it will not end with us. There is a great drama already in progress. Like every good story, there is the expectation of a good ending. The final words of the Nicene Creed points us forward to that hope.

In the previous chapter, I reviewed four models for understanding hope that provide helpful frameworks for my research. Yet these models do not outline a uniquely Christian understanding of hope. In order to engage in theological ethnography and in order for theological reflection to be integrated, the espoused and operant theologies of hope that the fieldwork revealed need to be set against a normative and operant theology of hope. This chapter begins to sketch a normative theology of hope by tracing early Christian hope until its formalization in the Nicene Creed.

## ESCHATOLOGY

The theology of hope is formally called eschatology, drawing from the Greek *eschatos*, which means "last." Eschatology is often described as being the study of last things. Yet, as many theologians have argued, Christian eschatology is so preoccupied with a particular goal—Greek *telos*—that it might make more sense to call it teleology. As Kent Brower notes, "Biblical eschatology may be defined as 'the direction and goal of God's active covenant faithfulness in and for his created order.'"[1]

The New Testament orients the Christian forward on the basis of an event in the past. The life, death, and resurrection of Jesus Christ have brought about a new and firm reason for hope. Paul writes of future bodily resurrection (Rom 8; 1 Cor 15), Peter of a new heavens and new earth (2 Pet 3:13), and John catches a vision of the joining together of heaven and earth, filled with the presence of God (Rev 21). The theological exposition of New Testament texts is the basis for shaping a theology of hope. But is important to explore how early Christian writers and church leaders interpreted these texts and shaped their vision of Christian hope.

## EARLY CHRISTIAN HOPE

***Diversity and commonality.*** Brian Daley provides a comprehensive survey of early Christian hope in his book *The Hope of the Early Church*. The diversity of perspectives he covers makes it difficult to speak of a singular hope. The range of images and ideas we see among early Christian writers, expressing their expectations for the future of the planet and individuals, saint and sinner, suggests that one might perhaps better speak of many facets of a rapidly developing, increasingly detailed Christian view of human destiny, of

---

[1] Kent E. Brower, "'Let the Reader Understand': Temple and Eschatology in Mark," in *The Reader Must Understand: Eschatology in Bible and Theology*, ed. Kent E. Brower and Mark W. Elliott (Downers Grove, IL: InterVarsity Press, 1997), 119.

many hopes—and many fears—enveloped within a single, growing, ever more complex tradition of early Christian faith and practice.[2]

But for all its variation, Daley is still able to discern a clear trajectory in the evolution of eschatological vision: from a sense of imminent apocalyptic crisis to a well-developed theology of creation, a future-oriented cosmology and anthropology; from a vivid expectation of the end of this historical order, followed by the raising of the dead and the creation of the wholly new human world, to a systematic doctrine of last things as the final piece in a Christ-centered view of history's whole; from an early focus on the community's hope for survival in the coming cosmic catastrophe, to a later preoccupation with the hope of the individual as he or she faces death.[3]

Daley qualifies even this evolution of thought as being too general to sufficiently account for the uniqueness of context that led "philosophers and polemicists, poets and spiritual writers, bishops in times of peace and prophets in times of persecution" to place different emphases on different aspects and to assimilate various elements in their own way.

Despite the limitations of general statements about dozens of different writers in different contexts, it can be helpful to identify common threads. The places of overlapping vision provide clues as to the core of early Christian hope. Daley points out that it is "clear from the beginning of Christian literature" that "hope for the future is an inseparable, integral dimension of Christian faith, and the implied condition of possibility for responsible Christian action in the world." In other words, while the specifics of what is being hoped for and how or when it will come about may vary, the presence of hope is undeniable within Christianity; it occupies a central place. Second, the patristic writers insist "in a crescendo of consensus" that Christians live with this hope "*within history*" and thus carry a sense of "realism."[4] Thus the centrality of hope and its quality of realism, which locates it within history, are part of the fabric of the Christian faith common to the early church.

***Common doctrine.*** Daley goes beyond this general common ground and attempts to outline common elements of early Christian eschatology as an

---

[2]Brian E. Daley, *The Hope of the Early Church: A Handbook of Patristic Eschatology*, 2nd ed. (Grand Rapids: Baker Academic, 2010), 216.
[3]Daley, *Hope of the Early Church*, 216.
[4]Daley, *Hope of the Early Church*, 217-18.

emerging doctrine. The first is what may be called a linear view of history. This stands in contradiction to the Gnostic repudiation of the temporal world and in contrast to Origen's musings about cyclical time. Orthodox Christian writers maintain a firm conviction that history has both an origin and an end, both "rooted in the plan and power of God."[5]

The second common element of patristic eschatology is *the resurrection of the body*. From second-century apologists, through Methodius, to Gregory of Nyssa and Augustine, early Christian theologians insisted on taking the biblical promise of resurrection literally.[6] Indeed, as Christopher Hall outlines in his work on the theology of the church fathers, many of these writers, particularly Athenagoras and Augustine, went to great lengths to show how God could take decomposed and even digested remains of a human and reconstitute them in an act of new creation to bring resurrection about. The body, because it was created by God, will be redeemed by God.

The resurrection of the body is closely related to another common element in early Christian eschatology, the prospect of judgment. This judgment, however, will be pronounced by God at the moment of death. This view is the seedbed for what in modern theology is thought of as an interim state between death and resurrection. Yet for the patristics, the details were less clear. Early theologians such as Justin and Irenaeus rejected the immortality of the soul and thus the view of the interim state as a sort of "shadowy existence in Hades"—the domain of the dead—or a kind of "sleep of souls," as in the Syriac tradition.[7] Later theologians from Tertullian on suggest that the person destined for eternal judgment begins experiencing it as a "soul" prior to bodily resurrection.

Nevertheless, because judgment was a common element of early Christian eschatology, so too was the related but distinct concept of retribution. Drawing from Jewish apocalyptic imagery while modifying it, "early Christian writers almost universally assumed that the final state of human existence, after God's judgment, will be permanent and perfect happiness for the good, and permanent, all-consuming misery for the wicked." By the fourth century, it became clear that the blessed and the damned received fates that relate to

---

[5]Daley, *Hope of the Early Church*, 219.
[6]Daley, *Hope of the Early Church*, 220.
[7]Daley, *Hope of the Early Church*, 220.

their proximity to God. Because humans are made for union with God, one is blessed for and with loving fellowship with him, and damned for and with the decisive turn away from him.[8]

One final common element Daley identifies in the doctrine of hope in the early church is the communion of the saints. While Augustine developed this view most clearly in *The City of God*, even early Christian theologians had a "general sense" that the departed were still somehow involved in the life of the church, whether by "praying for the living" or in "experiencing the benefit of their prayers." The point here is that salvation is communal and "ecclesial."[9]

***Disputed views.*** There are also common threads to the disagreement in patristic eschatology. Daley outlines five. First, there were a variety of opinions about the time and nearness of the world's end. One peculiar facet of this ambiguity about the timing of the end had to do with whether there would be a literal period of "earthly reward for the just before the dramatic denouement of history"—a millenarian hope. Yet while this view surfaced from time to time, it is worth noting that the majority of orthodox patristic writers rejected millenarianism as an overly literal reading of the Scriptures.[10]

Second, there was also continuing controversy about the materiality and physical character of the resurrection.[11] Origen was the strongest proponent of a spiritual body, while Methodius and Jerome were strong opponents of such a view. Though this was the subject of various debates in the Middle Ages, and, as we shall see below, is even in our day, the debate is not about whether there will be a resurrected body but rather what the resurrected body will be like.

Third is the extent of eschatological salvation. Origen, Gregory of Nyssa, and Evagrius held out hope that all "spiritual creatures" would be saved. Augustine took the other end of the discussion, assuming that the "majority of human beings will not be saved" and that even the "perseverance of believers in the life of grace" is not assured. Jerome fell between the two poles, arguing that all "Christian believers will experience the final mercy of God."[12]

---

[8]Daley, *Hope of the Early Church*, 220-21.
[9]Daley, *Hope of the Early Church*, 221.
[10]Daley, *Hope of the Early Church*, 221-22.
[11]Daley, *Hope of the Early Church*, 222.
[12]Daley, *Hope of the Early Church*, 222.

It is important to note that after Origen's day the hope of a wider salvation for all does not appear in the mainstream of theological thought, and where it does appear it is hotly contested.

Fourth, a variance of opinion emerges on the question of the possibility of change and progress for those whose final destiny has been determined.[13] Once again, Origen and Gregory of Nyssa depart from the view of the majority of ancient Christian writers. Origen and Gregory posit that since the state of blessedness is a "continual progress towards deeper union with God," souls after death could move from damnation to blessedness.

Related to the above issue is the fifth area of disagreement, the possibility of purgatory. Before purgatory was thought of as a separate, interim state in Western medieval theology, the concept of a "purgation from sin" emerged in the patristic era in the writings of Origen. Since suffering, in general, serves a medicinal purpose to gain wisdom and expiate sin, God might use a period of suffering after death to prepare souls for the presence of God. Gregory the Great, in the late sixth century, argued that souls who die in imperfection in "faith and virtue" must be "purged for a time in fire" before coming before God. Augustine, chronologically between Origen and Gregory, took a theological middle ground, considering such a view plausible but not promised.

***Different questions.*** Christopher Hall's summary of theology of the church fathers explores early Christian hope only in its focus on "the resurrection of the body and life everlasting."[14] From Hall's survey of Justin Martyr, Polycarp, Athenagoras, and Augustine, it becomes apparent that the church fathers were approaching the subject with particular questions. My reading of Hall's selections suggests a priority of four questions, listed here in no particular order:

+ What will the resurrected body be like?

+ How will God accomplish this given some peculiar and unusual circumstances?

+ On what basis can the Christian hope for resurrection?

+ Finally, what is bodily resurrection for?

---

[13]Daley, *Hope of the Early Church*, 222.

[14]Christopher A. Hall, *Learning Theology with the Church Fathers* (Downers Grove, IL: InterVarsity Press, 2002), 249.

Because the latter two questions relate closely to the paradigm of hope I am constructing for my research, I will give further attention to how early Christian theologians responded to them. The responses to the question of the basis for belief in bodily resurrection are rooted in the belief in both the incarnation and the resurrection of Jesus. Joanne McWilliam Dewart summarizes the argument made by Clement, one of the apostolic fathers: since Christians received salvation in the flesh, and since Christ who is "the means of salvation" was himself "enfleshed," then it is right that the "future reward should also be 'in the flesh.'" Ignatius, an early bishop and martyr, wrote that just as Christ "was truly raised from the dead, when His Father raised him up, [so] in similar fashion his Father will raise up in Christ Jesus us who believe in him."[15] These early writings form the seedbed of theology that was developed by later theologians of the church. The grounding for hope never wavered from the incarnation and resurrection of Jesus Christ.

The other question concerns to what end or for what purpose will God bring about bodily resurrection. Augustine rises to the task with particular eloquence and poetry. For him, the whole purpose of new, resurrected bodies is to behold God in his glory and beauty. With new physical bodies of the new creation, we shall "observe God in utter clarity and distinctness, seeing him present everywhere." Even if this vision is mediated through the "lives of believers and through creation itself," we will see God as he is. God "will be seen in the new heavens and the new earth, in the whole creation as it then will be; he will be seen in every body by means of bodies, wherever eyes of the spiritual body are directed with their penetrating gaze."[16]

***Normative theology: The Nicene Creed.*** The hope of the early church, as with other crucial aspects of early Christian theology, was codified by the Council of Nicaea (AD 325) and the Council of Constantinople (AD 381) in what we call the Nicene Creed. To understand Christianity in its own context is to see it as a movement that grew from Jewish roots. Luke Timothy Johnson, writing on the Nicene Creed, demonstrates that the Creed began as a variation of the Shema, the Deuteronomic confession of God as one (Deut 6:4-5). Johnson argues that the Creed is not "a late and violent imposition upon the

---

[15]Hall, *Learning Theology with the Church Fathers*, 250-51.
[16]Hall, *Learning Theology with the Church Fathers*, 272.

simple gospel story" but rather "a natural development of the Christian religion and the crises it faced from the start."[17] He outlines three specific challenges that occasioned the formulation of the Creed:

1. the challenge to define the experience of Jesus within and over against the shared story of Israel;

2. the challenge to clarify the complex understanding of God that was embedded in the resurrection experience; and

3. the challenge to correct misunderstandings of the newly emergent "Christian narrative" that was, at heart, a "story about Jesus."[18]

These challenges account for the Creed's trinitarian structure and the length of the section on Jesus. Thus the Creed is not a document of what a modern might call systematic theology. Such a designation would lead one to misconstrue it, and even to miscritique it. Thus looking for eschatology within the Creed may be fraught with pitfalls. My hope is that by providing a survey of early Christian writing from the church fathers, we find the necessary context for identifying eschatological phrases within the Creed. By that criteria, there are two key eschatological phrases in the Nicene Creed, one in the article related to Christ and the other in the article related to the church.

"He will come again in glory to judge the living and dead, and His kingdom shall have no end." This first creedal eschatological statement affirms the return of Christ, or his appearing, and the reality of a final judgment, which not only will occur but will be at least one of the reasons for Christ's appearing. It goes on to affirm that the reign of Christ, which is understood to have been inaugurated in his earthly life—though this is not made explicit in the Creed—will be consummated with a reign that will know no end.

"We look for the resurrection of the dead and the life of the world to come." This second eschatological statement in the Creed addresses the posture of the church. The church is to be a people who are straining forward even while our feet are in the moment. We *look* because we have reason to believe that things will not always be this way; we have hope. The content of this hope is made explicit in the final phrase: bodily resurrection and a new world. It

---

[17]Luke Timothy Johnson, *The Creed: What Christians Believe and Why It Matters* (New York: Image, 2003), 10.

[18]Johnson, *Creed*, 10-11.

should be noted here that while resurrection has received attention—even if it has been speculative—from the church fathers and modern systematic theologians alike, the nature of the world to come with relation to the physical universe has been largely ignored. Scientist and theologian David Wilkinson makes this point. This may be due to a lack of understanding of science, the difficulty of speaking about the cosmos from within it, or the perceived lack of practical value that such a study would produce.[19]

Nevertheless, these two phrases taken together provide a summation of early Christian eschatology, which I will refer to as creedal Christian hope. The creed confesses a future-oriented hope for the return of Christ, the full reign of Christ, the final judgment of the human race, the resurrection of the believer, and the new creation. Of particular interest to this study is the observation that the eschatology of the creed contains both *futurity*—Christ will come again; we look for the life of the world to come—and *materiality*—the body will be resurrected. When we begin to examine contemporary worship songs that worship leaders say are songs of hope, we will explore whether these songs contain elements of either futurity or materiality. But first, we need to move from the fourth century to our own day to examine what a formal theology of hope might look like.

[19]David Wilkinson, *Christian Eschatology and the Physical Universe* (London: T&T Clark, 2010), 24-25.

# 5

# WHAT IS CHRISTIAN HOPE?

## ESCHATOLOGY IN
## CONTEMPORARY THEOLOGY

## FORMAL THEOLOGY: JÜRGEN MOLTMANN
## AND N. T. WRIGHT

Creedal Christian hope needs to be articulated and explicated in each day for its day. This chapter moves from early Christian hope to the present by outlining key overlapping features of Christian eschatology in two theologians whose influence among evangelicals in the past several decades is notable in both the academy and the church. Renowned in the past century as being the theologian of hope, Jürgen Moltmann made eschatology no longer marginal but central to Christian theology. Wright took the next step, giving the New Testament vision of a redeemed creation a wider exposure. Arguably, no biblical scholar has done more to widen the reach of this view than Wright.[1]

The two scholars approach the subject from the perspective of different disciplines. Moltmann writes as a systematic theologian, Wright as a New Testament scholar with particular emphasis on Pauline theology. He has written extensively on subjects related to what may be called Christian origins. As such, Moltmann treats the topic more directly than Wright, though eschatology is a key feature in Wright's reading of Paul in particular and of the New Testament as a whole.

*Theology of Hope* was Moltmann's first significant theological work, and it reflects on how the resurrection of Jesus is central to Christian theology. Moltmann wrote even more extensively on eschatology in his work *The Coming of*

---

[1]J. Richard Middleton, *A New Heaven and a New Earth: Reclaiming Biblical Eschatology* (Grand Rapids: Baker Academic, 2014), 310.

*God*, focusing on personal eschatology, historical eschatology, and cosmic eschatology. Wright's most widely read work on Christian eschatology is a popular-level work called *Surprised by Hope*. Most of his writing on eschatology, however, comes in the context of his exposition of Pauline theology. Wright outlines the key features of Judaism as monotheism, election, and eschatology, and explores how Paul reshaped each around Jesus the Messiah and the Spirit. Though they appear in his smaller books on Paul, these three themes also provide the main structure of his two-volume work, *Paul and the Faithfulness of God*.[2] The rest of Wright's eschatology can also be found in his analysis of resurrection in his tome *The Resurrection of the Son of God*. Wright has recently brought his work on the historical Jesus and on Pauline theology together in his book based on his recent Gifford lectures, *History and Eschatology*, which provides a compact summation of how first century Jewish themes of temple, Sabbath, and image-bearer come to be fulfilled in and transformed by Jesus and the Spirit with particular implications for the development of Christian eschatology.

My goal in this chapter is to incorporate key insights from both theologians with the previous chapter's summation of creedal Christian hope in order to offer an expanded definition of creedal Christian hope. This definition will serve as a summary of both *normative* and *formal* theologies of hope. As such, it will function as standard against which to evaluate the hope uncovered through the fieldwork in the chapters that follow.

## OVERLAPPING VIEWS

Despite their different disciplines and approaches to the subject of Christian eschatology, there is considerable overlap in Moltmann's and Wright's respective eschatological visions. One might liken this to two people observing a city square from the windows of two different buildings; they are looking at the same scenes, but from different perspectives and angles, thus giving attention to different details and movements. I will outline six planes on which Moltmann and Wright overlap in their respective eschatologies.

*1. The primacy of Jewish eschatology.* Moltmann builds on the foundation of Jewish eschatology, carrying forward the theme of God's presence. As Richard Bauckham writes of Moltmann's eschatology: "The central expectation of

---

[2]N. T. Wright, *Paul and the Faithfulness of God*, vol. 2 (Minneapolis: Augsburg Fortress, 2013).

Jewish and Christian eschatology has always been the coming of God to his creation and the coming presence of God in his whole creation."[3] Moltmann employs the Jewish theological concepts of Sabbath and Shekinah to delineate God's presence now from God's eschatological presence. Sabbath is God's presence in time, and Shekinah is God's presence in space. Creation-in-the-beginning is finished in God's Sabbath; creation will be created anew so that it may become home of God's Shekinah. Sabbath and Shekinah thus are "related to one another as promise and fulfillment, beginning and completion." Time and space also are connected in this way: "Creation begins with time and is completed in space."[4]

Moltmann summarizes the Old Testament's vision of resurrection as an "unequivocal salvific hope" (Is 24–26) and as judgment (Dan 12), with the two perspectives found "side by side unharmonized." This is nuanced slightly by resurrection in the books of Maccabees as a "two-edged expectation, because one does not know to which side one will be called to account on Judgment Day." Moltmann surmises that the Jewish vision of hope is not about resurrection per se but rather what resurrection stands for: "the universal victory of God's righteousness and justice."[5]

Wright outlines three positions regarding the afterlife as seen in the Old Testament and proposes an explanation for how resurrection relates to each. While early Jewish eschatology taught that the dead were either resting with the ancestors or received by Yahweh into some continuing life, the later Jewish hope of resurrection is not a development out of the latter but rather a "radical development from within" the former.[6] This resurrection hope does not deny that a person goes to Sheol or "the dust" or "the grave"; but neither does it affirm that a "non-bodily post-mortem existence in the presence of YHWH is the final good" for which we hope.

Furthermore, Wright argues that resurrection as bodily resurrection for dead humans and resurrection as national restoration for exiled/suffering Israel are so closely intertwined that "it does not matter that we cannot

[3]Richard Bauckham, ed., *God Will Be All in All: The Eschatology of Jürgen Moltmann* (Minneapolis: Augsburg Fortress, 2001), 24.

[4]Jürgen Moltmann, *The Coming of God*, trans. Margaret Kohl (Minneapolis: Augsburg Fortress, 1996), 265-66.

[5]Moltmann, *Coming of God*, 268.

[6]N. T. Wright, *The Resurrection of the Son of God* (Minneapolis: Fortress, 2003), 124.

always tell which is meant, or even if a distinction is possible." This is evident first from the servant passages in Isaiah, where "the belief that Israel's god will restore the nation after exile" becomes the belief "that he will restore the nation's *representative* after death." "The earlier national hope thus transmutes, but perfectly comprehensibly, into the hope that Israel's god will do for a human being what Israel always hoped he would do for the nation as a whole." Eventually, this belief is also applied to the Messiah's people, which Wright grounds in Daniel 12, "where the nation's representative has become plural."[7]

Wright also refutes the claim that the hope of resurrection was a derivative of ancient Zoroastrianism or from Canaanite mythology. He argues that because the thrust of the resurrection passages is on Israel's unique status as the chosen people of the one creator God, to borrow imagery from pagan religions would be undermining the message. Even the relative lateness of resurrection in Jewish thought is itself a demonstration that Jews were not borrowing an image from pagan religions; instead, Wright sees resurrection as an imaginative contrast to the empires of Babylon and Syria and an evocative way of the prophets speaking of the end of exile and the renewal of covenant. Wright argues that resurrection in Jewish thought is both metonymy and metaphor. When resurrection refers to a literal prediction of one element in that restoration, it is a metonymy. When the belief in resurrection serves as "an image for the restoration of nation and land," it is functioning as a metaphor, such as in Ezekiel's vision of God breathing life into dry bones.[8]

Thus, for both Moltmann and Wright, Christian eschatology emerges from Jewish roots.

**2. The centrality of Christ's resurrection.** "Christianity stands or falls with the reality of the raising of Jesus from the dead by God," writes Moltmann in *Theology of Hope*. As a systematic theologian, Bauckham says, Moltmann links Christology with eschatology, viewing the two doctrines as existing in a "mutually interpretative relationship."[9] For Moltmann, eschatology begins with Christology, and Christology is completed or consummated in eschatology.

---

[7]Wright, *Resurrection of the Son of God*, 124.
[8]Wright, *Resurrection of the Son of God*, 124-28.
[9]Jürgen Moltmann, *Theology of Hope*, trans. James W. Leitch (Minneapolis: Augsburg Fortress, 1993), 165; Bauckham, *God Will Be All in All*, 2.

*Theology of Hope* outlines two key strands that explicate the essential mean-ing of the resurrection: identity and divine action. By identity Moltmann means that it was the same Jesus who was crucified who is now raised. Cross and resurrection represent total opposites—"death and life, the absence of God and the nearness of God, godforsakenness and the glory of God." Yet it was the same Jesus who experienced both. Thus, by "raising him to life, God created continuity in this radical discontinuity."[10]

Divine action refers to the resurrection as the fulfillment of God's escha-tological promise in the person of Jesus. Resurrection "represented the point at which Jewish hopes for the future became thoroughly eschatological, in envisaging a future in which even death will be overcome in God's new cre-ation." In raising Jesus from the dead, God guaranteed his promise by enact-ing it in Jesus. Furthermore, because Jesus "has been raised for the sake of the future eschatological resurrection of all the dead, the new creation of all reality, and the coming of God's kingdom of righteousness and glory," one must view the resurrection of Jesus as becoming the cause and grounds of this "universal future."[11] Almost thirty years after writing the above statement in *Theology of Hope*, Moltmann underscored it again in *The Coming of God:* "Christian faith in God is shaped by the experience of the dying and death of Christ, and by the appearances of the Christ who was raised."[12]

Wright also roots his theology of hope in the resurrection of Jesus, par-ticularly as Paul understood the resurrection. Paul believed two things that, for Wright, are only comprehensible as mutations within the Jewish worldview and not combinations of Jewish eschatology and something else. The first is that Paul believed the resurrection as a historical moment had divided in two: the resurrection (first) of the Messiah, and the resurrection of his people (at his parousia). Second, Paul argued that the resurrection would be bodily and would involve a transformation.

Resurrection is at the heart of the New Testament Christianity. "All the major books and strands, with the single exception of Hebrews, make resur-rection a central and important topic, and set it within a framework of Jewish thought about the one god as creator and judge," Wright says. In the centuries

---

[10]Richard Bauckham, *The Theology of Jurgen Moltmann* (Edinburgh: T&T Clark, 1995), 33.
[11]Bauckham, *Theology of Jürgen Moltmann*, 33-34.
[12]Moltmann, *Coming of God*, 69.

that followed, resurrection was "foundational to early Christianity in all forms known to us" with few exceptions. Against the pagan view that death was the end, Christianity "affirmed . . . the future bodily resurrection of all god's people." In contrast to the Jewish views of resurrection, Christianity "affirmed in great detail" (1) "that resurrection involved going through death and into a non-corruptible body the other side"; (2) that the Messiah was raised from the dead ahead of everyone else; and (3) that the resurrection allowed for an intermediate state of the denatured person being with the Lord until the resurrection. Furthermore, it is remarkable that Christianity found "new ways of speaking about what the resurrection involved and how it would come about" that Jewish texts and thought would not have envisioned. Why did this happen? Wright concludes it was due to being "decisively launched by, and formed around, the resurrection of Jesus himself"; the theology of resurrection was a result of early Christian witness that said that Jesus of Nazareth had been raised from the dead.[13]

For both Moltmann and Wright, Christian hope, and, indeed, Christianity itself, rises with the resurrection of Jesus Christ.

**3. The paradigm for the resurrection of the dead.** For both Moltmann and Wright, the resurrection of Jesus is not only central to our conception of hope; it is also paradigmatic for the resurrection of believers. Jesus' resurrection is how we understand what our resurrection bodies will be like. Furthermore, both see the future resurrection of the believer as central to Christian hope, just as the resurrection of Jesus is central to Christian theology. Future bodily resurrection is set in contrast to the immortality of the soul in Moltmann's writing, and in contrast to "going to heaven" in Wright's work. With a preacher's conviction and cadence, Moltmann writes:

> The immortality of the soul is an opinion—the resurrection of the dead is a hope. The first is a trust in something immortal in the human being, the second is a trust in the God who calls into being the things that are not, and makes the dead live. In trust in the immortal soul we accept death, and in a sense anticipate it. In trust in the life-creating God we await the conquest of death—"death is swallowed up in victory" (1 Cor. 15.54)—and an eternal life in which "death shall be no more" (Rev. 21.4). The immortal soul may welcome death as a friend, because

---

[13]Wright, *Resurrection of the Son of God*, 551-52.

death releases it from the earthly body; but for the resurrection hope, death is "the last enemy" (1 Cor. 15.26) of the living God and the creations of his love.[14]

For Moltmann, the crucial difference between belief in future bodily resurrection and belief in the immortality of the soul is the locus of trust. Resurrection requires trust in God; the immortality of the soul is the result of trust in self. One might also add that the first is an active hope in a dynamic object— God!—while the other is a passive hope in a static state of being.

Moltmann understands the resurrection of Christ to mean the "transformation of his whole, bodily, form" rather than the "survival of some eternal part of him," and therefore this physical bodily resurrection is the paradigm for the new creation of all things. Eschatology, then, is "emphatically not about the transcendence of immaterial and eternal aspects of creation [soul/spirit] over the bodily and mortal aspects. It is the new creation of the whole of this transient and bodily creation."[15]

Wright's thesis on the redemption of our bodies is simply this: "The risen Jesus is both the *model* for the Christian's future body and the *means* by which it comes about."[16] Like Moltmann, Wright finds modern Westerners to have more in common with Plato's dualism of material and immaterial than with Jewish creation theology, which affirmed the physical. Wright expounds on 1 Corinthians 15 as a key text, within which there are two crucial phrases: "physical body" and the "spiritual body." Wright finds these translations misleading:

> The contrast is between the present body, corruptible, decaying, and doomed to die, and the future body, incorruptible, undecaying, never to die again. The key adjectives, which are quoted endlessly in discussions of this topic, do not refer to a physical body and a nonphysical one. . . .
>
> The first word, *psychikos*, does not in any case mean anything like "physical" in our sense. For Greek speakers of Paul's day, the *psyche*, from which the word derives, means the soul, not the body.[17]

The deeper point linguistically for Wright is in the ending *–ikos,* which does not describe "*the material out of which things are made* but *the power or energy*

---

[14]Moltmann, *Coming of God*, 65-66.
[15]Bauckham, *God Will Be All in All*, 7.
[16]N. T. Wright, *Surprised by Hope: Rethinking Heaven, the Resurrection, and the Mission of the Church* (New York: HarperCollins, 2008), 149.
[17]Wright, *Surprised by Hope*, 155.

*that animates them."* Thus the contrast is really between the body that the soul powers versus the body that the spirit—God's Spirit—powers. As Wright puts it, the contrast is between *"corruptible physicality"* and *"incorruptible physicality."*[18]

Both Moltmann and Wright call us to look to the risen Jesus as the picture of what our embodied future will be. The best way to envision our future is to look at the future that has already occurred in Christ. His resurrected body is a paradigm for our future resurrection bodies.

**4. The paradigm for the renewal of creation.** The resurrection of Jesus is also paradigmatic, in both Moltmann's and Wright's views, for the new heavens and the new earth. For Moltmann, "There is no beginning of the world without the end of this old one, there is no kingdom of God without judgment on godlessness, there is no rebirth of the cosmos without 'the birth pangs of the End-time.'" Moltmann rejects both the view that creation will be annihilated and re-created and the view that the new creation will develop out of the old. Just as Christ was truly dead and his resurrection body did not develop out of the dead Christ, so the "new creation of all things does not issue from the history of the old creation." Instead, the end "hides a new beginning," while the new beginning is a genuinely "new creative act."[19]

In Moltmann's thought, the future bodily resurrection of the believer is connected to the renewal of the cosmos; one cannot happen without the other. "The two sides belong together: there is no resurrection of the dead without the new earth in which death will be no more," he writes. "Hope for the resurrection of the dead is therefore only the beginning of a hope for a cosmic new creation of all things and conditions." This forms the bridge in Moltmann's thought from "personal eschatology" to "cosmic eschatology." Without this bridge, Christian eschatology would devolve into a "gnostic doctrine of redemption," which advocates a "redemption *from* the world" not a "redemption *of* the world," a "deliverance of the soul from the body" and no longer "redemption of the body."[20]

Moltmann invokes the doctrines of God as Creator and as Redeemer as the basis for the link between personal eschatology and cosmic eschatology. The Creator God who rested from work of creation will redeem his creation

---

[18]Wright, *Surprised by Hope*, 155-56.
[19]Moltmann, *Coming of God*, 68-69, 234.
[20]Moltmann, *Coming of God*, 70.

and renew it in such a way that his presence can one day fully rest in his creation. The connection between creation and redemption, as between the aforementioned concepts of Sabbath and Shekinah, is God himself. "There are not two Gods, a Creator God and a Redeemer God. There is one God. It is for his sake that the unity of redemption and creation has to be thought."[21]

Wright emphasizes early Christians' practice of looking back at the first Easter in order to see what was coming. It was "precisely because of their very Jewish belief in God as creator and redeemer, and because they had seen this belief confirmed in the totally unexpected event of Jesus' resurrection, they also looked forward eagerly to an event yet to come in which what began at Easter would be completed." The resurrection of Jesus as a paradigm of the renewal of the cosmos is clear in Wright's mind: "What God did for Jesus at Easter he will do . . . for the entire cosmos."[22]

In contrast to Moltmann's move from personal eschatology outward to cosmic eschatology, Wright begins with what Easter means for the cosmos and moves inward to personal hope. Expositing 1 Corinthians 15, Wright links Paul's firstfruits language to Passover and Pentecost. In this light, Jesus' resurrection is both a kind of passing through the "Red Sea of death" and the defeat of sin and death as spiritual "slavemasters." Both the exodus and the resurrection are "an act of pure grace," not the result of some sort of progress. This is consonant with Moltmann's claim that the new does not emerge from the old as if it were latent within it as a possibility. Wright sums things up with one rather full sentence.

> What I am proposing is that the New Testament image of the future hope of the whole cosmos, grounded in the resurrection of Jesus, gives as coherent a picture as we need or could have of the future that is promised to the whole world, a future in which, under the sovereign and wise rule of creator God, decay and death will be done away with and a new creation born, to which the present will stand as mother to child."

Creation will experience redemption and renewal, both of which are "promised and guaranteed by the resurrection of Jesus from the dead."[23]

---

[21]Moltmann, *Coming of God*, 259.
[22]Wright, *Surprised by Hope*, 79, 99.
[23]Wright, *Surprised by Hope*, 98.

Both Moltmann and Wright build a bridge from the personal dimension of eschatology to a cosmic one. But they work toward the bridge from different sides. Where Moltmann sketches the vision of bodily resurrection and then constructs a backdrop befitting it, Wright paints the horizon of new creation and sets a new kind of human against it.

**5. *The insufficiency of secular and modern Christian eschatologies.*** If a common enemy makes two parties allies, then Moltmann and Wright would be comrades in arms in the fight against alternate eschatologies, specifically the secular ideal of progress and the popular Christian notion of a disembodied escape. Moltmann names the utopian myth of progress millenarianism, referring to the belief that humans can achieve peace. He names the dystopian fear of an inevitable end from which one seeks to escape apocalypticism. Peace and destruction come together in the Christian vision of death and resurrection. Bauckham sums up Moltmann's view this way:

> In relation to human history . . . the hope of redemption enables the future to
> be perceived neither in terms of *goal without rupture* (the one-sided seculariza-
> tion of the millenarian hope) nor in terms of *end without fulfillment* (the one-
> sided secularization of the apocalyptic expectation of catastrophe). It promotes
> neither then *"messianic presumption"* of utopian progressivism nor the *"apoca-
> lyptic resignation"* of fatalistic acceptance of inevitable catastrophe [citing Molt-
> mann, *Coming of God*, 192], both of which in their opposite ways aid and abet
> the modern historical project in deadly and destructive progress. By awakening
> hope in the power of God's redemptive future, it enables resistance to the power
> of history, anticipates a different future, alternative to that which the trends of
> past and present project, and in this way proves redemption already.[24]

What Moltmann calls millenarianist, Wright calls progressivist; but he does not have an exact analog to Moltmann's apocalypticist. Instead, Wright uses the term *dualist* to denote the hope of escape. The progressivist hopes for the fittest to survive, the strongest to conquer, and the best to win out. Though this can become a way to justify empire, it cannot account for evil. The dualist, on the other hand, is unconvinced that humans can change the world. Wright is far more scathing in his criticism of disembodied and escapist visions of Christian hope than he is of the secular myth of progress. Wright

---

[24]Bauckham, *God Will Be All in All*, 20.

dismantles the largely American fixation on a rapture with a blow-by-blow exegesis of the misunderstood texts.

Christian eschatology, for both Moltmann and Wright, serves as challenges and confrontations of rival eschatologies. Some of those rival eschatologies are secular; some are purportedly Christian but fall short.

**6. *The basis for the mission of the church.*** For both Moltmann and Wright, eschatology is not an esoteric or irrelevant doctrine, partly because of their belief about its impact on how the church understands it mission. Both scholars derive a kind of political theology from their eschatology, and Wright builds his vision of Christian ethics from the *telos* of Christian eschatology. Bauckham argues that Moltmann's interpretation of eschatology became widely influential precisely because of its "strongly practical thrust." Moltmann

> made Christian hope the motivating force for the church's missionary engagement with the world, especially for Christian involvement in the processes of social and political change. By opening the church to the eschatological future, it also opened the church to the world, casting the church in the role of an agent of eschatological unrest in society, whose task is to keep the world on the move towards the coming kingdom of God.[25]

This has been criticized by those who oppose liberation theology or who are uncomfortable with what they may perceive to be too much emphasis on the social over the moral or personal dimensions of salvation. Nevertheless, what must be noted is how action and vision are connected for Moltmann. If a Christian knows what Christ will do in the end, she is compelled to work in anticipation of it.

Wright makes a similar case in *Surprised by Hope*. Attempting to reframe mission, he writes:

> Living between the resurrection of Jesus and the final coming together of all things in heaven and earth means celebrating God's healing of his world not his abandoning of it; God's reclaiming of space as heaven and earth intersect once more; God's redeeming of time as years, weeks, and days speak the language of renewal; and God's redeeming of matter itself, in the sacraments, which point in turn to the renewal of the lives that are washed in baptism and fed with the Eucharist.

---

[25]Bauckham, *Theology of Jürgen Moltmann*, 30.

This mission cannot juxtapose "saving souls" and "doing good"; evangelism and justice belong together when mission is shaped by anticipation of the future.[26]

In an appendix critiquing what he believes are the two typical Easter sermons, Wright offers hints of what an Easter sermon *should* say and, by doing so, suggests how Christian mission might be reimagined in light of a more robust hope.

> Every act of love, every deed done in Christ and by the Spirit, every work of true creativity—doing justice, making peace, healing families, resisting temptation, seeking and winning true freedom—is an earthly event in a long history of things that *implement* Jesus's own resurrection and *anticipate* the final new creation and act as signposts of hope, point back to the first [resurrection] and on to the second [resurrection].[27]

Eschatology, for Moltmann and Wright, is not an abstract or irrelevant aspect of Christian theology. A robust vision of hope will inspire action here and now. While neither believes that Christian mission brings about the promised future, both believe in mission that is shaped by an eschatological vision.

## NOTABLE DIFFERENCES

*The reasons for renewing creation.* As mentioned above, Moltmann's cosmic eschatology includes a death and new beginning of creation. But his more radical claim is that the renewal of creation is not restoration but the perfection of creation. To make this clear, Moltmann presents two scenarios. The first is that creation was perfect from the beginning but was spoiled by human sin. In this scenario, grace is "the divine expedient designed to remedy the predicament of sin." Eschatology in this scenario is *restitutio in integrum*—"a return to the pristine beginning." The second scenario is that creation in the beginning was very good, which "does not mean that it was in the Greek sense perfect and without any future," but rather the Hebrew sense "that it was fitting, appropriate, corresponding to the Creator's will."[28] Hope is beyond redemption from sin and its consequences. Eschatology is *incipit vita nova*—"here a new life begins."

---

[26]Wright, *Surprised by Hope*, 264-65.
[27]Wright, *Surprised by Hope*, 294-95.
[28]Moltmann, *Coming of God*, 262, 264.

Even though the first scenario is an interpretation of cosmology that is common in many Western theological traditions, Moltmann finds it lacking because of its circularity. If one took circularity to be strictly true, "the circle of Christian drama of redemption would have to repeat itself to all eternity. The restoration of the original creation would have to be followed by the next Fall, and by the next redemption—the return of the same thing without end." Furthermore, Moltmann raises the question of how such a cyclical view would correspond to Paul's teaching that where sin abounds, grace abounds more (Rom 5:20). He argues that the "added value of grace is its power to end, not just actual sin, but even the possibility of sinning, not just actual death but even the being-able-to-die, as Augustine said." Hope, then, is "not directed to the 'restoration' of the original creation" but rather to "creation's final consummation." The "end is much more than the beginning."[29]

For Wright, creation needs to be renewed for three reasons. First, "the world is created good but *incomplete*." This is, as seen above, an area of agreement— even in language and perspective—with Moltmann. A nuance, though, is that Wright sees death as not being part of the original good creation but rather as an enemy that has its role as the result of sin. This view is in keeping with Christian tradition and belongs in Moltmann's first scenario above. Second, creation is subjected to slavery. Here, again, there are parallels for Wright with the children of Israel in Egypt. Creation will be free from its slavery when the people of God are glorified. Employing Pauline texts, Wright explains, "This is where Romans 8 dovetails with 1 Corinthians 15."[30] Third, creation is divided. One day, heaven and earth, as John the Revelator envisioned and Paul declared, will be joined together at last (Rev 21; Eph 1:12).

*The overlapping of ages and the inauguration of the kingdom of God.* Both Wright and Moltmann believe in an inaugurated eschatology, a kingdom of God that is both now and not yet. But for Moltmann, the rule of Christ from resurrection to new creation happens in two stages: the messianic rule now, and the millennial reign then.[31] During the millennial reign, two key things will occur: the martyrs who have died with Christ will live with him, and Israel will be raised and redeemed and form the messianic people of the

---

[29]Moltmann, *Coming of God*, 263-64.
[30]Wright, *Surprised by Hope*, 103.
[31]Bauckham, *God Will Be All in All*, 22.

messianic kingdom—along with Christians.[32] Moltmann sees this as a "transitional kingdom leading from this transitory world-time to the new world that is God's; it is not yet the kingdom of glory that Christ will hand back to the Father." Moltmann argues that the "transitional role of the millennium in historical eschatology" is parallel to "the intermediate state (between death and resurrection) in personal eschatology," though it must be noted that Moltmann rejects a "purgatory of any kind."[33] Moltmann also has no such parallel of a transitional role in cosmic eschatology as he does for his personal and historical eschatologies.

Wright is largely silent on a millennial period, leading many to conclude that he is an amillenialist. The best one can infer is that Wright reads the description of a millennial reign in Revelation as symbol and not code—a metaphor for living in the in-between that does not have a concrete referent.[34] Wright's refusal to map out anything that might resemble a timeline is a significant difference from Moltmann, whose process theology is as developed as it is controversial.

**Universal salvation.** Though he does not overtly express it, Moltmann leans toward a belief in ultimate universal salvation. In his view, God's redeeming act must be as comprehensive as his creative act if we are to see God as being faithful and gracious to his creation. God, Moltmann argues, would cease to be the creator if he left parts of his creation to perish; he would be a destroyer.[35]

Wright, however, does not even leave the door open for such a hope. Judgment, Wright says, is the "sovereign declaration that *this* is good and to be upheld and vindicated, and *that* is evil and to be condemned"; furthermore, judgment is "the only alternative to chaos." Yet Wright is uncomfortable with the traditional view—or distortions of it—that judgment is a sort of eternal torture chamber. He argues that when a being made in the image of God ceases to worship God, he or she gradually ceases to reflect the image of God. What results is a being that is less than human and therefore not only "beyond

---

[32]Moltmann, *Coming of God*, 195, 198-99.

[33]Bauckham, *God Will Be All in All*, 23.

[34]N. T. Wright, "Revelation and Christian Hope: Political Implications of the Revelation to John," episode 15 of *The N. T. Wright Podcast*, September 4, 2013, https://itunes.apple.com/us/podcast/revelation-christian-hope/id447840163.

[35]Richard Bauckham offers a rebuttal of this in his summary of Moltmann's eschatology in *God Will Be All in All*.

hope but also beyond pity."[36] He acknowledges the ambiguity about what this state of being would be. What is not left unclear, however, is the tragedy that some will in fact reject God's redemption and receive judgment as a result. This is not a contradiction to Christian hope but is in a sense a corollary to it.

## SUMMARY

Moltmann and Wright have overlapping yet different centers to their vision of Christian hope. The core of Christian hope for Moltmann is the presence of God; for Wright, it is the faithfulness of God. Moltmann, the systematician, emphasizes the coming of God as the great Shekinah that will fill the cosmos—hence the reason Bauckham's book on Moltmann's eschatology is called *God Will Be All in All*. The focus is on the presence of God coming and filling of all things. The cosmos will be completed and renewed to be fit for such a filling. Wright, the Pauline scholar, emphasizes the faithfulness of God. The covenant narrative is paramount for Wright. It is within that narrative that he finds God being faithful not only as Yahweh but on behalf of unfaithful Israel as well. It is this faithfulness that is good news for the whole world: God does not scrap his project (creation), forget his promise (the covenant with Abraham to bless all nations through his family), or abandon his people (Israel). While he certainly draws out themes such as victory from the resurrection, the resurrection is, for Wright, the consummate picture of the faithfulness of God.

## CONCLUSION AND CONNECTIONS

From the beginning, Christian hope was Christ centered: it was an expectation of a sure future secured by Christ's death and resurrection. The return of Christ will bring about the resurrection of the dead and the judgment of the living and the dead. This belief is articulated in the Nicene Creed's confession that Christ "will come again in glory to judge in the living and the dead" and that the church in the present looks forward to "the resurrection of the dead and the life of the world to come."

Moltmann and Wright make clear how Christian eschatology builds on a Jewish eschatology that is rooted in the faithfulness of God as both Creator

---

[36]Wright, *Surprised by Hope*, 178, 182.

and Covenant Keeper. Yet both Moltmann and Wright also demonstrate how radically new and different Christian eschatology is, precisely because it is shaped by the life, death, and specifically the resurrection of Jesus Christ. In a manner not altogether unlike Augustine's musings on the qualities of the resurrection body, Moltmann and Wright extend the work of early Christian theologians by reflecting on the nature of new creation and its relation to space and time.

It is worth noting that in N. T. Wright's most recent academic work, based on his Gifford Lectures in 2018, the dimensions of space and time in Christian eschatology come to a prominent focus. Wright argues that the Jewish themes of temple, Sabbath, and image-bearer are foundational to the Christian eschatology which developed. The temple provided a cosmology that imagined heaven and earth as overlapping and interlocking, not the split-level view of the ancient Epicureans or post-Enlightenment philosophers. The Sabbath imagined time as an overlapping of the ages, a way of foretasting the future rest in the present. Wright, drawing on work by Jon Levenson and Abraham Heschel, among others, affirms that what the Sabbath is to *time*, the temple is to *space*. But space and time are not the only key themes. The third is just as pivotal as the other two: the image-bearer. Human beings were set in the cosmic temple of creation as icons of the Creator-God, made to reflect and reveal his image. This human vocation was ultimately fulfilled not by Adam and Eve or by Israel's kings but by the true Messiah, Jesus Christ. In Wright's summation, "Temple-cosmology, Sabbath-eschatology and messianic anthropology formed a comprehensible whole. When reworked around Jesus and the spirit they made the fresh sense that the early Christians grasped".[37] It is not difficult to make the connections here with three of the dimensions of hope which I have outlined here: space, time, and agency.

Let us briefly review the ground we have covered thus far. Hope can be understood from several models. From a cognitive model, hope is a "positive motivational state"; it is oriented upward and forward; and it is based on "agency" and "pathway." Within an affective model, hope is the experience of positive emotions that result in a kind of optimism which functions as a motivation. The virtue-ethics model provides a link for the emotional

---

[37]N. T. Wright, *History and Eschatology* (Waco, TX: Baylor University Press, 2019), 179.

experience of hope to lead to the virtue or character of hopefulness. The phenomenological model provides a way of naming the structural elements of hope, focusing particularly on the grounds, the object, the hoper, and the act of hope. But theologically speaking, hope has to do not only with *who* and *how*, but also *where* and *when*. Following Moltmann and Wright, God's eschatological promises can be understood in terms of space and time. Drawing on historical Christian affirmations of hope, the most succinct line from early Christian communities is the one which ends the Nicene Creed: "We look for the resurrection of the dead and the life of the world to come." This provides the *what* of hope.

For the purposes of this project, I am defining creedal Christian hope in the contemporary context as follows: Christian hope is a confident assurance (act), grounded in God's promise and faithfulness as revealed in the Scriptures in general and in Christ in particular (grounds), that the triune God (agency) will bring about the "resurrection of the dead and the life of the world to come" (object) at Christ's appearing (time), making heaven and earth new and one (space), by means of what has already been accomplished at the resurrection of Jesus (pathway). To put it another way: the *who* is the triune God; the *what* is the resurrection of the dead and the world to come; the *how* is the resurrection of Christ; the *why* is the faithfulness of God in Christ; the *where* is both heaven and earth, made new; the *when* is to come and yet already.

With this as the working definition of hope, I turn now to culture, practice, and ethnography by examining the songs worship leaders named as songs of hope and by exploring how two congregations experience hope within the context of worship.

# PART 3

# EVANGELICALS, WORSHIP, AND HOPE

# 6

# HOPE ESPOUSED

## POPULAR EVANGELICAL ESCHATOLOGY

THE PREACHER BEGAN TO RAISE HIS VOICE as he spoke about the hope of the end times. Jesus is coming back, he said. But before he does, the devil is going to have his way. Things are going to get dark. The people shook their heads knowingly. "It already is dark out there!" "Amen," the people responded. "But it's gonna get worse!" He urged them to stay true to their faith and not to fall away. If they would remain faithful, then they would be rewarded by an escape. The hope for Christians, he said, is that we will be taken out of here before things got really bad. Jesus didn't want us to have to endure tribulation, he assured the saints. Amid the chorus of "Amens" from the people, a man seated near the back wondered whether anyone had considered that tribulation might be relative depending on where one lives. This sermon was being preached to an American congregation. *Aren't millions of Syrian Christians being driven from their homes on the other side of the world?* No one else in the church seemed to care. For them, interpreting the end times was about their comfort and safety.

This story is a composite of several moments from several different churches, but the scene is familiar. Eschatology in America is all about timeline charts and saints who will be airlifted before the persecution gets too beastly. How did it get to be this way? Why is the word *eschatology* so closely associated with the notion of a rapture? While we're at it, how did a fictional series of books based on the rapture become a runaway hit?

This chapter will begin with a brief sketch of the roots for popular evangelical eschatology, naming key historical turns and prominent preachers who intentionally or unintentionally perpetuated an incorrect or incomplete vision of the end. Then, I will outline prominent themes in popular evangelical eschatology by providing a taxonomy of four different evangelical visions of eschatology. The heart of the chapter is an examination of how pastors, worship leaders, and parishioners in the two churches in my fieldwork talk about Christian hope. By paying attention to sermons, interviews, and official statements from each church, along with focus group conversations, I will try to identity an espoused theology of hope in each church. This espoused theology will serve as the backdrop for understanding the chapters that follow on how hope is encoded in worship songs and experienced in worship services.

## POPULAR EVANGELICAL ESCHATOLOGY

***Searching for the roots of popular evangelical eschatology.*** Although theologians and biblical scholars of various denominational stripes affirm a restored and renewed creation, the theology at work in the lives of everyday Christians is often a distorted version of what I have termed creedal Christian hope. Take, for example, the preoccupation with heaven in the American imagination. Historian Gary Scott Smith notes a surge in books on heaven between 1970 and 2000, joining a growing number of books on near-death experiences. The very choice to focus Christian expectation on heaven is a shift from the materiality of creedal Christian hope outlined in the previous chapter. Quite often, no more is bodily resurrection or a redeemed and renewed creation the center of evangelical hope; instead it is a disembodied existence in an otherworldly place. Smith notes that throughout American history various authors have portrayed heaven as the antithesis of earth, highlighting its beauty, safety, abundance, and more. Bound up with the hope of heaven is the joy of being in God's presence and the comfort of being with loved ones.[1]

How did the hope of heaven come to eclipse, or at the very least become conflated with, the hope of resurrection and new creation? It is not an American story; it is much older than that. Richard Middleton offers a brief overview of eschatology in the history of the Western church. In his view, the first

---

[1]Gary Scott Smith, *Heaven in the American Imagination* (New York: Oxford University Press, 2011), 2, 227.

major unraveling of the hope of a renewed cosmos came through Augustine's reading of the millennium as a metaphor for the entire history of the church. The influence of Neoplatonism on his thinking can hardly be overstated, and thus "there is simply no redemption of the cosmos in Augustine's eschatology."[2] This resulted in a shifting center of Christian expectation. Caroline Walker Bynum writes that the hope of a "reconstituted universe" was completely absent by the fifth century, and "eschatological yearning" was no longer for a millennial age but was instead "increasingly focused on heaven."[3]

The hope of a redeemed cosmos is difficult to find in the theology of the Middle Ages. Walker Bynum writes, "Most late medieval Christians thought resurrection and the coming of the kingdom waited afar off in another space and time."[4] Though the hope of a new earth makes sporadic appearances in the works of both Martin Luther and John Calvin, there is not a conscious reflection on it; moreover, their preoccupation is with the redemption of people rather than creation as a whole. The revivals of the eighteenth and nineteenth centuries in the United States featured a postmillennial eschatology. This view looked for a thousand-year period of perfection, or at least of an amelioration of social conditions. Taught by Jonathan Edwards, George Whitefield, Charles Finney, and others, this view concerned only a temporary period, leading to a final state ushered in by the return of Christ. Middleton notes that even though the language of "new heaven and new earth" is used to describe this final state, it was more of a "picturesque way to speak of an acosmic final state than anything to be taken literally."[5] Historian Richard Tarnas surmises, "The early Christian belief that the Fall and Redemption pertained not just to man but to the entire cosmos, a doctrine already fading after the Reformation, now disappeared altogether: the process of salvation, if it had meaning at all, pertained solely to the personal relation between God and man."[6]

---

[2]J. Richard Middleton, *A New Heaven and a New Earth: Reclaiming Biblical Eschatology* (Grand Rapids: Baker Academic, 2014), 292.

[3]Carolyn Walker Bynum, *The Resurrection of the Body in Western Christianity, 200–1336* (New York: Columbia University Press, 1995), 13.

[4]Bynum, *Resurrection of the Body*, 14.

[5]Middleton, *New Heaven and a New Earth*, 295-97.

[6]Richard Tarnas, *The Passion of the Western Mind: Understanding the Ideas That Have Shaped Our World View* (New York: Ballantine Books, 1993), 306-7.

Perhaps no teaching has done more damage to the hope of bodily resurrection and a renewed creation than the rapture doctrine. Rapture teaching
arose from a framework for interpreting the Bible known as dispensationalism. Developed by Irish clergyman John Nelson Darby in the early 1800s,
dispensationalism divided human history into seven distinct time periods,
or dispensations. Darby also taught a premillennial view of the end times—the
belief that Christ will return to initiate the thousand-year reign and that there
will be no peace before it. The rapture, however, will be a secret and supernatural evacuation of all Christians on earth so that they will not have to
endure the great tribulation that precedes the return of Christ. This view was
spread by Darby himself at various prophecy conferences in North America
and Britain, and by American evangelist D. L. Moody, who used this belief
to provide a sense of urgency at his revival meetings. These end-times teach-
ings were also intertwined with advocacy for the Jewish restoration to Pales-
tine, as evidenced by the booklet *Jesus Is Coming*, written by William
Blackstone, a wealthy friend of Moody in the later 1800s. In the early twentieth century, it was the publication of the Scofield Reference Bible by Oxford
University Press that "gave near canonical status" to a dispensational premillennialism framework and the interpretation of biblical prophecies about
the last days or end times.[7] One theologian from Dallas Theological Seminary
even called the Scofield Bible "God's gift to the Church in the last days."[8] Such
a view is largely responsible for the current otherworldly and escapist views
of many North American evangelicals. This mix of rapture teaching and
Zionist zeal featured prominently in my fieldwork at Pathway Church, as will
be evident later in this chapter.

Historian Matthew Sutton also sees premillennialism as a key factor in
contemporary Christian visions of hope, but he makes a much bolder claim.
For him, apocalypticism—which began at the beginning of the twentieth
century with prophecy conferences in New York and Chicago, and became
the raw materials for evangelists such as Moody and, later, Billy Graham—
"provided radical evangelicals with a framework through which to interpret
their lives, their communities, and the future, which in turn often inspired,

---

[7]Middleton, *New Heaven and a New Earth*, 301-2.
[8]Quoted in Matthew Avery Sutton, *American Apocalypse: A History of Modern Evangelicalism*
  (Cambridge, MA: Belknap, 2014), 28.

influenced, and justified the choices they made." This end-times fervor helped American Christians make sense of the turmoil in the world in the twentieth century—two world wars, and then the threat of nuclear war—by situating it within the language of biblical prophecy. All these were simply birth pangs preparing the world for judgment and the return of Christ. This apocalyptic doom was only the backdrop for a blessed hope: escape was possible through Christ. Yet, paradoxically, this premillennial expectation did not lead to apathy or indifference but rather to "inspired fervent, relentless" action in the present.[9] In fact, Sutton's thesis is that apocalypticism is the key lens for understanding the rise of modern American evangelicalism with its pro-America, pro-Israel, right-wing worldview, politics, and social engagement. Though I found this precise conflation of influences at Pathway Church, this is too simplistic; the rise of modern evangelicalism cannot be explained through one lens. Nevertheless, the apocalyptic end of the world and the hope of a premillennial escape cannot be dismissed as an aberrant belief occurring on the margins of American Christianity.

**Taxonomy of evangelical eschatology.** Though I have focused on the escapist or otherworldly tendencies in popular eschatology, escapism is not the only paradigm of evangelical eschatology. As part of structuring my research, I created a taxonomy of evangelical eschatology. It began as a hypothesis, culling phrases from various end-times talks, popular Christian books, funeral sermons, and conversations with Christians over the course of nearly two decades in pastoral ministry, and then clustering them into four categories. I then used these categories in the survey taken by 966 worship leaders in North America. To get a sense of the denominational breakdown of the worship leaders, the survey provided the following options for church affiliation: Catholic, Anglican, Lutheran, Methodist, Presbyterian, Baptist, Assemblies of God, and Vineyard. I clustered Anglicans, Lutherans, and Methodists as mainline Protestant, and Assemblies of God and Vineyard as Pentecostals/charismatics for my research focus. Even so, Baptists remained the largest demographic. A breakdown by denominational cluster shows that about 43 percent of the respondents were Baptists, 26 percent were mainline Protestants (Methodists, Anglicans, and Lutherans), 21 percent Pentecostals and

---

[9]Sutton, *American Apocalypse*, 4, 22, 25.

charismatics (Assemblies of God and Vineyard), 5 percent Presbyterians, and 4 percent Catholic.[10]

My taxonomy of evangelical eschatology marks out four different yet potentially overlapping views: *new creation, explanation, evacuation,* and *compensation*. Smith's research on heaven in the American imagination would seem to confirm this taxonomy by providing summaries from various sermons and books on heaven. Hints of a *new-creation* view of hope are in the context of reunited relationships. Heaven is the place where the joy of being with loved ones is restored in a glorious reunion. The hope of *explanation* has come to the forefront as many Americans have experienced troubles, worries, and anxieties. Smith cites a prominent evangelical leader's assurance that "God would lovingly explain the reason" for every pain experienced on earth.[11] Smith also repeatedly points out the consistent assertion in American preaching and teaching that heaven is a destination, a place, and not "merely a state or a condition."[12] That heaven is viewed as an otherworldly place is underscored by the imagery used when talking about heaven: "celestial city," "refuge," "home," "haven," and more.[13] These are all examples of the view of hope I have called *evacuation*; they reflect a hope of escape, a hope that requires a different space from "here."[14]

The hope of *compensation*, which includes the notion of retribution for wickedness, is related to a desire for justice. This was more of a feature in the American imagination of heaven during the Civil War era and arose mostly from slaves. I will say more about this in contrast to the hope formed in comfortable contexts in the next chapter, but for now it is enough to note that it was the oppressed and abused in America—in particular, African slaves and their descendants—who expected heaven to provide "justice and compensation for their earthly exploitation and suffering." Yet even those who did not experience the same depth of suffering as slaves did look to heaven as an eternal reward.[15]

---

[10]I separated Presbyterians from other mainline denominations because one of the churches in my fieldwork was a Presbyterian church and I needed specific data from that denomination.

[11]Smith, *Heaven in the American Imagination*, 227, 297.

[12]Smith, *Heaven in the American Imagination*, 227 and 4, where he is quoting both R. A. Torrey and Billy Sunday.

[13]Smith, *Heaven in the American Imagination*, 3.

[14]See chapter five for an outline of the dimensions of hope, including "space."

[15]Smith, *Heaven in the American Imagination*, 227-28.

I did not use the terms from my taxonomy in the survey to reduce the tendency to give the perceived right answer. For example, my suspicion was that no one would willingly say their vision of hope was "evacuation." Thus, I developed statements that reflect each of these terms. For new creation, I used the sentence, "God will set it right one day"; for *explanation*, I said, "God will explain it to me one day"; for *evacuation*, I chose the sentence, "God will get me out of here one day"; and finally, for *compensation*, I said, "God will make it up to me one day." Because it is possible to hold more than one of these views, I designed the question to allow each respondent to rank the statements in the order of which brought the most hope. See figure 6.1 for the responses illustrating the breakdown of percentages of each group according to which statement they ranked number one.

- NEW CREATION: "God will set it right one day."
- EXPLANATION: "God will explain it to me one day."
- EVACUATION: "God will get me out of here one day."
- COMPENSATION: "God will make it up to me one day."

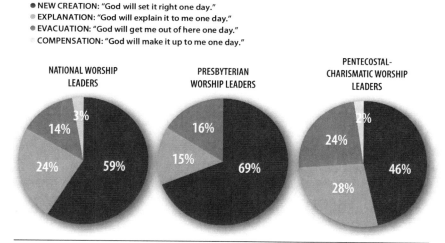

**Figure 6.1.** Taxonomy of hope: Evangelical worship leaders

Some initial observations: First, on a relatively minor note, it seems that no one is looking for God to "make it up to them." Evangelicals have a strong sense of the sovereignty of God. Their own emphasis on personal faith leads them to a posture of surrender. Second, it is striking that in what they claim to believe, evangelical worship leaders all prioritize the hope of new creation above all others. One reason for this may be that evangelicals hold a view of heaven that involves justice and restoration, even if it does not involve the redemption of materiality. Of course, it could also be that respondents were less comfortable with the other statements, as they imply a vision of heaven that has the self at the center, since the other statements include the word *me*. As noted above, throughout the centuries, even phrases such as "new heaven and new earth" have been treated as a metaphor for paradise beyond this world and not as a description of the redemption and renewal of this world. As I will demonstrate through my fieldwork below, it is possible to believe in new creation without believing in the redemption of this world and therefore of materiality. To put it in Helen Cameron's terms, one's espoused theology of hope may be of new creation while one's operant theology of hope is actually evacuation.

Third, it appears that Presbyterians are more likely to believe in new creation than the overall national worship leader group. More Presbyterian worship leaders ranked it as number one than their Pentecostal-charismatic counterparts. Fourth, Pentecostal-charismatics are more likely to believe in evacuation than other worship leaders. Though it was ranked third by most Pentecostal-charismatic respondents, more Pentecostal-charismatic worship leaders chose evacuation as the number one statement of hope than any other group of worship leaders. The last two of these observations are significant as a backdrop for my fieldwork. The themes of new creation and evacuation surface in the espoused theologies of River Valley and Pathway, respectively, as a later section in this chapter will show. I turn now from theoretical taxonomies to ethnography.

## ESPOUSED THEOLOGY: PASTORS AND WORSHIP LEADERS

In the two churches I studied, the pastors and worship leaders had their own ways of depicting Christian hope. The Pentecostal-charismatic church, Pathway, had done a series on the end times right before my research with it began. The goal of the series, according to the pastor who spoke, was to give hope. This was reiterated at various points in the series. One of the sermons in the series was on the rapture. With rhetorical flourish, the preacher insisted that believing in anything other than the rapture would not be a source of comfort. His conclusion, however, seemed almost out of place: "We need to be looking for the return of Jesus." These words nearly echo the creedal confession that "we look for the resurrection of the dead and the life of the world to come." But for the preacher, the return of Christ is conflated with our escape from tribulation. Such a conflation was evident in my interview with the worship pastor, Evan Osmond. I asked Osmond whether he thought most people in his congregation believed in the rapture or believed in Christ's return but not necessarily a rapture.

> "Oh sure, I would think everyone who is a Christ-follower [believe]s that the rapture is coming; but I don't hear that taught a ton, as far as that specific, the rapture itself. I would certainly think that most Christ-followers [at our church] would believe that Christ is coming again . . ."
>
> "But is there a rapture?" I clarified.
>
> "Yeah. I would certainly think so," he replied.

Our formal interview ended moments later, but the worship leader had a brief moment of panic, realizing that he had possibly confused the return of Christ with the rapture of the believer. Despite his clarification, it was evident that the mistake was not likely simply a verbal misstep; these two concepts are so closely intertwined that they are used almost interchangeably.

At the Presbyterian church I spent time in, River Valley, the pastor described being in hospital rooms with patients in tragic circumstances. When I asked him what he says or does in those moments, he said, "Most of what you do is a ministry of presence." He continued by saying that it is not often the time to quote Scripture or offer explanations. In fact, he said that even when people ask directly why God would let a particular tragedy happen, he will say, "I don't know. But I really believe that God is good, and I just have to tell you that I've been through this before and often we're just amazed at how good it can turn out, in the midst of horror." This is significant in light of my taxonomy of hope above; this pastor was refusing even human versions of the hope of explanation, pointing instead to the hope of redemption.

Like the pastor who preached on the rapture, this pastor also wanted hope to be a key takeaway from weekly worship. He told me that he wants there to be "a sense of joy, and a sense of hope" each week in the church's worship services because "what Satan markets most is desperation." He unpacked this more, talking about despair and paranoia. "Despair is really a sense that there is no hope." Paranoia, as he sees it, is "the sense that no matter what I see, no matter what, it will all go bad." By contrast, "faith is no matter what I see, it will all go good, it will all be fine." Both are related to a present circumstance;

one is bent by Satan toward "paranoia, despair, condemnation," and the other shapes it in light of God's sovereignty: "God is never caught off-guard. God never says, 'Boy, I didn't see that coming.' That's just not part of his nature. So even if *we* say that, there is this belief in me that there is a sovereign God who ultimately has got all of this figured out and plays to the win."

Here sovereignty is linked to victory. But in contrast with the prosperity gospel, this victory is in the future. In fact, it may be so far in the future as to be obscured by the trouble of the present. This way of speaking about sovereignty and victory makes clear the futurity of hope in his view. Because the conversation had clustered faith and hope together, I asked him how he would distinguish the two concepts. His answer was clear and confident: "Faith extended into the future is hope. . . . Hope is really my faith extended as far as I can extend it into the future. The picture is that God is at work now, but he's pushing us to trust him for tomorrow, too."

Despite the clear delineation of a futurity of hope, the Presbyterian pastor—Pastor Bob Slate—was ambiguous about the materiality of hope. He did not talk about new creation, or a new heaven and a new earth, or the restoration of all things. In fact, when he mentioned songs that epitomize Christian hope in part of his response to my question about the difference between faith and hope, he referenced "Before the Throne of God Above" and "We Shall Dance on the Streets That Are Golden." I took the opportunity to follow up by asking about what he sees as the "location of hope," since he had already addressed the timing of hope. He responded by talking about the experiential. "Hope in a lot of ways is an emotion and a realization. And that realization happens currently, here." Though he referenced the eschatological, he returned to the conviction that "Jesus is in charge and is on the throne" and therefore "I'm pretty sure tomorrow is going to be fine." "That's a statement of hope, isn't it?" he concluded. It may be that he misunderstood the question, or it may be that as a self-described "Christian mystic," he focuses on the experience of the "person, presence, and activities of Jesus."

How the experience of hope occurs in a service at River Valley involves both the head and the heart: "We need to use both the mind and the heart, and never forget the heart is the goal," Pastor Slate explained. Moving beyond the paradigm of the cognitive, he embraces the role of emotions in worship and is attentive to emotions even in his sermon writing and delivery: "I really believe that feelings are essential to emotion. When I preach I start at the mind and move to the heart," he told me. The distinction between feelings and emotions—parallel, perhaps, to the distinction I noted in chapter three between moods and emotions—reveals an understanding of emotions and human experience. He also described putting "parameters" on worship leader Allan Moody. Speaking about a closing song or a worship response song, Pastor Slate said he has told Moody that "even if it matches the theology of what I preach—it can't be in a minor key" or a song "that people don't know the words to." If it is sad or unfamiliar, the congregation "won't feel hopeful; they'll feel confusion, or they'll feel a bit of dissonance of life." That does not mean the song cannot be used; it just cannot be at the end of the service because he wants that to be a moment where people "can abandon a little bit of their brain" and be "engaged at a heart level."

But this desire to end with a positive and familiar song is more than service aesthetics for Pastor Slate. It is part of a "gospel liturgy." When I asked him at the end of the interview how often in his estimation people are conscious of their need for hope, he responded:

> I think they have need of it all the time, I think that they're not always conscious. But again, part of our gospel liturgy is that we start in the pit. Why is that? Because we need to see our situation in reality before we can see how amazingly helpful it can be. So, the whole movement of the liturgy [starts] in confession, in the brokenness, and then [moves] toward what Christ has done, and into what that means for us.

The pastors at each church had different ways of speaking about hope. At Pathway, it was otherworldly and apocalyptic. The focus was the rapture and final judgment. At River Valley, it was about trust in the sovereignty of God. Hope is the extension of faith outward into the future. Yet, neither pastor spoke about a material future. New creation and resurrection bodies were noticeably absent from the sermons I observed and the interviews I conducted.

## ESPOUSED THEOLOGY: WORSHIPERS AND DISCOURSE ON HOPE

*Pathway focus group.* In order to better understand how hope was expressed in the words of the people in each church, I formed a focus group at each.

One of the early questions I asked the group at Pathway was how they would describe Christian hope. Josh was the first to answer: "For me, it's seeing people who are older than me, who deal with the same stuff as me, who show me that . . . there is still a way, and there's something to still look forward to, and that I'm . . . not going to be defeated." Christian hope for him is a kind of assurance that we will overcome, though the emphasis seems to be more in this life than eschatological.

Mark echoed this sentiment in the question comparing comfort with hope: "Hope is that I know one way or another it's going to work out; it's going to be all right." Mark's response to the direct question about Christian hope, however, added a deeper layer. "Hope for me is . . ." He paused and switched his approach. "Things don't always work out the way we want it to work out, but we know that God's with us. The promise of his presence, that he's always going to be with us, to me, that's hope."

Jonah, saved out of drug addiction, spoke with a kind of gentle authenticity: "Christian hope for me . . . simply put . . . just takes the burden of worry away from everyday life, you know. . . . When I find myself in something that I'm worried about . . . I'm like, 'You know, I'm not going to be here very much longer' . . . well, you know . . . like, compared to eternity."

Sid, the oldest member of our group and a Christian for over sixty years, rooted hope in the Word of God. Comfort, for Sid, was "based on circumstances" and could come and go because "it's an emotional thing; it affects our emotions." "Hope, on the other hand," Sid insists, "is something that we can have in spite of circumstances. And it's eternal, 'cause it says so in the Word." He choked up with emotion while saying this.

Cindy, a Christian of over twenty-five years, echoed the necessity for Christian hope to be grounded in the Scriptures: "[Hope is] grounded in every word that God has spoken. It is . . . you know, 'cause you can have an empty hope . . ." Giving an example of this, she mimicked a voice: "'Oh, I hope for the best.' There's nothing to it . . . or you can hope for what God's Word consists of."

Christian hope, for the people of Pathway, seems to be about choosing to believe what the Bible says—that things will work out, that God is with us, and that we are not going to be here long anyway. To put it in terms of six of the seven dimensions of hope, the people in my focus group grasp the *act* of hoping as a confident assurance, even in the face of overwhelming odds. This act is possible because it is *grounded* in the faithfulness of God—though this character of God was never specifically named, it was implicit in their references to God's "promises" in his Word. The *agency* is attributed to God, though not in a trinitarian or explicitly Christian sense.

The *object* of their hope shows the greatest contrast with what I have outlined as creedal Christian hope. Much of the content of their hope had to do with things working out in the here and now, even if at some later date. It was about the stuff of their daily lives, not abstract or eschatological in any way. Only one member of the group referred to hope in relation to judgment. Bill, a Christian for over twelve years, three years of which were spent in full-time ministry as a pastor, and who is a student at a Christian university hosted at Pathway that offers mostly Bible and theology degrees, had this to say about hope: "[When] I think of Christian hope . . . I think of the finality of it all . . . the fact that we are never going to cease to exist, in one way, one form or another. . . . Hell is hot, and heaven is real." This is a well-worn saying, particularly in American Pentecostal circles. Bill added his own words to draw the connection between final judgment and hope: "And so, when I think of hope, I think of the hope in salvation, the hope of Jesus Christ. . . . He's coming back for us. That's Christian hope." If this view is shared among the congregation at Pathway, it would make sense of why, at the close of Pastor Johnny Edmonds's sermon about the rapture, he gave an altar call for salvation. The object of hope is salvation from judgment—gaining heaven and escaping hell.

Bill's statements may contain the most content related to eschatological hope because of his experience in ministry or his status as a student at the Christian university hosted on Pathway's campus. If so, we may be observing the shift from ordinary theology to a more formal theology. Pathway's official statement of faith includes a final article titled "Eschatology." It states: "We affirm the bodily, personal, second coming of the Lord Jesus Christ, the resurrection of the saints, the millennium, and the final judgment. The final judgment will determine the eternal status of both the saints and the unbelievers, determined by their relationship to Jesus Christ. We affirm with the Bible the final state of the new heavens and the new earth."

One might make the case that this is what the church officially believes as the *object* of its hope. Yet only one person in my focus group—the one undergoing formal theological training at a school affiliated with Pathway—referenced something like the content of this article, matching his espoused theology with the normative theology of his church and tradition. This may be due to the general lack of value Pathway—and the nondenominational Pentecostal-charismatic context to which it belongs—places on formal theological education. One former senior staff member remarked to me that other than a handful of staff members, most of the eight hundred staffers have a business background with no theological training. Thus the cultural norm at Pathway is not to speak in traditionally theological terms.

The *time* of hope for the people I interviewed at Pathway had to do largely with their lives now. Hope was about particular personal promises in their life—job, family, promotions, healing, and the like—coming to pass eventually, despite apparent opposition in the moment. It has a futurity to it, but only in a limited sense. The future was marked by months and years, not by the end of the eschaton. When hope was related to a far ahead future, it was only in reference to heaven and hell, as noted above.

The *space* of hope—the place where hope will come about—was also related to their daily lives. It was there, in their homes and workplaces, that God was going to come through for them. This is an important theme among charismatic Christians, that the power and promises of God can be active and applied in our lives today. Osmond, the worship pastor, explained it to me this way when describing his understanding of Christian hope:

> Christian hope is rooted in the eternal. But not only that; we have hope in heaven with God, but we can have abundant life today, here. It's not just living for that—it's not just scaring them into being a Christian so that when they die they go to heaven. When I was younger that was a lot of times where the message stopped. But instead there's so much more to having abundant living today.

But Osmond was quick to clarify what he meant by the abundant life. Rather than referencing a bigger house, a nicer car, a better job, or any of the other material markers of a "blessed life" often associated with a prosperity gospel, Osmond explained that what abundant living means to him is "a life that is giving, that is loving to others, kind; it's family." In fact, that is what shapes his approach to ministry at Pathway. Rather than the worship team functioning simply as a group of professionals gathered to do a job, Osmond wants it to be a family. "I want us to love each other and support each other. That's what Christian community should be like. That's what the church should be like, and I think we do a great job of that at Pathway."

**River Valley focus group.** I asked the same question that I had asked the group at Pathway to the group at River Valley: "What would you say hope is, as a Christian?" Darren, an older gentleman with a southern drawl, ventured a response: "I haven't thought this out very good, but I'll throw it out there," he laughed as he began. "To me, hope is positive. Hope is that we'll someday be in heaven with the Lord. . . . Hope is a way we can live our lives and feel good about it because we know we have our salvation." He had already said some key phrases. The location of hope was heaven. The reason for it was being "with the Lord." This identification of hope with the presence of the Lord is a consistent theme that showed up in my fieldwork with both Presbyterians and Pentecostal-charismatics. Even though each group may mean something slightly different by the term, it is clear that God's presence, both as it is felt in worship and as it will be known in an ultimate sense in heaven, is the primary focal point of hope.

Darren continued, speaking of hope now as a synonym for optimism—a tendency, as I showed in chapter three, that derives from psychological perspectives of hope: "You can either choose to be sad all the time, or you can choose to be positive. And I think hope gives us the positive way to go about our lives." Greg, another older man, offered a similar response. "Hope to me is that knowledge that no matter what happens . . . you will come out of it OK, to the best it can be." Not only was Greg speaking of hope as a kind of optimism, but he also focused its aim at heaven: "[Hope is the] knowledge that in the end of where you're gonna go. . . . You say, 'If I die tomorrow, I know where I'm going,' and it's a whole lot better than what we have here." Optimism about life in the present is ultimately justified because of the final destination: heaven. This represents a kind of evacuation view in my taxonomy, a generally positive attitude about life because we are not going to be here too long anyway.

Vicki provided a more God-centric rather than heaven-centric response:

> For me, I think hope is to really get it that God is in control no matter what your
> circumstances are, no matter what diagnosis you get, no matter what treatment
> you have to go through, no matter who you lose, no matter what your children
> are doing or not doing, or how messed up your grandchildren are, or having a
> fire and losing—all those things, everything that can just pull you down so much.
> To really know and hold on that God is in control, and that he blesses, and he is
> good, and he will work it out for our good—that to me is what hope is.

This came from a place of conviction. For Vicki, hope was rooted in God's sovereignty and goodness. The sense that God is in control is what anchors the people in my River Valley focus group; it is what makes their hope resilient. This view contains a strong sense of futurity while offering assurance in the present that God is both sovereign and good.

Milton and Diana, an older couple with a remarkable story of redemption, add another layer by describing a hope of deliverance. Milton recited a favorite piece of Scripture of theirs: "It's Isaiah 41:13, 'For I am the Lord your God who takes hold of your right hand, and says, "Do not fear. I will help you."'" Diana chimed in. "My feeling of hope is being on my knees and just reaching up, and, you know, 'Help!' Feeling like there's a hand of Christ come down, 'I gotcha. I have you.' . . . And that's Isaiah 41:13," she said as she quoted it again dramatically and with deep conviction. "That's hope." Here was a picture of hope that looked like confidence in God's deliverance. This is a theme that is consonant with Pastor Slate's description of God's redemption. Though it is not quite the new-creation view in my taxonomy, it is a view that contains futurity and has some connection to the present situation. Whereas Darren and Greg have a hope that is oriented toward the future but without implications for this life and its struggles, Milton and Diana have a view of hope that relates to God's salvation even as takes place in the present. It is future and redemptive. At the same time, the emphasis is on God's "hand" gripping them in the moment. Where Vicki spoke of God holding the situation in his hands, Milton and Diana derive hope from a personal picture; God is holding them in his hands. Thus, the stress here is not on God's sovereignty and therefore his transcendence; rather, it is on God's deliverance and therefore his immanence. God is near.

"I think it's a blessed assurance," Vicki chimed in at the very end, alluding to the words of the well-loved Fanny Crosby hymn: "Blessed assurance, Jesus is mine. Oh what a foretaste of glory divine." Indeed, for the group at River Valley, hope is found in the presence of Jesus, the sovereign and good God who is with them and who is holding them; this is the experience in advance of heaven.

## CONCLUSION AND CONNECTIONS

Through these interviews and focus group conversations, I discovered different but overlapping visions of hope in each church context. The kind of hope espoused in the Presbyterian church is closer to the new-creation view, though it lacks a strong statement of materiality, of the renewal and redemption of creation. The kind of hope espoused in the Pentecostal-charismatic church leans heavily toward the evacuation view, particularly because of the rapture teaching from the pulpit and because of the repeated focus on heaven and hell. In both churches, *heaven* was the word of choice when speaking of eternal hope. No one in either context brought up resurrection or a new heaven and a new earth.

What I discovered in each church were differences not only in the type of hope but in the correlation between what was espoused by leaders versus what was espoused by congregants. In the Presbyterian church, the pastor articulated a fuller version of Christian hope, even using key theological phrases such as "now, but not yet." The congregants in my focus group, however, did not articulate a vision of hope in formal or normative theological language; they spoke mainly of heaven and of God's deliverance and presence. In the Pentecostal-charismatic church, the language of hope used by leaders and by congregants seemed to be from the same lexicon. There was little discrepancy between a sermon on the end times and the way congregants spoke about eternity when asked about hope.

The distinction between espoused theology and operant theology is significant, particularly when doing ethnographic study. When a belief is asked about directly, people tend to give rehearsed answers or responses that they have inherited from church leaders. The desire to conform to group norms diminishes the chance of getting variegated answers within the same context.

In order to examine the operant theology of hope in each church context, I designed my fieldwork to give greater attention to the hope encoded in worship songs and experienced in worship services. The actual theology of hope may be found not in the words used to describe it, but in the songs we sing when we need hope and in the way we experience hope when we come together in worship.

# 7

# HOPE ENCODED

## EXAMINING CONTEMPORARY WORSHIP SONGS

PLANNING A FUNERAL HAS TO BE one of the more difficult parts of pastoral ministry. The minister is not free to fully attend to the grief of the living; she must also offer strength, clarity, and wisdom for the task at hand. Yet the goal is not to merely plug in elements of the service—which scriptures? which songs? which people to share memories of the beloved departed?—as if this were a fill-in-the-blank test. There are, inevitably, moments in a funeral planning meeting where people will break down and cry; they will trail off into a memory about their beloved mother's favorite hymn or the Bible verse their spouse used to recite often. Such a meeting is never really a planning meeting.

Pastors try to minimize the number of decisions for a family member to make in those moments. There is a sheet of recommended scriptures; there is a template for the service flow; there are recommendations for funeral homes and florists, for musicians and singers. But choosing the right songs, in my pastoral experience, is not a decision to default to the pastor on. Scrolling through a mental list of classic hymns and current worship songs, the family will often choose a well-loved hymn, such as "Amazing Grace" or "It Is Well," and a popular worship song, such as "Cornerstone" (which happens to also be a rewrite of a popular hymn).

What do we sing about when we sing about hope? What songs do we turn to when we need to be reminded of our hope? Funerals are not the only occasion for such songs. Whether we are walking in the valley of the shadow of death or have found ourselves in the miry pit, whether we are living in exile or standing amidst ruins, the psalmists of old knew we would need a song. The church needs songs of hope. The question I set out to explore in this chapter is, Do we have them?

## CULTURAL ANTHROPOLOGY AND RITUAL STUDIES

We turn now to the operant theology of hope in contemporary worship by focusing on the way hope is encoded in worship songs. In order to analyze this, I employed the help of ritual studies to shape my approach. It may seem odd to some, but singing as an act of collective worship is, in a very bare and technical sense, a ritual. Here I found Roy Rappaport's work helpful in defining the aspects of a ritual in order to set the stage for my research.

Rappaport, an American anthropologist whose work with the Tsembaga Maring people of New Guinea provides an extensive account of ritual, outlines what he deems the "obvious aspects of ritual." The first of these obvious aspects is *formality*, an adherence to forms. Formality may range from highly variant, where the performer may intersperse particular words or gestures at their own discretion, to highly invariant, where there is nearly nothing for a person to decide. A range is possible because even though invariance is implied in the adherence to forms, rituals are not absolutely invariant. There are often gaps in what is specified for a ritual, necessitating the exercise of choice of the part of the performer, the most fundamental of which is the choice of whether to participate. *Performance* is a second obvious aspect of ritual. If nothing is enacted, there is no ritual. Performing an act may not merely be an expression of something; a performance of a particular act is itself an "aspect of that which it is expressing." A third aspect of a ritual is that it is *noninstrumental*; that is, it does not need to accomplish anything. Though he would not call ritual merely a symbolic statement, Rappaport views ritual as more communication than action. Yet, drawing on J. L. Austin's work on speech-acts, Rappaport describes ritual as a saying that is in itself a doing.[1] Still, a ritual does not produce a "practical result on the external world."[2]

---

[1] Roy Rappaport, "The Obvious Aspects of Ritual," in *Ecology, Meaning, and Religion* (Berkeley, CA: North Atlantic Books, 1979), 173-74, 176-77.

[2] Roy A. Rappaport, *Ritual and Religion in the Making of Humanity* (Cambridge, UK: Cambridge University Press, 1999), 46.

Rappaport notes a ritual has been *encoded* by someone other than the performer. Performers follow orders that have been established by others, possibly even established by God. Where rituals are seen as being divinely prescribed, change is limited in both scope and content; only what is considered erroneous or inconsequential can be altered. Any attempt at invention, rather than reform, is met with resistance; and a new ritual, when introduced, is likely to be seen as a charade.[3] Thus, rituals composed completely of new elements are not often attempted and fail to be established. This explains one reason why contemporary worship resulted in the aforementioned worship wars.

If a ritual is an act of communication, then its messages must be analyzed. Rappaport delineates two types of messages that are transmitted in a ritual: canonical and indexical. Canonical messages are encoded into the ritual and tend to be highly invariant; indexical messages are conveyed by the performers and refer to their "physical, psychic, or even social state at the moment of performance." Canonical messages point to an enduring meaning; indexical messages refer to their immediate contexts. In a given performance, other messages may also be transmitted, but they are not likely to be incorporated into the ritual in a future performance. This aspect of rituals led to my specific focus on song lyrics. Lyrics are, generally speaking, an invariant aspect of the contemporary worship ritual. Furthermore, lyrics are a canonical message because they are pre-encoded; no worship song leaves sections with lyrical gaps to be filled by a worship leader or church.

Rappaport also argues that the performer "is not merely transmitting messages he finds encoded in the liturgy. He is participating in . . . the order to which his own body and breath give life."[4] Thus, a performer is both participating in and affirming of the ritual he performs. This participation and affirmation must be understood in terms of not only the ritual's convention but also its content. By "performing a liturgical order the performer accepts, and indicates to himself and to others that he accepts, whatever is encoded in the canons of the liturgical order in which he is participating."[5] This acceptance is itself a basic indexical message transmitted to the performer. In the act of singing with the congregation, worshipers are affirming the

---

[3]Rappaport, *Ritual and Religion*, 46.
[4]Rappaport, "Obvious Aspects of Ritual," 192.
[5]Rappaport, "Obvious Aspects of Ritual," 192-93.

canonical message of the song. Yet even this participation requires more exploration into what meaning is being ascribed to the ritual. For that, ethnography is required, which is what the next chapter will examine.

Interviews with the worship leaders at the fieldwork churches in the previous chapter and participant observation in the following chapter note a few of the indexical messages, but the focus of this chapter is on canonical messages. I have limited the scope of my research to the canonical messages encoded in lyrical content. Song lyrics are the most invariant aspect of contemporary worship songs. A worship team may change the key signature or even the chord progression as part of the creative musical expression, but lyrics are nearly never changed—at least, they shouldn't be without the permission of the writer and the publisher!—and are thus the most reliable way to examine canonical messages.

The majority of the chapter analyzes songs that worship leaders in North America say bring them and their churches hope, which I am referring to as songs of hope. I then compare the national data with responses from worship leaders in Pentecostal-charismatic churches and responses from worship leaders in Presbyterian churches. Breaking the analysis of encoded hope into sections that explore various dimensions of hope that were identified in chapters three, four, and five, I examine encoded space by looking at key song lyrics such as *heaven* and *earth*. I also assess encoded time by a detailed analysis of verbs for divine and human action. After noting a significant emphasis in these songs on the here and now, I offer possible explanations for this. I return to the analysis by investigating encoded agency as revealed by the nouns and pronouns used in the songs, paying attention to ratios of nouns and pronouns used for God versus the worshiper. I also compare the use of individual versus communal nouns and pronouns for the worshiper. In the final sections of the chapter, I examine the encoded hope based on responses to the same questions from the churches in my fieldwork.

## SONGS OF HOPE: SURVEY DATA

***Survey method and demographics.*** Several analyses of contemporary worship songs have been done. Pete Ward analyzed songbooks in *Selling Worship*; Lester Ruth has analyzed verbs and themes in the songs that have been listed in the CCLI Top 25 since the list began to be published over twenty-five years ago; and Matthew Westerholm has analyzed the eschatology of CCLI Top 25 songs in his recent dissertation.[6] While these studies have provided insight into contemporary worship music, the challenge with these lists is that they are influenced by market forces and consumer dynamics. A list such as the CCLI Top 25 may be representative of a particular era of worship music because it documents the popularity and widespread use of a song, but it lacks the kind of specificity my research required. I am not looking at how hope is manifest in popular worship songs; I wanted to know what songs people associate with the experience of hope. Furthermore, as Ward notes, "The analysis of songbooks"—and I would add of CCLI Top 25 lists—"in and of themselves is . . . slightly artificial, because in practice churches pick and choose from a range of sources."[7]

I employed a method known as free recall. Psychologists Carey Morewedge (Harvard University), Daniel Gilbert (Harvard University), and Timothy Wilson (University of Virginia) have demonstrated that free recall uncovers the best of times and the worst of times, rather than the most typical of times.[8] CCLI lists and worship songbook collections can show what the most typical songs are, but a free-recall question can reveal the most memorable song in terms of the hope the worshiper felt.

***Songs of hope: National worship leader responses.*** In partnership with Integrity Music, I asked worship leaders from its email distribution lists across North America to "Name a worship song that brought you hope in a time of despair." Then, later in the survey, I asked, "Name a song you sing at church that usually brings you hope." The first question (question 15) generated 844 song responses with 414 unique songs; the second question (question 25) generated 704 song responses with 319 unique songs.

Taking the top responses to both questions together, I discovered that each list had the same songs in the top five most-mentioned songs, albeit in slightly different order. I aggregated the mentions in these two lists by adding the mentions for each song and dividing them by two. The top five worship songs

---

[6]Pete Ward, *Selling Worship: How What We Sing Has Changed the Church* (Exeter, UK: Paternoster, 2005); Lester Ruth, "Some Similarities and Differences Between Historic Evangelical Hymns and Contemporary Worship Songs," *Artistic Theologian* 3 (2015): 68-86; Matthew Westerholm, "The Hour Is Coming and Is Now Here: The Doctrine of Inaugurated Eschatology in Contemporary Evangelical Worship Music" (PhD diss., Southern Baptist Theological Seminary, 2016).
[7]Pete Ward, *Liquid Ecclesiology: The Gospel and the Church* (Leiden, Netherlands: Brill, 2017), 153.
[8]Carey K. Morewedge, Daniel T. Gilbert, and Timothy D. Wilson, "The Least Likely of Times: How Remembering the Past Biases Forecasts of the Future," *Psychological Science* 16, no. 8 (2005): 626.

that were affirmed as bringing hope both at times of despair and in congregational worship are seen in table 7.1.

**Table 7.1.** Top songs of hope

| | |
|---|---|
| "Good Good Father" | 40.5 mentions |
| "It Is Well" | 24 mentions |
| "In Christ Alone" | 22.5 mentions |
| "No Longer Slaves" | 19.5 mentions |
| "Cornerstone" | 19 mentions |

***Songs of hope: Pentecostal-charismatic responses.*** In order to explore the responses from Pentecostal-charismatic worship leaders and Presbyterian worship leaders, I created comparisons of each subgroup with the larger survey respondents. I filtered out all responses except those from Assemblies of God and Vineyard churches, and clustered my findings of these Pentecostal-charismatic worship leaders. Repeating the same analysis as above, the summary of question 15, about a song that brought the worship leader hope in a time of despair, shows that out of 104 Pentecostal-charismatic worship leaders, 88 song responses were given, with 76 unique songs named. The summary of question 25, about a song sung at church that usually brings hope, yielded 83 song responses with 63 unique songs.

In aggregating the lists of songs mentioned two times or more in response to questions 15 and 25, six songs rise to the top. They are listed in table 7.2 below. Note that four songs from the above list from the entire worship leader base appear on this list: "Good Good Father," "It Is Well," " No Longer Slaves," and "Cornerstone."

**Table 7.2.** Top Pentecostal-charismatic songs of hope

| | |
|---|---|
| "It Is Well" | 3.5 mentions |
| "Good Good Father" | 3 mentions |
| "Great Are You Lord" | 3 mentions |
| "Still" | 3 mentions |
| "Cornerstone" | 2 mentions |
| "No Longer Slaves" | 2 mentions |

***Songs of hope: Presbyterian responses.*** When I filtered out all responses except those from worship leaders who identified their churches as Presbyterian, the song selection diversified even more. In response to the first question regarding a song that brought worship leaders hope, only two songs were mentioned twice. There were thirty-one unique songs named out of the thirty-three songs given. While there were fewer songs named in response to the question about a song they sing at church that brings hope, the percentage of unique songs rose slightly: twenty-six out of the twenty-seven total songs named were unique; only one was mentioned twice.

From both lists, worship leaders in Presbyterian churches named, on average, more than one song each. This is highest ratio of unique songs per worship leader in all three groups—the whole group, Pentecostal-charismatic worship leaders, and Presbyterian worship leaders. This may mean that Presbyterians are capable of finding hope from a larger array of songs than the average worship leader or the Pentecostal-charismatic worship leader, or it may mean that Presbyterians worship leaders have a wider array of songs that have hope encoded in them from which to choose. This survey data alone cannot provide that answer.

When I combined the songs given in response to both questions, I took the songs with the most total mentions and divided them by two. The average mentions of the top songs are shown in table 7.3.[9] Two songs on this list also appear on the list from the whole group of national worship leaders: "In Christ Alone" and "Cornerstone."

**Table 7.3.** Top Presbyterian songs of hope

|                                |               |
| ------------------------------ | ------------- |
| "In Christ Alone"              | 1.5 mentions  |
| "Boldly I Approach"            | 1 mention     |
| "Cornerstone"                  | 1 mention     |
| "Jesus, I My Cross Have Taken" | 1 mention     |
| "Still"                        | 1 mention     |

***Songs of hope: Initial observations.*** These three aggregated lists of songs that brought hope in some way formed the primary text for my analysis of how hope is encoded in contemporary worship songs. This metadata allowed me to compare patterns in the songs named by worship leaders across denominations with

---

[9]The number of mentions for each song is drastically lower here because of the smaller segment of responses and because of the large number of different songs named. The top song by mentions, "In Christ Alone," was named three times in the two questions; the others were only named twice.

the patterns in the songs named by Pentecostal-charismatic worship leaders and with the songs named by Presbyterian worship leaders.

A few observations may be made about all three lists, which result in nine total unique songs. First, "Cornerstone" is the only song that appears in the top songs on all three lists—the general worship leader responses, worship leaders at Pentecostal-charismatic churches, and worship leaders at Presbyterian churches. "In Christ Alone" shows up on two lists—the general worship leader list and the Presbyterian worship leader list. It is unclear what one ought to conclude about its absence from the Pentecostal-charismatic worship leader list. It is a song that emerged from Reformed contexts and that reflects Reformed theology.[10] That the largest segment of the general worship leader group in my survey are worship leaders at Baptist churches accounts for why the song shows up on the general list—many Baptists align with Reformed theology on many, though not all, points.[11] The one song that Presbyterians had in common with Pentecostal-charismatics was "Still." The only song unique to Pentecostal-charismatic worship leaders was "Great Are You Lord." There were two songs that only appear on the Presbyterian lists, "Boldly I Approach" and "Jesus, I My Cross Have Taken."

## ENCODED SPACE

Because space is a dimension of hope, it is important to examine where the action of the song is occurring and where is the worshiper directed to aim her hope. Hope in Christian theology can either be located *here* or *there*—earth or heaven. The worshiper is situated on earth, and worship is an action that turns us upward to God. Yet a remarkable number of these songs of hope specifically mention God's presence here.

"In Christ Alone" ends three of its four stanzas with a refrain that begins with the word *here*: "Here in the love of Christ I stand," "Here in the death of

---

[10] The line in the song about the "wrath of God" being "satisfied" on the "cross where Jesus died" has stirred no small controversy among Christians outside the Reformed tradition. It was even suggested that the line be changed in some hymnals and slide-presentation software to say "the love of God was magnified." But the songwriters themselves have rejected this suggestion, and Reformed theologians have doubled down on the line as being theologically necessary. All this may contribute to the reluctance of Pentecostal-charismatic worship leaders to use the song.

[11] See, for example, the popular blog collective thegospelcoalition.org, which features prominent Baptist pastors under the umbrella of a "gospel" centered approach—a phrase and framework that draws on Reformed theology as expressed in the neo-Reformed movement.

Christ I live," and "Here in the power of Christ I'll stand." Arguably, the *here* being referred to in each instance is not a geographical location but rather a theological one. Nevertheless, the point of emphasis seems to be that the love, life, and power of Christ are not distant realities to which one must travel but rather present and existential realities in which one "stands."

Earth is mentioned three times in the nine top songs of hope. First, in "It Is Well," a contemporary worship song that riffs off the classic hymn, the opening line reminds the worshiper that "Grander earth has quaked before." This appears to be a reference to the response of creation to its Creator walking on it and speaking to it, though it is unclear to which Gospel story this line refers. The implicit hope for the worshiper is that if the holy ground where Christ walked has responded to Jesus' voice before, surely the earth where we walk can as well. In fact, each earthly image—seas and mountains follow—is used to represent troubles of this present world that God can change here and now.[12] This is not unique to this song. Seas and storms are referenced in five of the nine songs, appearing seven times in all.

"Great Are You Lord," a song unique to the Pentecostal-charismatic list, uses *earth* as a reference not to the trouble in the world but to the creation that praises God. "And all the earth will shout Your praise, our hearts will cry, these bones will sing, 'Great are You Lord,'" the song exclaims. The final use of *earth* in these songs appears in "Jesus, I My Cross Have Taken," a song that only surfaced on the Presbyterian top-songs list. Here *earth* is used as an adjective, *earthly*, to refer to a temporal assignment that will one day end. "Soon shall close my earthly mission, swiftly pass my pilgrims days; Hope soon change to glad fruition, faith to sight and prayer to praise." *Earth* in these songs of hope refers to troubles in which God can intervene; creation, which can bring God praise; and a temporal place the worshiper will soon leave.

Heaven is mentioned four times, but in only one of the nine songs, a song unique to the Presbyterian list, "Jesus, I My Cross Have Taken." The opening stanza ends with the emphatic declaration that "God and heaven are still my own." The worshiper's hope is secure. Moreover, hope is not only a person (God) but also a place (heaven). The second stanza enumerates the worldly

---

[12]The first verse goes on to reference the "seas that are shaken and stirred" as being able to be "calmed and broken" for the "regard" of the worshiper. A second verse references the "mountain" in front of the worshiper as an object or obstacle that can be cast into the "midst of the sea."

people who make life difficult for the heaven-bound pilgrim, but the third stanza opens with the reminder that all these troubles only drive us to God's blessed presence. Even though "Life with bitter trials may press me, Heaven will bring me sweeter rest." The fourth stanza ends with a line that addresses the worshiper as a "Child of Heaven," admonishing her not to "fret." If this were not a clear enough orientation to a future place, the final stanza directs the worshiper onward and upward, pressing through the trials of the here and now.

> Onward then from grace to glory,
> Armed by faith and spurred by prayer;
> Heaven's eternal day's before me,
> God's own hand shall guide me there.

If seas and storms are metaphors of earthly woes, *throne* is a picture of the reign of God having the final say. The throne is an image of finality, of God's will being done, of evil being vanquished. *Throne* appears three times in two of the nine songs. "Cornerstone," the only song that appears on all three lists, ends its final verse with the image of the worshiper standing before God's throne.

> When He shall come with trumpet sound
> Oh, may I then in Him be found
> Dressed in His righteousness alone
> Faultless stand before the throne.

"Boldly I Approach" is the other song that employs the image of the throne. A song unique to the Presbyterian list, it envisages the worshiper coming to the throne not at a future time but in the present moment. The act of worship is an act that transports the worshiper from wherever he is to the heavenly throne. What is even more interesting is that both times the throne image is evoked, it is combined with a personal or familial metaphor, juxtaposing the sovereignty of God with the love of God. The song opens with this verse:

> By grace alone somehow I stand
> Where even angels fear to tread
> Invited by redeeming love
> Before the throne of God above

He pulls me close with nail-scarred hands
Into His everlasting arms.

The chorus, the centerpiece of the song, opens with the throne image but ends once again with the metaphor of the worshiper being held or welcomed into God's arms.

Boldly I approach Your throne
Blameless now I'm running home
By Your blood I come welcomed as Your own
Into the arms of majesty.

Moving beyond specific words and phrases, many of the top nine songs on the combined list have a general sense of immediacy and proximity. Even the use of *throne* in the above song illustrates how, even when the songs speak about God and heaven, they do so in a way that brings heaven down to earth, that makes God present here. "It Is Well" declares that "through it all my eyes are on You," giving not only a timeless quality to the moment but an immediacy to God. He is here, close enough for our eyes to see. "Good Good Father" imagines a God who is right here, close enough to hear his "tender whisper" in the "dead of night." "Still" begins with the premise that God is close enough for him to "hide" us under the cover of his "wings." Even "Boldly I Approach" places the worshiper "face to face with Love Himself." Only "In Christ Alone" and "Jesus, I My Cross Have Taken" contain a narrative progression, which is a concept I will explore in more detail below. "No Longer Slaves" evokes the imagery of Israel being led through the Red Sea to describe in an intensely personal way God's salvation of the individual worshiper:

You split the sea so I could walk right through it,
My fears were drowned in perfect love;
You rescued me so I could stand and sing,
I am a child of God.

The encoded space found in the songs that worship leaders named as songs of hope corresponds to the space where the same worship leaders locate their hope. Three of the twenty-five questions on the survey had to do with where the object of hope will arrive. I paired two statements and asked the worship leaders to pick the one that brought them more hope. Heaven is contrasted with earth. The responses are broken down by denominational cluster in figures 7.1, 7.2, and 7.3. The most interesting contrast is between figures 7.1 and 7.3. Though the majority of worship leaders affirmed their hope being in heaven's future arrival to earth, a majority also affirmed the claim that this world is not our home. It should be noted that Pentecostal-charismatic worship leaders were more drawn to this claim than Presbyterian worship leaders were. Finally, figure 7.2 demonstrates an overwhelming sense of hope from Christ's presence with us in our space rather than from his implied presence in heaven at the right hand of the Father or from his future glorious presence with us—even though that particular phrase, "Christ will come again in glory," is a direct line from the Nicene Creed.

## ENCODED TIME: VERB TENSES FOR DIVINE AND HUMAN ACTION

The sense of immediacy of access and proximity of place that has been traced in these songs of hope is only one dimension of encoded hope. The sense of space can be corroborated by a more technical analysis of the time dimension of hope. While locating the space of hope relies on a broad look

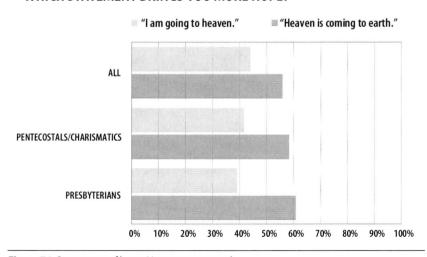

Figure 7.1. Statements of hope: Heaven versus earth

## "WHICH STATEMENT BRINGS YOU MORE HOPE?"

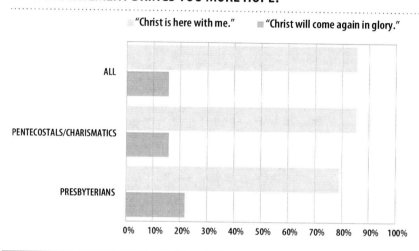

**Figure 7.2.** Statements of hope: Christ's presence versus Christ's return

## "WHICH STATEMENT BRINGS YOU MORE HOPE?"

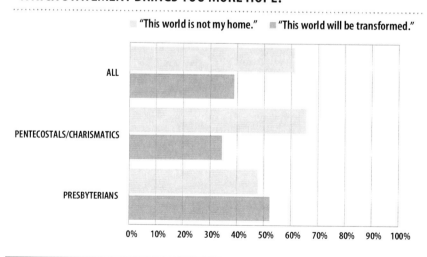

**Figure 7.3.** Statements of hope: The world as foreign versus the world transformed

at themes and keywords, an analysis of time can be revealed by a study of the verbs in these songs. Central to the question of how hope is encoded in songs is an analysis of verbs. A verb analysis allowed me to focus not so much on the type of action being sung about with reference to God and the worshiper but rather on the timing of the action. Verb tenses locate the action of both God and the worshiper in the past, present, or future. Because hope involves the dimension of time and specifically an orientation toward the future, I examined how much these songs are oriented toward the future.

I divided the verbs into three groups—divine and human action, human action, and divine action—and compared them by the lists on which the songs appear: general worship leaders, Pentecostal-charismatic worship leaders, and Presbyterian worship leaders. Three tables map the verb tenses of these songs of hope, beginning with verbs for both (table 7.4), then verbs of human action (table 7.5), and then verbs for divine action (table 7.6). It is significant to note in table 7.4 that both the subgroups sing about action in the past less than the general group. But most striking is the high percentage of verb tenses in the present tense from songs named by Pentecostal-charismatic worship leaders.

**Table 7.4.** Verbs for God and us in songs of hope

|  | In songs named by national worship leaders | In songs named by Presbyterian worship leaders | In songs named by Pentecostal-charismatic worship leaders |
|---|---|---|---|
| **Past tense** | 24% | 20% | 11% |
| **Present tense** | 59% | 61% | 68% |
| **Future tense** | 17% | 19% | 21% |

When the verbs of human action are separated out (table 7.5), the differences between the two shift slightly. Here the difference between the focus on the past is not pronounced, while the focus on the future is higher for Pentecostal-charismatic songs of hope. One also notes that the focus on the present is lower for Pentecostal-charismatic songs of hope. Pentecostal-charismatic songs of hope seem to have little trouble anticipating what the worshiper will do in the future.

**Table 7.5.** Verbs for us in songs of hope

| | In songs named by national worship leaders | In songs named by Presbyterian worship leaders | In songs named by Pentecostal-charismatic worship leaders |
|---|---|---|---|
| Past tense | 15% | 15% | 13% |
| Present tense | 67% | 66% | 58% |
| Future tense | 18% | 19% | 29% |

When the verbs for divine action are compared (table 7.6), the focus on the future is comparable. What is stunning—and this is the greatest discrepancy in the three graphs—is the lack of focus on the past and the strong focus on the present in Pentecostal-charismatic songs of hope. When it comes to singing about God, Pentecostal-charismatic worship leaders apparently derive very little hope from what God has done or what God will do. They are fixated instead on what God is doing. Because it is puzzling how a song can be said to bring hope when there is so little reference to the future, whether ours or the one that God will bring, it is worth exploring further a few possible explanations for why this is the case.

**Table 7.6.** Verbs for God in songs of hope

| | In songs named by national worship leaders | In songs named by Presbyterian worship leaders | In songs named by Pentecostal-charismatic worship leaders |
|---|---|---|---|
| Past tense | 33% | 27% | 8% |
| Present tense | 52% | 55% | 81% |
| Future tense | 15% | 18% | 11% |

## POSSIBLE EXPLANATIONS FOR A HERE-AND-NOW FOCUS

How can there be hope when there is no orientation toward the future? Below are three possible explanations. Each explanation represents a plausible hypothesis, the beginnings of which are explored in my research, but which requires further investigation in future studies. These explanations are to be understood as layers that may coexist. All three explanations may be working at the same time, contributing to the focus of the aforementioned songs on the present tense.

*Worship and the character of God.* A simple explanation for the focus on the present tense may be that the nature of Christian worship is to focus on who God is rather than what God will do. This does not negate an orientation toward the future; it may simply mean that confidence for the future is grounded in the unchanging nature of who God is. An example of this can be found in a cursory examination of early Christian worship songs. A pair of ancient hymns not derived from either the Psalms or the New Testament texts are found in the writings of the Cappadocian theologians of the fourth century. The first is known as the *Phos hilaron*, meaning "Joyous Light." The second, which is also better known in the West, is *Gloria in excelsis*. The first was used in evening prayer, the second in morning prayer. The *Phos hilaron* contains only three verbs in its English translation found in Andrew McGowan's text on ancient Christian worship.[13] Two of the verbs denote action from the church, and one from the cosmos; there are no verbs for action from God. All three verbs are in the present tense. Each verb is italicized below:

> Joyous Light of the holy glory of the immortal Father,
> Heavenly, holy, blessed Jesus Christ;
> *Coming* to the setting of the sun, *seeing* the evening light,
> We *hymn* Father, Son, and Holy Spirit, God.
> It *is* right for You at all times to *be* praised with blessed voices,
> Son of God, the Giver of life. Therefore, the cosmos *glorifies* you.[14]

The second hymn, *Gloria in excelsis*, contains twelve verbs—five that denote human action, five which denote divine action, and two, the first and the last, that are ascriptions of glory to God. All are in the present tense. Once again, I have used McGowan's translation and italicized the verbs below for emphasis:

> Glory *be* to God in the highest,
> and upon earth, peace, goodwill among human beings.
> We *praise* you, we *hymn* you, we *bless* you, we *glorify* you,
> we *adore* you by your great High Priest;
> You, true God, sole and unbegotten, the only inaccessible one,
> Because of your great glory, Lord, heavenly King, God the Father Almighty;
> O Lord God, the Father of the Lord, the immaculate Lamb,
> who *takes* away the sin of the world, *receive* our prayer,
> You who *are enthroned* upon the cherubim.

---

[13]Andrew B. McGowan, *Ancient Christian Worship* (Grand Rapids: Baker Academic, 2014).
[14]McGowan, *Ancient Christian Worship*, 126.

For you only *are* holy, you only *are* the Lord, God and Father of Jesus,
the Christ, God of all created nature, our King, by whom glory,
honor, and worship *are* to you.[15]

This is not to say that all ancient Christian worship was in the present tense. Much more detailed study would be required before such claims could be made. McGowan even notes that the Syrian church in the fourth century composed hymns that "told stories in narrative form," "with the women's and men's choirs taking the parts of biblical characters."[16] Other Syrian hymns were "explicitly doctrinal and pedagogical in character."[17] Nonetheless, it cannot be overlooked that many of the contemporary worship songs listed above in the survey are simply following a long tradition of singing about who God is, praising God for his being Father or Cornerstone. The perpetuity of God's reign, God's holiness, and more may form at least part of the reason why contemporary worship songs contain so many verbs in the present tense.

Compare the first hymn, the *Phos hilaron*, for example, with "Great Are You Lord," one of the top six songs that Pentecostal-charismatic worship leaders named as a song of hope. The first verse opens with a series of statements about what God does, culminating in the praise of who God is:

You give life,
You are love,
You bring light to the darkness
You give hope,
You restore every heart that is broken
Great are you Lord.

Praising God for who he is, as his character and nature are made manifest by his divine actions, is a longstanding Christian practice.

***Contemporary songwriters, spirituals, and the perfect present.*** Another possible explanation for the focus on the present in contemporary worship songs of hope is that the "present" is relatively pain-free for both the worship songwriter and many of the worship leaders I surveyed. The top five songs in my aggregated list (fig. 7.4) were written in Atlanta, Georgia ("Good Good

---

[15]McGowan, Ancient Christian Worship, 127.
[16]McGowan, Ancient Christian Worship, 128.
[17]McGowan, Ancient Christian Worship, 128.

Father"); Redding, California ("It Is Well"); Nashville ("Great Are You Lord"); Sydney, Australia ("Still," "Cornerstone"); and Sophia, North Carolina ("No Longer Slaves"). Though these are not necessarily places of affluence, they are, broadly speaking, places of ease. A word of caution about this hypothesis: I have no way of knowing the precise circumstances of these writers when they were writing these songs. They are, by all accounts, genuinely godly and humble people. They may have been experiencing personally trying times that provoked these songs of worship and trust. The attempt to compare their immediate social context with that of other writers—for example, as you will see, with those who wrote slave spirituals in the American South—is not meant to cast a disparaging light on any of these contemporary writers. It is simply to suggest that our situations and surroundings may affect the way we sing about hope. It is possible that contemporary worship songs of hope can dwell on the present because life is good right now, for both songwriter and worshiper. Focusing on the present tense is a luxury of the privileged.

These songs stand in contrast with the slave spirituals. "The spiritual," James Cone argues, "is the spirit of the people struggling to be free; it is their religion, their source of strength in a time of trouble. And if one does not know what trouble is, then the spiritual cannot be understood." Cone suggests that the spirituals were not about a "'spiritual' freedom" but an "eschatological freedom grounded in the events of the historical present, affirming that even now God's future is inconsistent with the realities of slavery." Though this theological language is not explicit in spirituals, Cone insists that the "expectation of the future of God, grounded in the resurrection of Jesus . . . was the central theological focus of black religious experience." The rhetoric of the songs and the sermons of black preachers, taken together, makes clear that the grounds and object of hope were eschatological. By eschatology, Cone means not simply the future return of Christ but the past resurrection of Christ, since it is the resurrection that shapes our hope at his return. Thus Cone writes, "The resurrection was an eschatological event which permeated both the present and future history of black slaves." In fact, it was because "the black slave was confident that God's eschatological liberation would be fully revealed in Jesus's Second Coming" that "he could sing songs of joy and happiness while living in bondage." Cone continues by asserting that this "hope in a radically new future, defined solely by God the Liberator," is manifest in spirituals through their language about place and time—two categories that Moltmann outlines as key dimensions of Christian hope.[18]

The spirituals are full of references to heaven, a place where "the oppressed would 'lay down dat heavy load'"; "a place where slaves would put on their robes, take up their harps, and put on their shoes and wings." It was a "home indeed, where slaves would sit down by Jesus, eat at the welcome table, sing and shout, because there would be nobody there to turn them out"; it was "God's eschatological promise," where there would be "no more sadness, no more sorrow, and no more hunger." But heaven was not simply a place of future hope; it was also a metaphor that inspired action in the present. Heaven, in spirituals, "served functionally to liberate the black mind from the existing values of white society, enabling black slaves to think their own thoughts and do their own things." Cone gives some examples of what the language about heaven came to signify.

> For Tubman and Douglass, heaven meant the risk of escape to the North and Canada; for Nat Turner, it was a vision from above that broke into the minds of believers, giving them courage and the power to take up arms against slave masters and mistresses. And for others, heaven was a perspective on the present, a spiritual, a song about "another world . . . not made with hands."

The *time* of hope was set in the future even as it inspired action in the present. Black slaves used an "apocalyptic imagination" to express their "anticipation of God's new future." Such imagery emphasized that the reality of God's future could not be contained in our present. They "stressed the utter distinction between present and future."[19] This is why black eschatology meant an affirmation of life after death.

Black eschatology in spirituals also had to do with judgment and justice at the return of Christ. Cone, with forceful voice, writes:

> The spirituals speak not only of what Jesus has done and is doing for blacks in slavery. Jesus was understood as holding the keys of Judgment, and therefore the full consummation of God's salvation will take place outside of the historical sphere. Jesus is the Son of God who dwells in heaven. And he is coming again;

---

[18]James Cone, *The Spirituals and the Blues*, 2nd ed. (Maryknoll, NY: Orbis Books, 1992), 30, 42, 50, 52, 88.

[19]Cone, *Spirituals and the Blues*, 86, 88-90.

but this time "he ain't coming to die." He is coming to complete God's will to set free "the poor, black, and wasted." He will take them home to be with him.[20]

From Cone's analysis, the grounds, space, time, and agency of Christian hope in the spirituals are made clear. Setting this against my analysis of the songs that contemporary worship leaders say bring them hope, the *agency* of hope is consistent—it is God who brings about the hoped-for reality—and the *grounds* may be comparable, but the *space* and *time* of hope are remarkably dissimilar. If the futurity of spirituals is clear because of a difficult present, it is plausible that contemporary songs of hope are fixated on the present because life is mostly good here and now.

*Postmodernism and the loss of narrative.* The lack of narrative in the songs that people chose as songs of hope is part of a larger trend in contemporary worship songs. Worship historian Lester Ruth compares contemporary worship songs with what Stephen Marini calls historically significant American evangelical hymns. One notable difference is in the eschatology encoded in the songs. "The sense of our ultimate destiny in EH [Evangelical Hymns] is delayed and mediated by key biblical types. One day our sojourn through the wilderness will be done, we will pass over the river, and enter into the Promised Land or heavenly city." By contrast, "the sense of fulfilment in CWS [Contemporary Worship Songs] is immediate."[21]

Ruth is reluctant to make absolute claims about why the difference exists, since the two bodies of songs originate from dozens of writers. Yet he makes two observations. First, the historic contexts are different in terms of the sense of frailty or vulnerability. Modern medicine, among other things, has extended human life and mitigated the fear of death, and with it a "corresponding fear of the wrath of God": "Longer lives, consumerist expectations, and a middle-class lifestyle for lyricist and congregation alike have created a desire for immediate fulfilment. We do not sojourn, we arrive. We now flee from meaninglessness, not an impending judgment. Recent songs tend to reflect this shift." This is consonant with the above hypothesis of a perfect present accounting for the fixation on life in the present tense. Second, Ruth observes a shift from a pilgrimage paradigm, the epitome of which is enshrined in John

---

[20]Cone, *Spirituals and the Blues*, 51.
[21]Ruth, "Some Similarities and Differences," 69, 75.

Bunyan's *Pilgrim's Progress*, to an end-times paradigm. Discipleship is no longer "a long journey toward our final destiny" but rather a faithful waiting for the imminent return of Christ. Ruth remarks that early contemporary worship songs arose out of the Jesus people movement, in which an eschatology of escapism and an impending return of Christ featured prominently, and out of which came a movement of worship songs called "Maranatha! Music"—meaning, "Come, Lord Jesus!"[22]

Yet the lack of narrative is hardly noticed because meaning no longer derives primarily from the story told by sermons and worship songs but from the worshiper's experience. In Martin Stringer's observations of a Baptist church, he notes that stories featured prominently in their sermons. Hymns in this context, Stringer argues, either become stories themselves or "triggers for the recalling of stories. . . . One line of a hymn has the potential to conjure up a whole series of biblical stories." Stringer posits that there are three stories in a worship event: the story that we bring to worship and that affects what we hear in worship; the new stories that we hear in worship, either from Scripture or from leaders; and the story of the interaction or merger of those two stories. This third story is the story of how worship speaks to us, which Stringer says is an instance of an instantaneous superimposition of both our own story and the liturgical story, which results in a flow of meaning or emotion between the two.[23]

This merging of personal story and the stories supplied in worship makes up at least part of what is named as the experiential dimension of contemporary worship. Catholic liturgical theologian Aidan Kavanagh asserts that "what is unknowable in worship is essentially experiential."[24] Stringer concludes that the act of worship is best understood as a space without meaning (in a linguistic sense). Individuals who come to worship have no imperative need to fill that space with meaning. Rather, they fill it in an experiential, "significance" kind of way.

It is this experiential dimension that makes it possible to have truncated narratives in contemporary worship. The encoded story in the songs that

---

[22]Ruth, "Some Similarities and Differences," 76.

[23]Martin D. Stringer, *On the Perception of Worship* (Birmingham, UK: University of Birmingham Press, 1999), 104-5.

[24]Quoted in Stringer, *On the Perception of Worship*, 107.

people say bring them hope is anemic in both origin and ending points. The encoded story has very little to say about the beginning of hope and the telos, or goal, of hope. Yet worshipers supply meaning by bringing their personal story to bear on the lyrics of the song.

This loss of narrative in contemporary worship songs must also be situated within wider cultural trends. Philosopher Charles Taylor maps how our secular age came to be. As Taylor sees it, it is more than a subtraction story, an account of how people simply stopped believing in God. Rather, it is, as James K. A. Smith puts it, "a sum, created by addition, a product of intellectual multiplication." Mapping out Taylor's thesis of the story of immanentization, Smith highlights several shifts. One is the loss of what Taylor calls further purpose. Both "agents and social institutions lived with a sense of a *telos* that was eternal." Another shift seems an inevitable result of the first; it is a loss of the "idea that God was planning a transformation of human beings which would take them beyond the limitations which inhere in their present condition."[25] Without a grand telos or an eschatological vision, the story humans narrate and inhabit is much smaller. It may be that the truncated salvation narratives encoded in contemporary worship songs are a product of this secular age.

That worship leaders and songwriters are shaped or affected by the loss of narrative in culture at large is evidenced by their responses to other questions on my survey. Four of my twenty-five questions had to do with the time dimension of hope. I placed a pair of statements before the worship leaders and asked them to choose which one brought them more hope. Both statements are arguably true from a theological perspective. My assumption is that Christians privilege certain aspects of their faith above others, and I wanted to know which statement of the sets of pairs represented a more deeply held belief. By asking which one brought more hope, I was also attempting to discover which statement would be given priority when writing or selecting songs that could bring hope. My assumption here is that a worship leader will look for songs that reflect the belief or beliefs in which the worship leader finds the most hope. Thus, the personal theology of the worship leader skews which songs he or she perceives to be songs of hope.

---

[25]James K. A. Smith, *How (Not) to Be Secular* (Grand Rapids: Eerdmans, 2014), 26, 48-50. See Charles Taylor, *A Secular Age* (Cambridge, MA: Belknap, 2007).

In the following graphs, I display the responses of the whole group in comparison with Pentecostal-charismatic worship leaders and Presbyterian worship leaders. In the first pair of statements (fig.7.4), the majority of worship leaders—more than 70 percent—in each cluster find hope from the statement "God will make all things well in the end." Their hope is oriented toward the future.

## "WHICH STATEMENT BRINGS YOU MORE HOPE?"

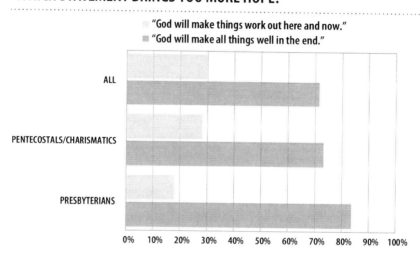

**Figure 7.4.** Statements of hope: All things present versus all things future

In the next three questions related to the time orientation of hope, however, worship leaders, irrespective of denominational identity, chose the statement rooted in the present tense. The relatively small difference between the responses of Pentecostal-charismatic worship leaders and those of the larger group of worship leaders is interesting given that worship leaders in Pentecostal-charismatic churches account for only 23 percent of the total group. This may possibly be due to the influence of charismatic theology beyond churches that identify as Pentecostal or charismatic, possibly through contemporary worship songs, as mentioned in chapter two. What is most striking in figure 7.5 is the difference in responses between Presbyterians and Pentecostal-charismatics. Of the four questions related to time, this pair of statements—about victory—showed the greatest disparity in response. Presbyterians seem much more reluctant to find hope in the belief that victory is ours now.

## "WHICH STATEMENT BRINGS YOU MORE HOPE?"

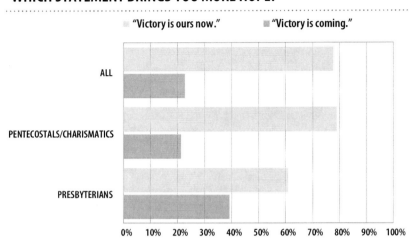

**Figure 7.5.** Statements of hope: Present victory versus future victory

The final two graphs of the remaining pairs of statements in my survey related to the time dimension of hope illustrate the hope that worship leaders derive not only from statements related to the present tense but also from statements that relate to them as individuals. The first of the following two pairs of statements (fig. 7.6), sets the assertion that "It is well with my soul"

## "WHICH STATEMENT BRINGS YOU MORE HOPE?"

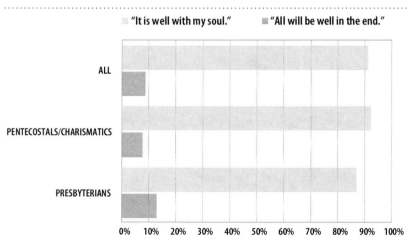

**Figure 7.6.** Statements of hope: Well with my soul versus well in the future

in contrast to the expectation that "All will be well in the end." Worship leaders of all denominational stripes overwhelmingly favored the more personal of the two assertions. Of the four time-oriented questions, this had the highest leaning one way or another—and it leans heavily toward the present and the personal.

The final pair of statements (fig. 7.7) is perhaps the most stunning. Though this graph was displayed earlier with reference to encoded space, it is worth noting here that a phrase from the Creed is set against a present-tense assertion of Christ's presence with the individual. Once again, both may be defended as theologically viable and biblically grounded. Yet one is an exact phrase in the Creed, oriented toward Christian hope and the expectation of Christ's return, and the other is an existential claim. It is not the future return of Christ that will bring about the consummation of salvation and the restoration of all things that inspires hope; it is the presence of Christ with the individual. The experience of Christ by the individual in the here and now has subverted the sense of futurity and consequently contributed to a loss of narrative.

The focus on the here and now, in both space and time, of the worship leaders surveyed can be seen in figure 7.8. I took all seven questions relating to space and time, aggregated the percentages, divided them by the

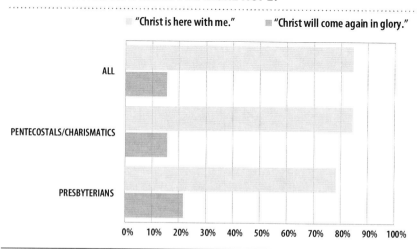

## "WHICH STATEMENT BRINGS YOU MORE HOPE?"

**Figure 7.7.** Statements of hope: Present versus future

number of questions relating to space (three) and time (four), and plotted them as seen in figure 7.8.

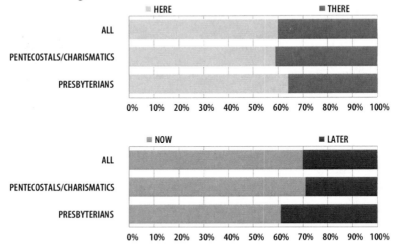

**Figure 7.8.** Hope in space and time

If we are looking for explanations for why worship leaders chose songs as songs of hope that seem to be overly fixated on the present tense, we may look to the nature of worship songs themselves—singing about God means singing about a present-ongoing state of being; we may look to the context of the writers and worshipers—situations of relative privilege and ease; and, we may look to the cultural shift toward a loss of narrative in postmodernism. All these are just hypotheses; they would need to be tested and explored. They may also all be at work at once, and the work of distinguishing one contributing factor from another is complex, if possible at all.

## ENCODED AGENCY

***Nouns and pronouns: God or us?*** Since agency is another key dimension of hope, I also examined nouns and pronouns in these songs to determine who the primary actors are in the songs of hope. My primary delineation was between nouns and pronouns that refer to the worshiper and those that refer to God. As evidenced from table 7.7, the results were as anticipated. Each grouping revealed comparable percentage breakdowns of nouns and pronouns; the percentage splits were nearly even. Notably, direct comparison between the songs named by Pentecostal-charismatics and those named by Presbyterians revealed an identical split.

**Table 7.7.** Pronouns and nouns in songs of hope: Human versus divine

|  | In songs named by national worship leaders | In songs named by Presbyterian worship leaders | In songs named by Pentecostal-charismatic worship leaders |
|---|---|---|---|
| Human | 44% | 47% | 47% |
| Divine | 56% | 53% | 53% |

While the percentages of nouns and pronouns are nearly evenly divided between those that refer to God and those that refer to the worshiper, it would not be accurate to suggest based on this that worship leaders view God and humans as having equal weight in the agency of hope. In fact, when I asked them in the survey a question related to agency, the answers were unequivocally tipped toward divine agency (see fig. 7.9). Each group had at least 83 percent of its constituents answer the question in a way that acknowledged human futility. Whatever humans can do, they cannot repair the mess the world is in.

This is also borne out by a closer look at the song lyrics. "Christ alone" is the "cornerstone"; the "weak" are "made strong" only in the "Savior's love." "It

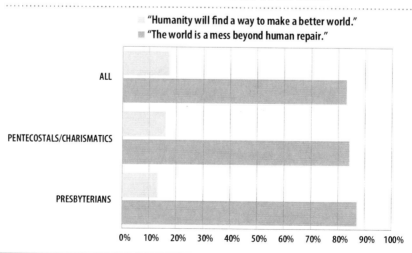

## "PICK THE STATEMENT THAT BEST REFLECTS YOUR VIEW."

**Figure 7.9.** Agency in songs of hope: Human versus divine

is well" because the "waves and wind still know His name." It is God who "split the seas" so we could "walk right through it"; it is God's "perfect love" that drowns our fears; it is God who "rescued" us so that we can "stand and sing." "In Christ alone" our "hope is found"; it is Jesus who "commands my destiny," so much so that no "power of hell" and "no scheme of man" could ever "pluck me from his hand"; and when we do die, it is because Christ "calls" us "home." Even the song "Still," which pictures the worshiper soaring above the storm, reminds us that we are soaring with God the Father, who is the "King over the flood," and thus we can "be still and know" he is God. It is God who gives life and brings "light to the darkness"; it is God who gives "hope" and restores "every heart that is broken"; moreover, it is God's very breath that is "in our lungs." God is "the one who fights for me," who "shields my soul eternally." The lyrical content of each of these songs of hope clearly places the agency of hope in God's hands.

The one song that comes close to emphasizing the strength of the worshiper in conquering challenges is one from the Presbyterian list, "Jesus, I My Cross Have Taken." In the fourth stanza, the hymn writer addresses his own soul: "Take my soul His full salvation, conquer every sin and care." Yet in the lines that follow, worshipers are admonished to think about the Spirit dwelling within them, the Father who loves them, and the Savior who died to win them. Thus, even the admonishment to conquer is grounded in the agency of the triune God.

***Pronouns: Individual or communal?*** The most interesting data came from a closer look at the pronouns that refer to the worshiper. While this does not relate specifically to agency, it does shed light on the way worship leaders—and perhaps the worshipers in the congregations they represent—experience hope. The pronouns that refer to the worshiper are overwhelmingly singular, as table 7.8 displays. Ninety-five to ninety-eight percent of the pronouns in these songs of hope are individual rather than communal, singular rather than plural. When is hope is felt most deeply, it is experienced most personally. There is nothing in the lyrics to indicate an exclusiveness to the hope being offered or experienced. It is not private. But the heavy emphasis on the individual means, at the very least, that worship leaders can experience hope regardless of what others experience. Their sense of well-being is not directly or explicitly related to the well-being of others. So long as the worshiper feels that God is "coming through" for him, there is hope. Hope may not be privatized, but it certainly has been detached from the community.

**Table 7.8.** Pronouns in songs of hope: Individual versus communal

|  | In songs named by national worship leaders | In songs named by Presbyterian worship leaders | In songs named by Pentecostal-charismatic worship leaders |
|---|---|---|---|
| Individual | 95% | 98% | 95% |
| Communal | 5% | 2% | 5% |

## ENCODED HOPE AT LOCAL CHURCHES

*Verbs for divine and human action.* In each of the two churches I studied as part of my fieldwork, I replicated a version of the survey taken by the national worship leaders. The questions regarding hope asked for a song that brought hope in a time of despair and for a song they sing at church that brings them hope. Because the contexts are significantly different—the national survey was given to worship leaders, while the fieldwork surveys were given to laypeople—I am cautious about trying to make any connections between the two very different types of data. My aim is simply to set the local within the larger context of national trends, both general and denominational.

As seen in table 7.9, a general verb analysis of the top three songs at Pathway reveals very similar results to the national Pentecostal-charismatic worship leaders. The focus on the past is identical. But there is one glaring difference: future-tense verbs are completely missing in the songs named by the focus group at Pathway Church. The present-tense verbs absorb the difference, skewing these songs even further toward the immediate.

**Table 7.9.** Verbs for God and us in songs of hope

|  | In songs named by Pentecostal-charismatic worship leaders | In songs named by laypeople at Pathway Church |
|---|---|---|
| Past tense | 11% | 11% |
| Present tense | 68% | 89% |
| Future tense | 21% | 0% |

When the verbs are separated out as verbs relating to divine action (table 7.10), we see a slightly different picture. The focus group at Pathway finds hope in singing about God's action in the past more so than the national group of Pentecostal-charismatic worship leaders and consequently sings about God in the present slightly less. Again, for the focus group, hope is apparently not found in singing about what God will do.

**Table 7.10.** Verbs for God in songs of hope

| | In songs named by Pentecostal-charismatic worship leaders | In songs named by laypeople at Pathway Church |
|---|---|---|
| Past tense | 8% | 24% |
| Present tense | 81% | 76% |
| Future tense | 11% | 0% |

When we examine verbs for human action (table 7.11), we find the most dramatic difference. Here there are only present-tense verbs. The Pathway focus group finds the most hope when singing about what they are doing and experiencing in the moment. Nothing in their own past matters; nothing in their own future is of consequence. It is all about this present moment in the presence of God.

**Table 7.11.** Verbs for us in songs of hope

| | In songs named by Pentecostal-charismatic worship leaders | In songs named by laypeople at Pathway Church |
|---|---|---|
| Past tense | 13% | 0% |
| Present tense | 58% | 100% |
| Future tense | 29% | 0% |

The number of survey respondents at River Valley Presbyterian Church was significantly larger than that of Pathway Church, but the same number of songs appeared at the top of the list: three. When the verbs for both divine and human action in River Valley's songs of hope are examined, a comparatively balanced picture emerges (table 7.12). These songs focus less on the present tense—nearly half as much—as the songs named by national Presbyterian worship leaders. While the focus on the future is comparable, it is the orientation toward the past that is significantly higher than the songs from the national list. In fact, the songs chosen by River Valley congregants are more than twice as much about the past than those chosen by the national Presbyterian worship leaders.

**Table 7.12.** Verbs for God and us in songs of hope

|  | In songs named by Presbyterian worship leaders | In songs named by laypeople at River Valley Presbyterian Church |
|---|---|---|
| Past tense | 20% | 48% |
| Present tense | 61% | 32% |
| Future tense | 19% | 20% |

When the verbs are split out to reveal divine action, the ratio remains more or less the same (table 7.13). The focus on the future is comparable. The orientation toward the present is about half as much in the songs from nationwide Presbyterian worship leaders. Again, the preoccupation with the past is evidenced by past-tense verbs, which more than double in percentage those in the songs of the nationwide Presbyterian worship leaders. In fact, singing about what God has done is what River Valley congregants sing about most when they sing about God and experience hope. What God is doing or will do is, by comparison, of little use for their experience of hope.

**Table 7.13.** Verbs for God in songs of hope

|  | In songs named by Presbyterian worship leaders | In songs named by laypeople at River Valley Presbyterian Church |
|---|---|---|
| Past tense | 27% | 62% |
| Present tense | 55% | 23% |
| Future tense | 18% | 15% |

The ratios lessen slightly when examining the verbs of human action (table 7.14). Unlike the songs from the nationwide group of Presbyterian worship leaders, the songs of hope from River Valley do not have a clear priority of verb tense when singing about the worshiper. Singing about the worshiper's action in the moment has the edge, at 42 percent, but singing about the worshiper's action in the past is not far behind, at 33 percent. The worshiper's future action is not much further behind that, at 25 percent.

**Table 7.14.** Verbs for us in songs of hope

|  | In songs named by Presbyterian worship leaders | In songs named by laypeople at River Valley Presbyterian Church |
|---|---|---|
| Past tense | 15% | 33% |
| Present tense | 66% | 42% |
| Future tense | 19% | 25% |

When the verbs of the songs of hope from both of the churches in my fieldwork are placed side by side, the differences become even more obvious. In tables 7.15, 7.16, and 7.17, it is evident that the Presbyterian church in my fieldwork finds hope in songs that sing about the past, present, and future in a more evenly distributed way than in the songs in which the Pentecostal-charismatic church in my fieldwork finds hope. Relatively speaking, both groups find hope in songs that speak of God's action in the past more than the worshiper's action in the past. But clearly the most significant difference has to do with the orientation of these songs toward the future. The worshipers at River Valley Presbyterian church find hope in songs that speak of the future, specifically of what God will do in the future, but more so in what they will do in the future. The worshipers at Pathway have no apparent need to sing about the future in order to find hope. There are no future-tense verbs in the songs that bring them hope. Furthermore, there are no past-tense verbs with regard to the worshiper.

**Table 7.15.** Verbs for God and us in songs of hope

|  | In songs named by laypeople at Pathway Church | In songs named by laypeople at River Valley Presbyterian Church |
|---|---|---|
| Past tense | 11% | 48% |
| Present tense | 89% | 32% |
| Future tense | 0% | 20% |

**Table 7.16.** Verbs for God in songs of hope

|  | In songs named by laypeople at Pathway Church | In songs named by laypeople at River Valley Presbyterian Church |
|---|---|---|
| Past tense | 24% | 62% |
| Present tense | 76% | 23% |
| Future tense | 0% | 15% |

**Table 7.17.** Verbs for us in songs of hope

|  | In songs named by laypeople at Pathway Church | In songs named by laypeople at River Valley Presbyterian Church |
|---|---|---|
| Past tense | 0% | 33% |
| Present tense | 100% | 42% |
| Future tense | 0% | 25% |

*Nouns and pronouns.* It is necessary to set the nouns and pronouns of the songs listed from each fieldwork church within the context of the songs from the national survey. I have compared them against the songs from the general group, and against songs by their closest denominational affiliation or affiliations (tables 7.18, 7.19, 7.21, and 7.22). Nothing unexpected appears from the comparison of nouns and pronouns that refer to God versus those that refer to the worshiper. In fact, in the comparison between River Valley and Pathway (table 7.20), the percentages are nearly identical. The only comparison of note is when individual versus communal pronouns are set side by side (table 7.23). Here it appears that River Valley's songs of hope favor communal pronouns significantly more than the songs from national Presbyterian worship leaders. By contrast, the songs of hope from Pathway seem to favor communal pronouns only slightly more than the songs from national Pentecostal-charismatic worship leaders.

**Table 7.18.** Pronouns and nouns in Presbyterians' songs of hope: Human versus divine

|  | In songs named by Presbyterian worship leaders | In songs named by laypeople at River Valley Presbyterian Church |
|---|---|---|
| Human | 47% | 43% |
| Divine | 53% | 57% |

**Table 7.19.** Pronouns and nouns in charismatics' songs of hope: Human versus divine

|  | In songs named by Pentecostal-charismatic worship leaders | In songs named by laypeople at Pathway Church |
|---|---|---|
| Human | 47% | 46% |
| Divine | 53% | 54% |

**Table 7.20.** Pronouns and nouns in the laypeople's songs of hope: Human versus divine

|  | In songs named by laypeople at Pathway Church | In songs named by laypeople at River Valley Presbyterian Church |
|---|---|---|
| Human | 46% | 43% |
| Divine | 54% | 57% |

**Table 7.21.** Pronouns in Presbyterians' songs of hope: Individual versus communal

|  | In songs named by Presbyterian worship leaders | In songs named by laypeople at River Valley Presbyterian Church |
|---|---|---|
| Individual | 98% | 71% |
| Communal | 2% | 29% |

**Table 7.22.** Pronouns in charismatics' songs of hope: Individual versus communal

|              | In songs named by Pentecostal-charismatic worship leaders | In songs named by laypeople at Pathway Church |
|--------------|-----------------------------------------------------------|-----------------------------------------------|
| Individual   | 95%                                                       | 92%                                           |
| Communal     | 5%                                                        | 8%                                            |

**Table 7.23.** Pronouns in the laypeople's songs of hope: Individual versus communal

|              | In songs named by laypeople at Pathway Church | In songs named by laypeople at River Valley Presbyterian Church |
|--------------|-----------------------------------------------|-----------------------------------------------------------------|
| Individual   | 92%                                           | 71%                                                             |
| Communal     | 8%                                            | 23%                                                            |

## CONCLUSION AND CONNECTIONS

The result of this analysis of encoded hope in songs that worship leaders say bring them and their churches hope is that the operant theology of hope among worship leaders in North America focuses on immediacy and intimacy and lacks a future orientation and a narrative sense. This focus on the here and now may be due to the tendency of Christian worship to sing about God in the present tense, to the comfortable conditions of contemporary worship songwriters and worship leaders in North America, and/or to the wider loss of narrative in a postmodern era. These songs of hope also sing about what the worshiper is doing as much as they do about what God has done, is doing, or will do, though they are clear that the agency of hope is God's. Finally, these songs are written from the perspective of the individual rather than the community. These trends are replicated within the churches in my fieldwork, although with differences of degrees.

While an analysis of these song lyrics and themes may lead to a hypothesis that the quality of hope in contemporary worship is weak, the songs themselves are different from the experience of the worship service. This significant distinction, drawn from ritual studies, is highlighted in the beginning of this chapter, where I note that the ritual is separate from the performance of it. The distinction between a ritual and its performance also underscores the need for discourse analysis, as Stringer argues, in order to explore how personal stories supply meaning to the encoded hope of a song. It is to the experience of hope in contemporary worship services and the discourse about that experience that we turn now.

# 8

# HOPE EXPERIENCED

## EXPLORING CONTEMPORARY
## WORSHIP SERVICES

I WILL NEVER FORGET the worship service that Wednesday night. Three days earlier, a gunman had opened fire on our campus, taking the lives of two teenage girls in the parking lot and wounding a few others. He was apprehended by a security guard, then took his own life. Our church hallway, which hours earlier had been filled with laughter and conversation, now was stained with blood. All this had occurred just thirteen months after the founding senior pastor at our church had been caught in a sordid affair that made headlines around the world. A new leader was chosen ten months after the scandal, and we were just beginning to heal.

Then, this. Violence. Tragedy. Death. Pastor Brady Boyd called the church together on a Wednesday night. He didn't wait a week; he knew we needed to be with each other. We needed to weep; we needed to grieve. We needed to pray and be reminded of the Scriptures. We needed to *sing*. We found just the right anthem in a song, "Overcome," written by Jon Egan, one of our brilliant worship leaders and songwriters at the church.

> Savior, worthy of honor and glory
> Worthy of all our praise
> You overcame.
> Jesus, awesome in power forever
> Awesome and great is your name
> You overcame.

With tears running down our faces, we belted out the chorus from the depths of our being. And then came the bridge. Hope, set to music.

We will overcome,

By the blood of the Lamb and the word of our testimony

Everyone, overcome.

Over and over, we sang, until the room erupted with praise and hope overflowed in our hearts. This would not be the end.

This chapter is about how we experience hope when we gather in worship. What happens when Christians come together at church? Is hope a something we should expect to experience in worship? Drawing on the models for hope outlined in chapters three, four, and five, I studied the experience of hope in congregational worship. To explore hope from a phenomenological angle that pays attention to both the cognitive and affective aspects, I designed my fieldwork research with two churches to focus on the worshipers and their experience of God during the service. The main part of this chapter consists of a long section on each of the two churches I visited in my fieldwork, making specific connections to the social sciences in each section. Broadly speaking, Pathway's experience of hope tends toward the affective model, while River Valley's aligns more with the cognitive model. Having said that, I am conscious that, as Ralph Hood writes, a religious experience is a "subjective appreciation that is neither merely affect or cognition, but a more totalization of what it is that has happened or occurred."[26] Furthermore, with Alexis Abernathy and Charlotte Witvliet, I affirm that the "sacred involves both emotions and cognitions," thus making it "complicated to separate the emotional and cognitive dimensions of spiritual experience from the emotional reactions to it."[27] The final three sections of the chapter deal with the experience of hope fulfilled and hope deferred, and how the members of my focus group from each church might move from hopeful feelings to the virtue of hope.

Before beginning the exploration of my fieldwork with each congregation, it will be helpful to describe the rationale for my approach.

---

[26] Ralph Hood, *Handbook of Religious Experience* (Birmingham, AL: Religious Education Press, 1995), 3.

[27] Alexis D. Abernethy and Charlotte vanOyen Witvliet, "A Study of Transformation in Worship: Psychological, Cultural, and Psychophysiological Perspectives," in *Worship That Changes Lives: Multidisciplinary and Congregational Perspectives on Spiritual Transformation*, ed. Alexis D. Abernethy (Grand Rapids: Baker Academic, 2008), 200.

## ETHNOGRAPHY OF CONGREGATIONS

My approach has been influenced by Martin Stringer's ethnographic study of congregational worship, *On the Perception of Worship*. Stringer studied four congregations: an independent church, a Baptist church, an Anglican church, and a Roman Catholic church. In Stringer's view, the study of congregational worship has usually been undertaken from one of three stances: the "informed celebrant" (Aidan Kavanagh), the "paranoid altar server" (Keiren Flanagan), and the "concerned lay person" (Robert Cotton and Kenneth Stevenson).[28] Yet few studies attempt to understand worship from the perspective of the worshiper. To accomplish this goal, Stringer attended services as a participant observer, analyzed sermon transcripts, and took notes on discussion groups.

Stringer's contribution to the ethnographic study of worship is his identification of various discourses. He names four primary categories: *individual discourse*—the view of what is occurring in worship from the unique individual perspective; *communal or collective discourse*—the shared view of worship by a particular congregation, owing to a common history and tendency to attract people of common thinking and temperament; *official discourse*—the kind of "language and understanding" of worship "that is given status and authority within the congregation" such as liturgical texts, prayers, sermons, and more; and *unofficial discourse*—all other conversations outside worship settings that provide a kind of "folk view" of the congregation.[29] The significance of each discourse is found in its relation to other discourses. Stringer concludes that the dialogical relationship between discourses is so complex that it is "practically impossible to say what any one liturgical performance means for any one individual at any one time," let alone trying to decipher "what worship means to a particular congregation." Yet an analysis of the discourses in a congregation about worship is not fruitless. These discourses can shape the kind of meaning and the ways that meaning is generated from within a worship service.[30]

---

[28]Martin D. Stringer, *On the Perception of Worship* (Birmingham, UK: University of Birmingham Press, 1999), 62, 75. Each of these views are expounded on and cited in Stringer's work.

[29]Stringer, *On the Perception of Worship*, 66-74.

[30]Stringer, *On the Perception of Worship*, 75.

The necessity of discourses in providing meaning for the act of worship arises out of Stringer's belief that the ritualized act contains no meaning on its own. Here Stringer is building on Caroline Humphrey and James Laidlaw's analysis of ritual. Unlike Rappaport, Humphrey and Laidlaw find very few common features in what may be called rituals. Instead they prefer to think not in terms of rituals as a logically separate kind of activity but rather in terms of ritualization, a quality that can be applied to wide range of ordinary activities "such that it defines a particular way of doing things."[31] Thus meaning is given to an act by a community. Yet, because meaning is difficult to parse from the multiple discourses mentioned above, Stringer concludes that the focus of ethnographic work ought to be on the experience of worship rather than on its meaning in an abstract sense.[32]

Stringer's conclusions shaped my approach to the fieldwork. I designed ways to engage the various discourses at each church. Through interviews with pastors and worship leaders, I interacted with official discourse, while participant observation allowed me to pay attention to unofficial discourse. The focus groups were designed to elicit collective discourse while also making room for individual discourse to occur. In this way, I allowed the various discourses to shape the meaning of participation in the ritual of congregational worship. In fact, the discourses helped my interpretation of the data from the encoded canonical messages of song lyrics. The meaning-making work of discourse analysis identified not only the espoused theology of hope at each church but also the operant theology—or theologies—of hope.

I also put the words and narrated experiences from the focus groups in conversation with literature from the social sciences on ritual, emotion, and collective behavior as part of an analysis of unofficial and collective discourses. In the final sections, which combine insights from both churches, I mark the discovery of a resilient hope, which results from transferring agency and pathway to God. Finally, in an effort to connect the experience of hope with the virtue-ethics model of hope described in chapter four, I explore the resilient hope I discovered in both focus groups in light of the processes of prospection, affective adaptation, and virtue formation.

---

[31]Stringer, *On the Perception of Worship*, 201.
[32]Stringer, *On the Perception of Worship*, 76, 205.

My goal with the focus groups at each church was to try to find indirect ways into the subject of hope in worship so as to avoid eliciting responses that were conditioned by their knowledge of my research interest. I spent multiple hours with both focus groups talking about what drew them to start attending the church, what they think is happening in corporate worship, and how they experience hope in the midst of congregational worship. I also asked them how they defined hope, whether they had experienced disappointment with God after experiencing hope in worship, and whether they had found a way to prevent hope from fading.

## PATHWAY CHURCH: ENCOUNTERS AND EXPERIENCES IN THE PRESENCE OF GOD

**Personal encounters.** Worship at Pathway Church is seen primarily as an experience with God. As a church that describes itself as Pentecostal and charismatic, it is no surprise that its dominant paradigm for congregational worship is the one I called "worship as encounter" in chapter two. My focus group was a cross-section of ages, from a few single people in their twenties, to married couples in their thirties and forties, to an older man in his seventies. About 20 percent of the group were African Americans while the rest were of European descent. When I asked the group what they would guess the worship team's goal for the congregation is in the worship time, Mark, a man in his mid-forties, answered without hesitation: "experiencing God." After listening to a handful of others, Julie affirmed that she would echo what had been said and then offered the perspective she would have of congregational worship if she were the one leading:

> I would want to just usher in the presence of God, and allow people to experience it, and to have an actual connection with God, to actually experience him, connect with him.... [Someone in the group] said [for] hope to be experienced, but [I would want] just [for] that love to be experienced, for God's presence to be so overwhelming that everyone feels it, and has that connection, that communication, that meeting, that encounter with God.

She used the word *experience* four times; a related word, *connection*, twice; and other personal words such as *feel*, *communication*, and *encounter* a total of three times. Nine out of sixty-four words in her opening remarks about the goal of congregational worship were words drawn from the language of relationship, of personhood and encounter.

The language of encounter in charismatic worship is an outworking of the refusal to objectify God, to treat God as a cosmic "It." This flows from a paradigm of two persons interacting with each other dynamically and dialogically. Julie's language of encounter here is significant because according to the criteria offered by religious historian Kate Bowler, Pathway is a prosperity-gospel megachurch, which reduces God merely to a means to human ends.[33] The language of personal encounter, in contrast, demonstrates a dynamic relationship between God and the worshiper, each capable of being moved by the other, making God no mere object.

Julie and Mark were not alone in using the language of experience to describe what occurs during worship. When talking about what drew her to Pathway, Carol said it was the people. But she specifically mentioned that when she does not feel like coming, it is the "freedom that is in this church" that draws her. The staff and the people at Pathway, she said, have obviously "experienced that freedom."

Bill described times when he is "not feeling the presence of the Lord" as him worshiping "individually." Note that he mentioned this as an anomaly, as a departure from an expected outcome. Here he was going off the unofficial script at Pathway that people come in and sense God's presence in worship in a personal and individual way. He rescued the narrative, however, by sharing his remedy to such an occurrence:

> Sometimes when I'm not feeling the presence of the Lord as I'm worshiping individually, sometimes what I do is I just open up my eyes and I start looking at all the saints, everybody else with their hands up, and that actually does some-

---

[33]Kate Bowler, in her book *Blessed*, identifies four unifying features of the prosperity gospel: faith—an "activator, a power that unleashes spiritual forces and turns the spoken word into reality"; wealth—faith is demonstrated in material increase; health—faith is demonstrated in physical well-being (thus "material reality is the measure of success of immaterial faith"); and victory—faith is to be marked by victory. Bowler also distinguishes between "hard prosperity" and "soft prosperity" by how outcomes are evaluated: hard prosperity evaluates faith by immediate and specific outcomes; soft prosperity evaluates faith more gently and with a more "roundabout" approach—a general sense of victory and blessing without the specifics such as physical healing or financial increase. Pathway would fit under the "soft prosperity" designation. See Kate Bowler, *Blessed: A History of the American Prosperity Gospel* (New York: Oxford University Press, 2013), 7-8 and 239-48.

thing to me; just . . . watching everybody else experiencing God even when I'm not maybe experiencing God that way I want to experience him at the moment. Something about opening up my eyes and seeing everybody else experiencing God does something for me, and it changes me from the inside out.

Bill uses the words *feeling* or *experience* and *experiencing* five times in ninety-one words. It accounts for five of the twelve verbs in this description. When the congregants at Pathway speak about what is occurring in congregational worship, they speak about an experience that they can feel.

This is often contrasted with how things were at their previous church. Christopher, a man in his early fifties, talked about coming from a Baptist church to Pathway and of how the "whole Holy Spirit thing" was new to him and to his family. Likewise, Carol bemoaned the fact that even though people at her old Baptist church believed in the Holy Spirit, or at the very least had "heard of the Holy Spirit," not a lot of them "knew you could experience the Holy Spirit."

This emphasis on experiencing the Holy Spirit is not unique to Pathway. In fact, as I showed earlier, the Spirit has been central in Pentecostal and charismatic traditions for decades, with encounter as a primary paradigm. After extensive analysis of songbooks in the UK from the 1960s to the 1990s, Pete Ward at Durham concludes that in charismatic spirituality, contemporary worship songs are not only "narratives of encounter" but also "the means to a personal encounter with God." In singing, the worshiper expresses praise, adoration, devotion, and love to God. In turn, God, through the Holy Spirit, communicates his presence to the worshiper. "Intimacy is . . . both expressive and experiential."[34]

This focus on encounter reflects a change, even in the relatively short history of contemporary worship. Ward notes that in the *Youth Praise* songs of the 1960s, the focus used to be an event in the past, either conversion or baptism or the in-filling of the Holy Spirit. But the "charismatic experience moved evangelical Christians into a more immediate and experiential understanding of worship," in which the focus of the activity of God is in the present. Not only is an encounter to be experienced in the present, but it is expected to be normative, as referenced above in Bill's comments about the implied abnormality

---

[34]Pete Ward, *Selling Worship: How What We Sing Has Changed the Church* (Exeter, UK: Paternoster, 2005), 198-99, 202-3.

of being in worship and not feeling God's presence. Whereas experiences with God were either initiatory or occasional, they are now expected to be normative for the worshiper.[35] Worshipers now describe, disdainfully, going to church and "just singing" as opposed to "really worshipping."[36]

This emphasis on a relational encounter is a distinctive of charismatic worship. Yet, it is spreading in the wider evangelical Christian circle. One evidence of this is the soaring popularity of the song "Holy Spirit." Written by two young, charismatic worship leaders, the song specifically asks that the Holy Spirit would "let" the worshiper "become more aware" of his presence," and that the Spirit would "let" them "experience the glory of [God's] goodness." It is certainly not the first song to ask for such things. Yet no song that made such a request had ever achieved the kind of popularity that this song has. It is the first song in the CCLI US Top 25 to use the word *experience*.[37]

**Feeling God: Experience and emotion.** How does a worshiper at Pathway know whether she has experienced God in worship? If experiencing God is central to the purpose of congregational worship, then each worshiper must be gauging this each time she comes to church. I have already noted that this experience with God is something that worshipers feel. But what is that emotion like? How does the presence of God feel?

Arlie Hochschild, a sociologist at the University of California, Berkeley, has written about the "managed heart." Emotion, as Hochschild understands it, is a "bodily orientation to an imaginary act" and therefore has a signal function, warning us or alerting us to where we stand in relation to inner or outer events. Because emotion has a signal function, it is a way of locating our viewpoint or position. It is also a way that we try to locate someone else's position or viewpoint. Yet its signal function is culturally shaped. Hochschild argues that emotion is "more permeable to cultural influence than organismic theorists have thought," but "more substantial than some interactional theorists have thought."[38]

---

[35]Ward, *Selling Worship*, 200, 203.

[36]Gordon Adnams, "'Really Worshipping' Not 'Just Singing,'" in *Christian Congregational Music: Performance, Identity and Experience*, ed. Monique Ingalls, Carolyn Landau, and Tom Wagner (Surrey, UK: Ashgate, 2013), 186.

[37]Lester Ruth (@jl_ruth), "New CCLI top-25 song 'Holy Spirit' uses word 'experience' for the first time among top songs since 1989," Twitter, February 27, 2015, https://twitter.com/jl_ruth/status /571385209981022209.

[38]Arlie Russell Hochschild, *The Managed Heart: Commercialization of Human Feeling*, 2nd ed. (Berkeley: University of California Press, 2003), 28.

The signal function of emotion is complicated because of what Hochschild calls surface acting and deep acting. Surface acting involves disguising what we feel and pretending to feel what we do not. In surface acting, we may deceive others, but we do not deceive ourselves. Deep acting, on the other hand, requires deceiving ourselves. In deep acting, a person changes himself by "taking over the levers of feeling production."[39] In short, surface acting changes the display; deep acting changes the emotion.

The need to act, whether in a surface or deep way, arises out of culturally shaped norms. Hochschild calls these norms and expectations *feeling rules*. We discover the feeling rules of a group when confronted by direct statements such as, "You should be ashamed," or, "You have no right to feel. . . ." They are even revealed by disguised questions such as, "Don't you love . . . ?" or, "Aren't you thrilled about . . . ?"[40]

In daily life, we run up against these feeling rules any time we sense a gap between the perceived ideal feeling and the actual feeling we are experiencing. There may also be misfitting feelings, such as sadness at a wedding, or the lack of sadness or even the wrong amount of sadness at a funeral. In relationships that are more tightly knit, the parties involved are required to do more emotion work; yet that work is increasingly more unconscious in close relationships.

The congregants in my focus group at Pathway were not always aware of the feeling rules at Pathway. In fact, the ones who had been there longer were less able to stand apart from the pastors and worship leaders and name the unspoken rules of emotion in worship. The three people in the focus group who were relatively new to Pathway—Betty, Bill, and Josh—felt the most freedom to admit a departure from the norm, a violation of an unsaid feeling rule. It is important to note, however, as Hochschild does, that even the conscious choice to violate a feeling rule is not a changing of the rule, for it needs the rule to be present and clear in order to make a statement by breaking it.

Betty seemed conscious of this as she responded to a question I asked about a time when any member of our focus group had walked into church in a negative emotional state and left in a more positive one. "Can I talk about a time when maybe it didn't happen?" she ventured. Taking the group's silence

---

[39]Hochschild, *Managed Heart*, 33.
[40]Hochschild, *Managed Heart*, 58.

as sufficient permission, she continued. "When I first came here, I thought the music was too loud." She quickly qualified her perception, which was a clear deviation from the feeling rules, with a conformity to a different group norm at Pathway—the mysterious knowing that something is the will of God: "But I knew I was supposed to be here. So, it was a bit tortuous, but I came every Sunday even though I still thought it was too loud—'cause I'm not a noise person; I don't do concerts." After peppering in another positive affirmation about Pathway—specifically about how she enjoyed the messages from the beginning—she returned to her struggle with the music, admitting, "It really took about three months for me to be really kind of be able to tolerate it. . . . And even now, three years later, I'm not a big worshiper, and it doesn't have that profound effect on me, and I'm still usually waiting for it to end—and it's funny because I can tell when they go a little long."

The group was not sure how to respond to this. She was the only one who expressed any negative experience stemming from the worship itself. Others admitted being angry about something else when they came into the service; but Betty was breaking the rules significantly by saying that she was not moved in a particular way by the worship time. Perhaps as the relative newcomer, one who had not yet bonded as deeply with the church, she was not as willing to acquiesce to the unspoken rules.

***God vibrations: Emotion, energy, and collective behavior.*** When I asked the group to describe what made corporate worship—gathering together in church to worship—significant compared to listening to the same songs at home or in the car, the word *energy* was mentioned several times. "One of the things we noticed," Christopher said, "the very first time we came to Pathway was all of the energy. You just sense God's presence in a very real way. I get completely enveloped." Julie, his wife, added more detail and enthusiasm:

> The excitement is contagious; it's absolutely contagious. When everyone around you is screaming and shouting for God, and praising him—you've hit an emotional standpoint [sic]. You've got people all around crying. That energy—you can't *not* feel the presence of the Holy Spirit; you can't *not* feel the presence of God; you get goose bumps. You can get those feelings by yourself, but there's an energy that comes in that corporate worship settings.

Julie was prioritizing her feelings, yet there is validity to Julie's appraisal. There is an energy that comes in corporate worship settings. Randall Collins, drawing on both Emile Durkheim and Irving Goffman, describes what happens when "human bodies are together in the same place." There is a "physical attunement: currents of feeling, a sense of wariness or interest, a palpable change in the atmosphere." "The bodies," Collins says, "are paying attention to each other, whether at first there is any great conscious awareness of it or not." Durkheim argues that once bodies are together, collective effervescence—the "process of intensification of shared experiences"—may occur.[41] Collective effervescence is such a "strong, shared emotional experience" that it "connects participants to the collective and its identity and goals."[42] In fact, Collins argues, collective effervescence will result in "group solidarity, emotional energy, symbols of social relationship, and standards of morality."

Moreover, Collins argues that humans are seekers of emotional energy, in particular, which he defines as a "socially derived . . . feeling of confidence, courage to take action, [and] boldness in taking initiative." Gaining more emotional energy, according to Collins, is the goal of social interaction. Thus, the creation of more and new options for "social action and affiliation" is fueled by this innate desire to gain and spread emotional energy. The people, groups, or activities that "effectively produce Emotional Energy are more attractive and successful."[43]

How do groups produce emotional energy through their rituals? Collins draws on interaction ritual theory to outline four criteria that if followed results in collective effervescence and high amounts of emotional energy: high number of participants assembled, high barriers for excluding outsiders, mutual focus of attention, and shared emotional mood.[44] In some settings, there are what Collins calls "energy stars"—people who can actually create a mutual focus of attention, and therefore create a shared emotional mood.[45] Energy stars are closely related to rituals that successfully produce high levels of emotional energy.

---

[41]Randall Collins, *Interaction Ritual Chains* (Princeton, NJ: Princeton University Press, 2004), 34-35.
[42]James K. Wellman Jr., Katie E. Corcoran, and Kate Stockly-Meyerdirk, "'God Is Like a Drug . . .': Explaining Interaction Ritual Chains in American Mega-churches," *Eastern Sociological Society* 29, no. 3 (2014): 652.
[43]Wellman, Corcoran, and Stockly-Meyerdirk, "'God Is Like,'" 652.
[44]Collins, *Interaction Ritual Theory*, 48.
[45]Wellman, Corcoran, and Stockly-Meyerdirk, "'God Is Like,'" 653.

The worship space at the campus at Pathway where I conducted my fieldwork was a large rectangular room with over a thousand seats. The large screens in the front of the room gave close views of the worship team—the energy stars—and occasional panoramic shots of the congregation. Jason Wollschleger discovered that congregations with worship services that produced more collective effervescence had higher rates of church attendance because people will keep returning to rituals that give them higher levels of emotional energy.[46] The large sanctuaries of megachurches with cameras that help people see one another feed into a form of interaction—albeit a tacit one—making people feel like they are "where the action is."[47] The effect of cameras and screens on an already large room may be that they intensify the sense of a large assembly, thus far exceeding the first criteria of producing emotional energy.

The second component for producing emotional energy is high barriers. James Wellman Jr., Katie Corcoran, and Kate Stockly-Meyerdirk argue that megachurches have intentionally low barriers. They are quick to note, however, that there are several kinds of barriers. The Episcopal Church has low barriers in its theology but high barriers in its liturgy. Megachurches are the reverse. They leverage cultural capital from the culture at large by creating an atmosphere in the lobby that resembles a Starbucks and by playing music in the stylistic genre range of what may be heard on the radio. Thus megachurches require very little "cultural membership capital" of people—when guests come, they find the scene and sounds and feel to be familiar. This is generally true of churches than adopt contemporary worship, as demonstrated in chapter two, but it is especially true at megachurches. Because this ease of adaptability can be perceived as a low barrier and thus a contradiction to Collins's theory, Wellman, Corcoran, and Stockly-Meyerdirk seem to contradict Collins's second criteria for emotional energy, that of high barriers for excluding outsiders. They argue that since collective effervescence is amplified when more individuals are participating, having lower barriers is better than having clear boundaries if those boundaries work to lower the number of participants. Lower barriers mean higher attendance, and higher attendance is the chief ingredient for producing emotional energy.

---

[46]Jason Wollschleger, "Interaction Ritual Chains and Religious Participation," *Sociological Forum* 27, no. 4 (2012): 896-912.
[47]Wellman, Corcoran, and Stockly-Meyerdirk, "'God Is Like,'" 653, 657.

Wellman, Corcoran, and Stockly-Meyerdirk need not make this case, however. The high barriers of theology found in megachurches are not hidden or peripheral to the life and worship of the church. Megachurch preaching tends to place a high value on the authority of Scripture and to fall in line with conservative positions. Moreover, people who attend megachurches are more likely to hold theologically conservative or traditional views. Though these data points are not demonstrations of causation, comparisons from a Baylor Religion Study led by Rodney Stark in 2007 showed higher commitment and traditional theology in megachurches than in smaller congregations.[48] These serve as high barriers to outsiders.

Pathway confirms the Baylor study by its conformity to traditional doctrines regarding eternity and the afterlife. During my research, I noticed a particularly strong and public affirmation of belief in hell. In a sermon on the rapture, an influential pastor second only to the senior pastor at Pathway, Johnny Edmonds, demonstrated the moral decay of America by rattling off a statistic from the hip: "Half of churches do not believe in a literal hell and a literal devil." The congregation, already incredulous, was ready for his oratorical knockout punch: "If the Bible is lying to us about hell, you think it's telling us the truth about heaven? . . . If one thing in this book is wrong, how can we trust anything in it?" He offered an unsubstantiated claim that Jesus talked more about hell than he did about heaven and concluded this segment of the sermon with a forceful, rhetorical question: "Is Jesus a liar?"

You may recall the quote from Bill, from my focus group, in chapter six, responding to a question regarding the nature of Christian hope by talking about the finality of judgment and "the fact that we are never going to cease to exist, in one way, one form or another." "Hell is hot," he states, "and heaven is real." The prominence of such strong views on judgment, hell, and the afterlife surely cannot be considered a low barrier, as Wellman, Corcoran, and Stockly-Meyerdirk imagine. I contend that megachurches, particularly in the Pentecostal-charismatic streams, fit more closely within

---

[48]Stark's study, in which megachurches are defined as having more than one thousand members and small congregations fewer than one hundred, shows higher percentages of people at megachurches tithing, attending a Bible study, attending services more often, and believing in orthodox but controversial Christian doctrines such as the existence of heaven and hell. See Rodney Stark, *What Americans Really Believe* (Waco, TX: Baylor University Press, 2008), 46-47.

Collins's paradigm of emotional energy than Wellman, Corcoran, and Stockly-Meyerdirk imagine.

Wellman, Corcoran, and Stockly-Meyerdirk lump the third and fourth ingredients of successful ritual chain interactions together since the two items, a mutual focus of attention and a shared mood, "interact dynamically to create cumulative effects." In general, the songs result in a kind of emotional participation that is so astounding that Wellman, Corcoran, and Stockly-Meyerdirk have coined a term for it: "a *connectic* experience: a multi-sensory mélange of sensory input." But it is not just the music that produces this effect; it is also the preaching. In fact, Wellman, Corcoran, and Stockly-Meyerdirk view worship as setting the appropriate mood for the pastor to provide "mutual entrainment" in shared values or convictions.[49] Thus they conclude:

> The combination of the qualitative and quantitative data clearly demonstrates that megachurches succeed in creating successful interaction rituals. The processual ingredients of the large-scale worship services, enhanced by the pastor as an emotional energy star, and supplemented with small-group participation create an effective interaction ritual chain, promoting collective effervescence and EE [emotional energy], membership feelings, membership symbols, feelings of morality, and a heightened sense of spirituality.[50]

The reality, seen clearly at Pathway, is that worship leaders and preachers are key performers in a fairly predictable script. Timothy Nelson, who spent twelve months doing ethnographic research on an African Methodist Episcopal church in the American South, suggests fixed characteristics of the kind of collective behavior that happens in emotional services. For Nelson, there are four key differences between the required behavioral norms in emotional services versus those in nonemotional services (formal, liturgical services):

1. Ambiguity of Role: No one knows who should be the one to "say Amen," or stand, or shout. But they know somebody should.

2. Expectation of Climax: The arc of the emotional engagement is supposed to build in intensity as the service progresses.

3. Resistance to Visibility: Because it is unclear who should play what role, and because someone has to take the first step to increase the degree

---

[49]Wellman, Corcoran, and Stockly-Meyerdirk, "'God Is Like,'" 660-61.
[50]Wellman, Corcoran, and Stockly-Meyerdirk, "'God Is Like,'" 667.

of intensity in response, that individual will stand out. This visibility has the potential to create a barrier to individuals.

4. Responsibility of Key Performers: The key performers—such as the preacher and the worship leader—take on the responsibility to help the congregation surmount these barriers.[51]

Collective behavior in emotional services, by Nelson's analysis, works like a feedback loop. Performers use the particular resources of music (drums and rhythm feature prominently) and language to evoke a response from the congregation. The response "increases in *intensity* and *quality* of the performer's actions, which in turn evoke a greater congregational response." This circular reaction is a hallmark of collective behavior and involves an "oscillating movement toward higher levels of intensity and participation."[52]

Collective behavior, Nelson argues, also requires the transfer of control. The emotional service is thus a joint creation produced by the performer and the congregation. The key dynamic that makes this possible—and indeed, makes all collective behaviors possible—is the individual's willingness to "transfer control" to the group.

Without consciously referring to emotional energy, several members of the focus group at Pathway described being drawn to the church because of the energy they felt there. Jonah, who has been a Christian for two years, was no stranger to church life growing up. He recalls the worship led by a choir in the Baptist church he attended as a child, comparing it to the energy he now feels in worship at Pathway:

> I remember [a] long time ago my mom used to force me to go to church. It was a Baptist church; you had people in the choir singing; everyone stood up singing. But looking back on it now, it was all so clinical; it was all so cold, like it was something you were just supposed to do. Here, I remember the first time I came—everybody started singing, and I could see people with their hands up. That used to bother me, but, well, that was when I wasn't a Christian. Now that I am, I get it. I didn't know anything about the Holy Spirit either.

---

[51]Timothy J. Nelson, "Sacrifice of Praise: Emotion and Collective Participation in an African-American Worship Service," *Sociology of Religion* 57, no. 4 (1996): 388-91.

[52]Nelson, "Sacrifice of Praise," 392.

Jonah brought his point home by comparing being at church with being at a "baseball game or hockey game." Sure, one can watch at home and become engaged, but when actually there, "It can just take you over; you feel the vibration, you feel the energy in the air, the people, it brings your worship level to just a whole 'nother level."

To be clear, neither the fact that worship at Pathway involves well-known elements for producing and sustaining emotional energy nor the observation that the worship services follow the pattern of other emotional services negates the possibility that the worshipers are encountering God's presence. What the members of the focus group at Pathway describe as their experience of the Holy Spirit is not invalidated or called into question because sociological explanations for those phenomena exist.

## RIVER VALLEY CHURCH

*The message in the music.* Worship at River Valley is programmed to coordinate with the season of the church's liturgical year and with the textual or topical series through which the pastor is preaching. In this way, River Valley, a Presbyterian church, fits the general pattern of churches within the Reformed tradition and approaches congregational worship through what I called the formation paradigm in chapter two. My focus group, composed of people in their sixties and seventies of European descent, all seemed particularly attentive to the lyrics of the songs they sang.

When I asked the group what they thought the worship team's goal was for the congregation each week, the conversation went immediately to lyrics and the meaning of the songs. Milton, who described himself as having been a Christian all his life but a "practicing Christian" only the past decade or so, talked about the way Allan Moody, the worship leader at River Valley, introduces new songs and then repeats them over the next few weeks. Milton finds that to be a helpful practice since it takes until the third or fourth time to "really get to the meaning." Worship songs, Milton added, really "touch" him, and he listens closely to the words.

The lyrics are also important to the group because of the way they relate to the sermon. Milton, again, noted this: "Moody makes an effort to tie the songs and the music into the message. And there have been times when I've really wondered if he has written those lyrics himself. . . . I've wondered, you know, it was so perfect; it was just so perfectly aligned with Bob's message, or whoever was preaching . . . that day."

The theme of the music relating to the message surfaced in comments from two others in the group. There was a clear value of the cognitive dimensions of worship. The people in the focus group want to be able to comprehend the meaning and the message of the music. Furthermore, they want the meaning and the message of the music to be consistent with the message that is preached. Thus, the prioritization of the cognitive dimension of worship is seen in the congregation's desire for both comprehension and consistency.

**Be still and know: Silence and simplicity.** The setting of the Saturday evening service is designed to be understated. The large sanctuary is sectioned off to only allow seating on one wing. Cards with the service order—their own created liturgy—rest on a music stand near the pews for people to take. Candles are lit and placed on one side of the wing of seats, and the lights are dimmed for the effect of warmth. The service leader and preacher stand not on a stage or platform but on the floor. The instrumentation of the band is usually a grand piano, acoustic guitar, cello or upright bass, and a stripped-down drum kit with a djembe or other hand percussion taking the place of a full rack of toms—and even then, the drummer plays with brushes or rods, not sticks. Everything about the atmosphere is designed to make the worshiper exhale and slow down. In fact, Greg, who seemed to be the least versed in Christian culture or language, described coming into service carrying burdens or things he had been "bombarded with," even as a retired man. He physically exhaled to demonstrate the feeling of relief, and talked about his own physical posture beginning to change: "Yeah . . . you can kinda feel your shoulders relax."

When I asked my focus group what drew them to the church, Milton, who has been attending River Valley for the past four years, said that with regard to worship services themselves, what drew him was the way "it kind of strips away all the pomp and circumstance of some services and gets right to the heart of it." Though he acknowledged that it is "not for everyone," he enjoys the "contemplative" and "quiet" quality of the service because of the way it allows time "to really focus on worship rather than all the external things."

Darren, who moved to Colorado from Arkansas, where he and his wife had attended a Presbyterian Church (USA) church, described being at an

Evangelical Presbyterian Church church now as a "significant change." When I asked Darren how long he had been a Christian, he responded with Southern charm and the drawl to match: "I guess I've been a Christian since I was born!" The group laughed. Yet the significance for Darren in being part of an Evangelical Presbyterian Church church instead of a Presbyterian Church (USA) church is in what the *E* stands for in the acronym for the denomination: evangelical. Though he did not say it this way, it became evident when he described the biggest difference—and one he now enjoys—is that River Valley is "much more Bible-based." This prioritization of the Bible as an authoritative text is, as I noted in chapters two and six, a characteristic of evangelicalism. But that was not all that drew Darren to the church. He and his wife also appreciate the quietness, the space for reflection, and weekly communion at the evening service—all things that are different from the Sunday morning services at River Valley. "I like it because I love the candlelight. It's more contemplative. . . . And the time to be quiet and reflect is very meaningful. . . . And I like taking communion every single time. And I love going up and taking, breaking the bread—it's very powerful."

Greg struggled to find a way to describe what he thought Moody sought to achieve through the music each week.[53] It was clear, however, that Greg did not care for music that feels coercive or designed to produce a particularly energetic emotional response. This is interesting especially for the way it sets the group at River Valley in contrast to the group at Pathway, where energy is a big part of why people like to attend.

> I think we've been in churches where the worship leader or the song leader brings . . . the music along to more crescendo, and . . . you know, wants you to start doing the jubilation, and—I'm not there. . . . I like the way [Allan's] music is, to me, is pertinent to what's coming on. . . . We're not trying to get . . . people all jumping and shouting and [trails off]. This is just a nice progression of music, and it's pertinent to . . . the message, and it's . . . just enjoyable. It goes with the meditation of the evening.

Greg is expressing the very opposite of an "expectation of climax," one of the components of an emotional worship service. Yet, the other elements

---

[53]When I asked Greg how long he had been a Christian, he responded, "To my knowledge, I've been a believer all my life—being raised in a Christian home and such."

necessary for the cultivation of emotional energy according to Collins are still very much present: there are relatively high numbers of people assembled (though in the hundreds compared with thousands at Pathway), high barriers to outsiders, a mutual focus of attention, and a shared emotional mood. Even though the shared mood is more subdued, it is still shared.

**Getting real: Informality, authenticity, and community.** Another theme that emerged in my conversations with the focus group were the related themes of informality, authenticity, and community. In Christian terms, the word *fellowship* is sometimes used to describe the sense of openness and closeness to one another that can be fostered in a group of believers. Various members of the group shared how the Saturday evening service's informality—relative to the Sunday morning services at River Valley—facilitates authenticity, vulnerability, and community.

Greg believes that even the senior pastor, Bob Slate, is "probably a little more open in this service because of the smallness." The service runs about seventy-five to one hundred people in attendance. Greg referenced its size to make his point. "It's just your own little community that on Sunday morning you don't have." Milton chimed in, "It's like a large small group!" The group heartily agreed. I asked a clarifying question about Bob's preaching, inquiring whether it had a different tone to it on Saturday evenings. "He's more real" and "Very transparent" were a few of the comments made, in addition to jokes about his wearing jeans and comments about the congregation's physical proximity to the pastor as he preaches from the floor with a music stand—as opposed to on the stage behind a pulpit on Sunday mornings.

The informality embodied by the pastor, and encoded in and engendered by the service structure, fosters a sense of vulnerability and closeness as a faith community. This sense of community within the congregation is in itself one of the factors that drew people to the church. Vicki, who also described herself as someone who has been a Christian all her life—"I was raised in a Christian home, and I've really loved the Lord since I was very, very little"— talks about the mix of ages within the congregation as a specific aspect of the community that drew her to the church:

> Partly for me, that difference [between the Saturday evening service and the Sunday morning services] is having a more mixed age group—I love that. I

love having older people. And, I am an "older people" now [laughter follows]. No, and children too. I love that diversity of age, for one thing. I love the—there's much more interaction in this service. And you don't feel dumb about it. You know, you don't feel so embarrassed to speak. And . . . they try to really engage people, like in prayer especially. I would say I've noticed that more than anything else. A vast difference.

The element in the service that facilitates authenticity and vulnerability within the community most effectively and consistently, however, is not the preaching or the music but the time of prayer. Almost every week in the service, there is a "prayers of the people" section where people from the congregation voice a brief prayer request and the rest of the people listen in agreement. At first, some members of the congregation were skeptical about this practice. Greg shared his perspective: "Just thinking back to when we first started— some of the prayer time we had when we first started was very . . . Some of the regulars—I'll put it that way—including me, were holding back, you know." Then Greg folded his arms and reenacted the posture and words that were reflective of his response at the time: "Let's see where this is going." Laughter followed Greg's dramatization.

Nevertheless, people eventually became more comfortable with it. Vicki added that now "you feel safe speaking up." Diana, Milton's wife, pointed out that the part of the safety comes from knowing that one is not alone in the issues one faces. She said, in fact, that it is "surprising how many of us have the same issues. . . . You know, you don't want the . . . whole congregation to really know—but in this little group, it feels safe. You're not alone." Milton described how the pastor will at times ask for people to pray for someone dealing with a particular issue, and though one might guess that there would not be many who would respond, Milton said that about "eighty or ninety percent of the people have a name of somebody that are dealing with that issue that he asked for prayer about."

Vicki, not wanting to be critical of the Sunday morning service and its structured approach—because "there are people who need that kind of structure and that kind of service"—nevertheless appreciates the freedom to have unscripted prayers from the congregation during the service. When asked to describe Sunday mornings, Milton responded, "Structured. Pomp and circumstance," referring to the robes, choir, and organ.

Milton described coming to church knowing about a "devastating situation" in which a friend found himself. The sermon and the time for prayers of the people in that evening's service provided an openness and an opportunity for Milton to pray for his friend. This would not have been possible, in Milton's estimation, during the Sunday morning services: "And nothing against the services tomorrow, but because it's so structured, and, you know, you're not usually going to get that opportunity . . . just to have quiet time, and this forces you to have quietness."

This preference for the informal and the personal is similar to one of Nelson's behavioral norms in "emotional services": the ambiguity of role. It could also be argued that even though the leadership style of both pastor and worship leader are deliberately more understated in the Saturday evening service than on Sunday mornings at River Valley, the importance of both pastor and worship leader as key performers remain high. Even though Pathway seems to be more the outwardly emotional service, full of emotional energy, the technical use of both terms—"emotional services" and "emotional energy"— vis-à-vis Nelson and Collins respectively reveals that *both* Pathway and River Valley have emotional services that produce emotional energy, even though the shared mood may be different kinds of emotions, from upbeat to reflective.

## HOPE FULFILLED: PROMISE AND PROSPECTION

I asked the focus groups at each church to talk about times when God had done something they had hoped he would do. I told them it could be big or small. Both groups had stories, but at Pathway, the stories were hard to stop. One woman shared a story about hoping that her youngest child would come to a decision of faith. At a recent church youth camp, it seemed that he had made a step in that direction. Another man shared a similar story about being frustrated with his son, only to realize that God wanted him to help lead his son to faith. Neither of these initial stories were quite the stories of promise and fulfillment I had been looking for, but I waited.

Julie, always willing to share, began by saying that she was trying to "just think of one," implying that God had come through for her so many times. She told a couple of short stories about two of her children needing medical interventions early in life, and the Lord guiding them to the right procedures for them. "We just prayed, and God said, 'Do this,' and we did it, and he's been fine ever since." Her second story was especially arresting. "Our third was a NICU baby, and she had to pass this test to be able to go home, and, her levels kept dropping during her test, and we just prayed, and said, 'Nope . . . her last test, she'll be a seventy-five and she'd going home today.' And her last test, she was a seventy-five, and she went home."

Daniel Gilbert and Timothy Wilson write about prospection, the ability to "experience the future" in the present. The act of prospection relies on *simulation*, which Gilbert and Wilson define as a "mental representation of a future event." This is to be distinguished from *memory*, a "mental representation of a past event," and *perception*, a mental representation of a present event. Two things are necessary for the simulation to be useful for prospecting emotions. First, the mental representation of the event in the future, the prospection, must match the mental representation of the event when it is eventually experienced in the present, perception. In other words, the event must occur as the person imagined it would. Second, the contextual factors of the prospection must match the contextual factors of the perception. If both these conditions are met, then the "hedonic experience," the emotions and feelings of pleasure or pain, of the imagined event will match the hedonic experience of the actual event. In Gilbert's and Wilson's words, "Simulations allow people to 'preview' events and to 'prefeel' the pleasures and pains those events will produce."[54]

Julie predicted that by the end of the day she was going to experience something like relief and gratitude that the ordeal was over because her daughter was going home. Julie was confident that last test would not require them to stay an extra night. Julie was right not only about how she would feel; she was right about the circumstance that she had predicted. Notice that for Julie, her mental representation of the outcome of the test matched the actual outcome of the test later that day, and therefore her anticipated feeling of relief was in fact her experienced feeling by the day's end. What she had hoped for had occurred, more or less as she had imagined it.

One fascinating aspect of what Gilbert and Wilson describe as the contextual factors for the simulation has to do with how the sense of anticipated

---

[54]Daniel T. Gilbert and Timothy D. Wilson, "Prospection: Experiencing the Future," *Science* 317, no. 5843 (2007): 1351-52.

pleasure or pain can be affected by the "events that are occurring in the present, the thoughts we are having in the present, our present bodily states," and more.[55] For example, we "feel better when we imagine going to the theatre than to the dentist, but we feel better imagining either event on a sunny day than on a rainy day, or when we are well rather than ill." This is precisely where the atmosphere of congregational worship can influence prospection. If the mood of the worship service is positive, the simulations one creates in one's mind of a future event are likely to produce more strongly positive hedonic effects that if one were to simulate the event in an ordinary moment of the day. In a particularly powerful story, one member of the Pathway focus group recounted an emotional breakthrough that occurred not only in a time of congregational worship but also through a vision that occurred in that worship service of being at the beach with Jesus.

> There was an actual worship experience. I was at a [prayer and worship] service, and just in a pit of despair, agony, pain, suffering, and I was like, "God I need you; I need you more than ever. I need you to show up. I need to feel your presence in a way that I've never felt your presence before. I am at a rock bottom," and I honestly have no idea what song we were singing, but I got the first vision that God's ever given me, and he came, and all I for like the next twenty minutes, I just remember having a personal encounter with him. We were walking down a beach together—'cause that's like my happy place; if I could choose any place to be, it would be on the beach—and we were just walking down the beach, and he was like, "I got you, and I'm carrying you, and you don't need to worry; I'm right here." I just remember falling to my knees, and crying, but leaving so filled with hope. Because at my bottom, God showed up in a visual, tangible way.

In this situation, no future event was imagined; it was a change of negative emotions that was needed, the breaking of despair. In a favorable context— congregational worship, which this focus group member had earlier said she loves—she experienced a vision, which is a kind of simulated perception, simulated because it occurs in the mind but perception because it occurs in the present, of another even more favorable context, her "happy place," the beach. The context gets even stronger in positive associations; God began to

---

[55]Gilbert and Wilson, "Prospection," 1352.

talk to her, saying words that she had longed to hear. This experience narrates a progression from a favorable general context to an imagined context with strong positive associations to an extremely powerful context of an encounter with God. The change in her emotional state from despair to hope is an unsurprising outcome.

At River Valley, there were no stories of specifically thinking about or imagining situations that congregants were facing during times of congregational worship. In fact, one member of the group, Milton, said that he preferred to just be silent during the service. Nevertheless, there were a few personal stories of "God coming through," though they were not connected to the times of congregational worship. Diana recounted a particularly moving story about feeling lonely at the holidays because of her estranged relationship with her son and because of her husband Milton's lack of relationship with his children. They had gotten married late in life—a second marriage for each of them—and were struggling to make their peace with the emptiness of their new home. In effort to move beyond their own loneliness, they began hosting a small group through the church. One day, a young family came over to join the group. Eventually, a relationship began to build. The older couple, Milton and Diana, decided to go out on a limb and offer to be like grandparents to the kids and extended family to the young couple. The couple was moved by this because Denver was a new city for them and not near either of their families. Diana was emotional as she recounted how they all came over to spend Mother's Day together and how the kids call them "Pippy and Poppy" as their grandparents of sorts.

Perhaps what is most noteworthy about this story as it relates to my research is that the thing that was hoped for—a family to fill their home on special days—was supplied through relationships and the community within their church. The stories at Pathway of God acting in a way that fulfilled their hope tended toward the ecstatic or what congregants may call the supernatural. This fits the worldview of Pentecostal-charismatics. God is at work in the heavenly realm bringing about changes on earth. But at River Valley, God seems to be at work on earth through other human beings; it is incarnational. Where members of the Pathway focus group described visions and divine encounters—again, consistent with the paradigm I have called in chapter two "encounter"—members of the River Valley focus group described human encounters through which God met them. My intent here is not to praise one over the other; it is simply to note this difference not only in the mode of meeting with God—mystical versus relational—but to note which aspect of the congregational worship service fulfilled this hope, music versus fellowship.

## HOPE DEFERRED: PROSPECTION AND ADAPTATION

In the same focus-group meetings at each church where we discussed a time when God came through, I also asked each group to talk about a time when God did not do the specific thing they were hoping he would. At Pathway, several people seized the opportunity to share openly about struggles that they had faced. This vulnerability about personal suffering contradicts Bowler's sketch of prosperity-gospel churches as lacking a vocabulary for hardship. The people in my Pathway focus group were not living in denial or running to triumphalism; they were honest about disappointment but resilient in their hope in God.

Mark, a Christian for over fifteen years, opened up about a recent struggle to get pregnant. Mark and his wife were in a second marriage with no children together.

> Several months ago . . . we had been praying for my wife. She had a tubal ligation done, so we had got that reversed back in April [this interview was done in August of the same year]. We were just praying for a baby. . . . Her mom talked her into getting the tubal ligation done, and then we had that reversed 'cause she really wanted to have a baby. . . . We found out in June she was pregnant, then . . . probably three or four weeks ago, we went in for a sonogram, and they saw the sack, the placenta, everything was there, except there was no heartbeat . . . no baby. . . . You know, it was really hard. It was hard on me; it was really hard on my wife.

This was the first time that afternoon that someone in the Pathway focus group had been willing to express negative emotions about an experience. Yet the group seemed empathetic; Mark was not out of line for expressing this, even though it seemed to be outside the normal "feeling rules" for the group. "We talked to [the campus pastor] . . . and we said, . . . 'Will you pray for us?' We prayed, and we just really believed God that when we went back to the doctor the next week there was going to be a baby there, there was going to be a heartbeat. We went back, and there wasn't. There wasn't a heartbeat." The group was quiet and attentive, feeling Mark's pain, sensing the emotion in his voice as he narrated the story. Perhaps in an effort to prevent the group meeting from descending into despair, or perhaps because of his own discomfort with being overly sad, Mark began to pick up the tone of the story.

> But the first time we went in there, my wife was devastated. And I was devastated, and I was like, you know . . . it's just a really hard thing to go through. But, when we went back in the second time, we really hoped to, you know, thought that, you know, there will be a baby here. But there wasn't, but we had a peace. I mean, it was just like, I mean I can't tell you how much of a peace we had when we went back there. The week that we were getting ready to go back to the doctor, Pastor Ted Ralph [a pastor who had been on staff at Pathway and was now a senior pastor at another church] spoke on his message, "When God says no," and it was just a really, really timely message, you know, for both of us.

As noted earlier, Pathway Church is at the very least on the spectrum of what Kate Bowler calls soft prosperity gospel. It would not teach that there is a way to guarantee health and wealth, but it tends to emphasize divine blessing in material terms. Yet it is noteworthy that it was a speaker at Pathway who gave language to the disappointment Mark and his wife were experiencing. As a result, Mark was able to, like the psalmists, move from lament to trust.

> You know, because sometimes we don't know . . . and I just told my wife, you know, I said, "We're just going to trust God. We don't know what's going on here. But we're just going to trust God." And the other thing is, that somehow, it just brought us closer together, you know . . . it just brought both of us so much closer together. So, we didn't get what we were praying for, but God really gave us a peace about it, and it really did something, I don't know, really rekindled something in our marriage.

Luke, a single guy built like a football player, shared a story about a recent relationship ending, prefacing with the suggestion that sometimes "it's easier to remember the [prayers God] didn't answer than the ones he did." Luke recounted a story about being engaged and then coming clean to his fiancée about a struggle in his life out of obedience to the Lord but then having his fiancée break up with him and walk away. During the breakup, he read the Bible, prayed, and felt like the relationship was going to come back. "And it never came about—ever. And I just kept telling myself over and over, 'I believe in God, I know you're in it.'" Finally, he came to the point of having to let her go. He seemed pretty self-aware of the hurt he had caused her, which led her to completely cut off the relationship in a way that was hurtful to him. It took him nine months to a year to eventually get over it: "But in getting that 'no,' I wouldn't change it, right? At all. For everything that I learned in that year. . . . But I don't know why it's easier to remember the 'no' than the 'yes.' Maybe it's a bigger lesson in the 'no' than in the 'yes.'" Julie chimed in that we remember the pain most because that is what "the enemy" wants us to focus on instead of remembering "our faith" and staying "focused on the victory." But Luke did not want to minimize the pain or to overemphasize the devil's work, pointing instead again to the lessons he learned during his time of hardship and to the sovereignty of God: "Whatever he [God] wants, he gets."

One might say that at River Valley, the confidence level in God's ability to come through was even higher. When I asked the River Valley focus group to name a time when God did not come through, Diana promptly responded that it had not happened yet. She was quick to clarify that she does not believe in a vending-machine God who exists to do her bidding.

Milton chimed in to frame the question in terms of how one understands prayer. This was an astute theological move. In his book on prayer, well-known Presbyterian pastor Tim Keller says, "God will either give us what we ask or give us what we would have asked if we knew everything he knows."[56] Milton did not reference Keller, but he described in essence Keller's view. If prayer is understood as a way of participating in God's will arriving on earth as it is in heaven, then surrender is as much a part of prayer as asking.

I will return to this trust in God that leads to a resilient hope in both the Presbyterian focus group at River Valley and the Pentecostal-charismatic focus group at Pathway at the end of the next section. For now, I note that resilience is a quality of the hope found in both contexts; both demonstrated a hope that can withstand disappointment. At times, this resilience is seen

---

[56]Timothy Keller, *Prayer: Experiencing Awe and Intimacy with God* (New York: Dutton, 2014), 228.

even in reframing disappointment to not be a disappointment directed at God at all.

## FROM FEELING TO VIRTUE: PERSISTENCE AND RESILIENCE

*Moving from moods to traits.* This resilience is significant because it is a link between the feeling of hope and the virtue of hope, as outlined in chapter three. Recall that Christian philosopher Bob Roberts argued that "real, spiritual hope" is not something that is felt "only in church, with the help of a vaulted ceiling, the unctuous preaching of Easter, and the resounding chords of 'Christ the Lord Is Risen Today.'" The feeling or experience of hope must develop into a "character trait" that is "characterized by 'endurance,'" which Roberts defines as "the ability to feel the emotion even in situations that don't seem very propitious for it."[57]

However, Roberts believes that the ornamental aspects of a worship service, from architecture to colors to music, can create the appropriate moods as a step toward awakening the right emotions. "These features of the service are not just aesthetically fitting, but encourage moods in us that foster Christian emotions. So these aesthetic or ornamental features of the service serve partially as aids to our having the Christian emotions in the midst of the worship service." Nevertheless, Roberts is aware that there are dangers to this strategy. Mood setting can be so powerful that the moods themselves may be mistaken for Christian emotions. The passing emotional states precipitated by these aesthetic aspects of the service may be mistaken for genuine expressions of Christian emotions. The above may result in the Christian being "partially immunized against real Christianity by being made complacent about their spirituality." Thus Roberts is skeptical about what worship services can achieve toward the end of developing hope as a virtue. The engineering of a service, along with its architecture and decoration, delivery of sermon, and more, may "skew the emphasis away from the character building" and toward "experiences."[58]

Yet once a Christian learns to distinguish "Christian emotions" from moods or passing emotional states, he can be taught to not merely experience hope

---

[57]Robert C. Roberts, *Spiritual Emotions* (Grand Rapids: Eerdmans, 2007), 19.
[58]Roberts, *Spiritual Emotions*, 156, 163.

in the worship service but to become a hopeful person: "The hope he experiences in the service should become a deeply etched hopefulness, a character trait that he carries into the most diverse and unconducive situations of his life, situations where the environment, unlike the church, does not at all predispose him to hope."[59] In fact, the toughness of the world is a tutor for turning the experience of hope into the character of hopefulness.

**When the feelings fade.** One of the ways the experience of hope in worship is tested is when the feelings begin to fade. Gilbert and Wilson call this affective adaptation. It is the result of people beginning to "'explain away' these events, transforming them from extraordinary events that grab attention into ordinary events which do not."[60] The Pathway focus group related several stories of this occurring. Carol from the Pathway focus group saw the devil as the one behind such normalizing:

> I think God ministers to you so much through worship that sometimes you don't even need a message. Sometimes you just need to be in the worship music, and he'll do that . . . and so you're so like on this, kind of like, worship high, I guess you could say. And then, like, in a few days, when you get away from that, sometimes . . . Satan will start putting these thoughts in your head, like, "You're never going to get through that trouble," you know, "You're never going to get over that."

Gilbert and Wilson name explanation as only the first half of a weakening affective experience; adaptation is the second half of it. Once the events are reappraised with a different narrative—"I was just making that up" or "I must have been emotional from being so tired"—then a person adapts the experience or event by attending to it less and thereby experiencing weaker affective reactions. But the Pathway focus group has shown that the reverse is also true. By attending to the experience—by recalling it, remembering it, reimagining it in prayer—the worshiper is able to reexperience the affective reactions. Carol concluded her story above by simply saying, "But then I always have to go back to what I experienced, how big I experienced God in that place of worship, and that's all it takes is an instant." Luke does not think reliving the

---

[59]Roberts, *Spiritual Emotions*, 156-57.
[60]Timothy D. Wilson and Daniel T. Gilbert, "Explaining Away: A Model of Affective Adaptation," *Perspectives on Psychological Science* 3, no. 5 (2008): 370.

experience is even necessary since it is easy to simply re-create the atmosphere of congregational worship: "You can almost, like, re-create 'em [experiences of hope in worship] by even just another time of worship. . . . It may be a song, but there's just something about when you just surrender your heart, and it's just you." Julie agrees: "What I have noticed is that if I have turned back on my music and start to worship, it [the experience and the accompanying feelings] will immediately come back." Thus, the hope experienced acquires resilience through reliving or re-creating the experience.

***Adjusting and trusting.*** In chapter three, I outlined Snyder's cognitive theory of hope as the result of both agency and pathway, willpower and way power. From my question above to each focus group about a time when God did not bring about something they had hoped for, I discovered that many of them had experienced situations where they had lost a sense of control or agency and were disappointed about things taking a turn that was different from the pathway they had imagined. "Mine never go through like I think they're gonna go through; it never lines up how I pretty much think it's going to line up," Josh from the Pathway group shrugged.

The most stunning example of this experience came from the Pathway group. In Mark's account of the custody battle he and his wife endured, they had a promise from God that the process would not require a battle, and yet it did.

> God spoke to us a promise, and we were like, "OK, we're gonna walk into court and this is going to happen." And we went to court every two months, you know, so, and the judge basically wouldn't do anything. But we were like, we got a promise from God. "God, what is going on here?" You know, like, "You told us that this is gonna happen," and then we go to court and go to court, like thousands and thousands of dollars, and nothing would happen.

By the end of his story, however, Mark had appraised the situation not as an instance where God had not come through but where God had kept his word, but in a different way.

> It happened exactly what God—God literally spoke to us and said, "You're not even going to have to fight a battle." And we were trying to fight a battle the entire time, and I think God really was working on us. We kept going back in. And then we walk into court in February of this year, and he wasn't there, and

the judge was like, "Well, what do you guys want?" You know, and . . . our lawyer wrote up a custody order, and we got exactly—I mean exactly—what God promised us.

I did not get a chance to find out what Mark meant by that—whether the custody outcome was what they had hoped to get or whether the process itself was ultimately not a battle.

What makes the hope experienced in charismatic worship have this quality of resilience? How is it adaptable to different outcomes and processes? One reason may be that the worshipers in the Pentecostal-charismatic church stress divine agency rather than human agency. Their own powerlessness is irrelevant because God is all-powerful. Moreover, they believe that God will bring his power to bear on their behalf. Bowler may consider this an instance of soft prosperity gospel, that God is working toward our ends; but this belief is fertile ground for hope. Second, the worshipers in my focus group appeared to trust divine pathways more than the ones they devise or imagine. As Josh shared, "There's always a different way around it, but the end result is usually the same." Finally, it is not just that God may have a different path for bringing about their desired end; it is that they believe that God may have other good goals in mind, such as inner transformation. Mark's conclusion to their arduous and no doubt expensive custody battle was, "We want the end result, but we don't want the transformation that God does in us along the way." Thus the hope experienced is resilient because it is rooted in divine agency, divine pathway, and perhaps even divine goodness.

But Pentecostal-charismatics are not the only Christians with a resilient hope that they experience in worship. The Presbyterians also described situations that did not go according to plan. Diana described being troubled by her difficult relationship with her estranged son. She had prayed many times about it, asking the Lord to restore it. One night, she was awakened in the early hours of the morning by what she felt had to have been the Lord. She sensed God telling her to release the relationship to him and to trust him with her son's life. "I just wanted to know that he was OK," she said. "And I felt the Lord said that he was OK." I asked her whether she ever wavered from that, whether days or weeks later she doubted the assurance that had filled her that night. She said no. In fact, that vision became a source of inspiration not only for her but also for many others. She wrote down the vision and printed out copies of it to take with her to prisons where she ministers to inmates.

This written account of her divine vision is what Gilbert might call an explanation, the third step of affective adaptation. But whereas Gilbert describes explanation as the process of transforming "extraordinary events that grab attention into ordinary events which do not," my focus group at River Valley shows that explanation can work in the opposite direction.[61] An explanation of transforming ordinary events into extraordinary events reinforces the affect or the emotional experience of the event. Diana believed that God spoke to her that night; she reinforced the event with a written narrative that was repeated in multiple settings. Each repetition allowed her to reexperience the emotions, a kind of attending to the original event, in Gilbert's terms. It is also worth noting that while for Pathway attending to the event involved music and thus the more affective aspects of the original experience, the focus group at River Valley used a cognitive approach to attending to the original experience of hope. Whether affective or cognitive, this revisiting of the experience contributed to the resiliency of the hope that came from it.

## SUMMARY AND CONCLUSION

How do evangelicals experience hope in contemporary worship services? From my participant observation, interviews, and meetings with a focus group at both Pathway Church and River Valley Presbyterian Church, I made four observations. First, by exploring the experience of hope in two very different congregational worship contexts, I discovered that worshipers are able to draw hope through a variety of means. At Pathway, emotion is crucial. Worshipers' experience of God is positively affected by the energy in the room, the music, and their own emotional response. At River Valley, the informality of the evening service, the silence, and space for contemplation allow a more cognitive engagement with God through the message and the offering of prayers. Yet both are technically emotional services that produce a kind of emotional energy, the latter of which is not dissimilar from the affective model of hope.

---

[61]Wilson and Gilbert, "Explaining Away," 370.

Second, in both churches, hope in God was adaptive to their circumstances. When things went as hoped, they gave God the credit; when they did not, they trusted him anyway. People in both churches recounted times when God came through for them, and both groups were relatively buoyant even when things did not go as they had hoped. No one in either group hinted at losing faith in God or questioning God's ways.

Third, neither group provided anything like an eschatological vision of hope. They spoke about heaven when they die or circumstances in their immediate future. Thus, the experience of hope, while memorable and significant, is not like creedal Christian hope. If it had a future orientation, it did not deal with the material creation; if it related to the materiality of life issues—sickness, relational discord, financial trouble, or the like—it had no long-range future dimension to it. Hope was either about things improving now or about getting to heaven soon. This may be described as a therapeutic hope, a hope that helped people feel better about life and its challenges.

This is not to be dismissed as insignificant, however, because of the fourth observation. This hope, even if it is not eschatological in its orientation toward the future, is still theological in its grounding in relation to God. For the Pentecostal-charismatic group, agency and pathway are turned over to God because of belief in God's supernatural power; for the Presbyterian group, agency and pathway are ascribed to God because of the belief in God's sovereignty. Yet for both groups, resilient hope is the result of being grounded in divine agency and pathway.

These observations add a much-needed nuance to the research that is focused solely on songs. As my own work in the previous chapter shows, if worship were the sum of the lyrics we sing, there would be grounds for concern. But much of the hand-wringing about contemporary worship has neglected a study of the actual experience of a worship service. Here, in two very different churches with overlapping demographic context and theological convictions, we find a hope that is experienced consistently, through variant means, and with a resilient quality, though it is not nearly a robust Christian eschatology. Our final section will deal with that discrepancy and chart a way forward for preachers, worship leaders, and songwriters.

# PART 4

# THE SPIRIT AND
# THE CHURCH

# 9

# THE SPIRIT OF HOPE

HOW CAN THE SONGS that are said to bring hope be so poor in their eschatological quality while the experience of hope in worship services in which such songs are sung be so rich? It may seem as if the research I have presented in chapter seven and chapter eight is at odds. This is precisely why a methodology that involves both quantitative and qualitative research methods helps present a nuanced analysis of a situation. If we were only to count verbs and pronouns and survey responses, one might conclude that contemporary worship is poisoning the well of Christian practice and robbing the church of the hope so vital to the Christian life. Yet, conversely, if we were only to listen to Christians self-report their experiences in church, one might assume there is nothing for pastors or worship leaders or worship songwriters to change; all is well and working properly. But by setting the analysis of songs and services side by side, by looking at both the text and the performance of the ritual of contemporary worship, we arrive at a more complex appraisal of both.

Let me summarize five key observations from my fieldwork, drawing out the most significant themes and trends. This will help show where the two components of the research intersect and interrogate each other. The remainder of the chapter after that will be an attempt to construct a threefold theological reflection on the questions and tensions raised by the research.

## SUMMARY OBSERVATIONS

First, by my study of songs that people, worship leaders and congregants alike, said brought them hope, I discovered an extraordinary focus on the present tense and the proximate space. Through there was some differentiation between the general evangelical base and the Presbyterian and

Pentecostal-charismatic responses, the overall trend was to sing about things that are occurring here and now. I suggested several possible reasons in chapter seven that this might be the case, from the relatively comfortable conditions of the songwriters and the worshipers to the postmodern deconstruction of metanarrative. Threads from each of these surfaced in the official, unofficial, and collective discourses with parishioners and leaders through interviews and focus groups. There was not a compelling reason to privilege one of these explanations over the others, nor is there reason to believe that the list of explanations is exhaustive.

Second, these songs of hope are expressed from the perspective of the individual rather than the congregation. In other words, where there are pronouns referring to the worshiper, they are overwhelmingly in the singular case. Once again, the evangelical propensity for personal faith shows in these songs. The individualization of faith and the privatization of a relationship with God are often blamed as the reason for the heavy dose of singular personal pronouns. Yet there has not been sufficient work in comparing the use of singular pronouns in the Psalms with the usage in contemporary worship songs. Even a comparison between the early Christian hymns found in the New Testament—the Benedictus, Magnificat, and Nunc Dimitis—all are written from the perspective of an individual: Zachariah, Mary, and Simeon respectively. One might make the case that the individual "I" when sung in a congregation becomes a collective "we" before God. Nevertheless, this does raise theological and ecclesiological questions, since it seems the worshipers in my focus groups can experience hope without any reference to what their community of faith is experiencing.

Third, the experience of hope seems to be strongly correlated with congregational worship. In fact, the times when worshipers did not experience any sort of uplift as a result of gathering at church were rare and noteworthy. My questions approached the subject from various angles by asking about things such as what drew people to church, what keeps them coming, and times when they have come to church feeling down but left feeling better. Everyone in my focus groups at both churches provided some basis for viewing the worship service as an experience that had an overall positive effect on them. In this sense, whether hope was experienced was of less interest to me than the kind of hope that was experienced.

Fourth, the hope possessed by many in both focus groups may be described as an adaptive or resilient hope. Despite setbacks, despite things not working out as they had hoped, the people in my focus groups seemed to maintain their hope in God. Their hope was not overly attached to a particular outcome so that when that outcome did not occur they fell into despair. They were able to keep singing, keep praying, and keep showing up at worship services because their hope was anchored in God rather than in themselves.

Finally, as mentioned in the conclusion to chapter eight, though the hope encoded in songs and experienced in services was not necessarily eschatological in quality, it was still theological in nature. It was not clearly oriented toward the future, much less a future hope of bodily resurrection and new creation. Yet, it was still oriented Godward. It was not self-obsessed, nor was it reflective of the self-help spirit of the age, as some have accused contemporary worship of being. It was unashamedly Christ oriented.

What are we to make of all this? This leads us now to a final, critical piece of theological reflection.

## THEOLOGICAL REFLECTION: HOPE AND THE HOLY SPIRIT

I want to shape this summary reflection around three questions:

1. How could the experience of hope be consistent when the encoded hope was so theologically weak?

2. Why does the experience of God's presence produce hope?

3. In what ways is the Spirit present and active in congregational worship?

Though there are certainly other questions raised by the research in chapters seven and eight, these questions are the ones that seem to me most puzzling and pressing. In each case, I propose that an aspect of pneumatology, a theology of the Holy Spirit, will be illuminating and instructive.

Let me say a few brief words here about why I am proposing engaging in a robust theology of the Spirit in this final piece of theological reflection. This choice of a theology of the Spirit here is not incidental. The Spirit is not ancillary to the church, and a theology of the Spirit is not peripheral to the church's life. Oftentimes, conversation about the Holy Spirit—particularly about the gifts of the Spirit or an experience of the Spirit—presume that this is treading beyond the basics, as though the Spirit were the curriculum of an extra-credit course. I think it is worth saying here that the witness of the Scriptures and of the Creed say that the Spirit is at the very heart of the church's life, worship, and mission. There is no confession of Christ as Lord without the Spirit (1 Cor 12:3); there is no building up of the body of Christ without the Spirit (1 Cor 12; 14; Rom 13); and there is no mission without the Spirit's power (this is at least one of the themes of the book of Acts, beginning with Acts 1:8).

It is not insignificant that the Nicene Creed speaks of the church within the article on the Holy Spirit. The creed is organized by the persons of the Trinity. In the context of confessing the Spirit as Lord, as having spoken through the prophets, and as being worshiped and glorified, the creed leads us to confess our belief in the church. The church is where the life of the Spirit takes shape.

There are those who would like to speak of the Spirit without speaking of the church. They want to emphasize the mystical and the experiential without the communal or even the institutional. The Spirit is *out there* somewhere, unpredictable and wild. These people would rather not gather consistently with a wider group of believers—certainly not people who are not already in their circle of friends. Their justification for their esoteric and eccentric practices are that they are following the Spirit. But what the Spirit is doing, indeed, what the Spirit has always done, is to form believers into a new family; the Holy Spirit forms kingdom communities, congregations. On the other side are people who love the church and all its traditions but have forgotten that the power is not in the forms but in the Spirit. It is the Holy Spirit who is the Giver of life, as the creed says. It is not an institution or a ritual that sustains a church. It is the Spirit who makes our spiritual formation happen (Gal 5:16-23); it is the Spirit who empowers our mission in the world (Acts 1:8); and it is the Spirit who animates our prayer and practices so that they glorify God and edify the church (Rom 8; 1 Cor 12; 14). There is no speaking of the church without also speaking of the Spirit. So in engaging in theological reflection on the church's contemporary worship practices, we turn now to speak of the Spirit.

***The Spirit as God's eschatological presence.*** We begin with the question of disparity between the content of the worship songs and the experience in worship services. One of the more puzzling results of my research was the apparent dissonance between the encoded hope and the experienced hope. The encoded hope of contemporary worship songs lacks narrative or much of a future orientation. Yet the experience of hope was reliable and resilient. This was surprising. How are we to reconcile the two? I propose it is by looking afresh at what it means to experience the presence of God.

There are several unlikely pieces that combine to give us a fuller picture. First, remember that the center of eschatology for Jürgen Moltmann is the presence of God. Though Moltmann was thinking of the eschatological presence of God, the final filling of the renewed creation with God's Shekinah, his focus on presence is a key to understanding the way hope is encoded and experienced in contemporary worship. In the future, it is the presence of God that will renew all things. The ultimate hope of the world is in the fully manifest presence of God. Putting it in those terms links us to the second part of the picture I am trying to paint. *Manifest presence* is a key term in how Pentecostal-charismatics think about corporate worship. Recall that the focus on the presence of God in contemporary worship is a key contribution of the Pentecostal roots of the contemporary worship movement, as demonstrated in chapter two. Moreover, a sociological analysis of worship in a global context suggests that "the Charismatic meeting, complete with 'worship time,' powerful, emotive and biblical preaching, and the manifestation of the Spirit in some dramatic form" is "the most common form of Christian worship in the contemporary world."[1]

Contemporary worship, shaped as it is by a charismatic expectation of God's presence made manifest by the Holy Spirit, produces hope by giving the worshiper a foretaste of the future, a future that is God's presence filling all in all. What I am proposing here is that a theology of *the Spirit as God's eschatological presence in* the gathered church is the intersection between the presence of God in Moltmann's eschatology and in the presence of God that is experienced in contemporary worship services. New Testament scholar and son of an Assemblies of God pastor Gordon Fee summarized his extensive study of the Spirit in Pauline theology by describing the Holy Spirit as "the *experienced, empowering* return of God's own *personal presence* in and among us, who enables us to live as a radically eschatological people in the present world while we await the consummation." Fee sets his understanding

---

[1]Martin D. Stringer, *A Sociological History of Christian Worship* (Cambridge, UK: Cambridge University Press, 2005), 233-34.

of the Spirit in Paul's theology within the framework of an already/not yet eschatology. In fact, Fee argues that for Paul, "neither his own experience of the Spirit nor his perception of that experience makes sense apart from the perspective of the fulfilled promise and salvation as already but not yet." It is the outpouring of the Spirit which signaled the beginning of the new age and the "guarantee of its final consummation."[2] Fee focuses on Paul's imagery for the Spirit as the down payment, firstfruits, and seal, each emphasizing either "the present evidence of future realities or . . . the assurance of the final glory, or both of these simultaneously."[3]

That phrase, "the present evidence of future realities," is precisely what I discovered in how evangelicals experience hope in contemporary worship services. They are experiencing present evidences of future realities. If the ultimate future reality is, as Moltmann argues, that the presence of God will fill the earth so fully and gloriously so as to make it new; if, as Gordon Fee argues, the Holy Spirit is the experience of that future in the present; and if, as Pentecostals and charismatics have believed, congregational worship—the gathered church—is the location of the presence of God through the Holy Spirit, then it follows that congregational worship would be a prime setting for the experience of hope.

But here is the key implication of this proposal: for this experience of hope to occur, the songs need not be specifically about that hope; they simply need to be songs of worship that make the worshiper aware of God's presence.[4] This may be the most powerful theological reason why songs that are more about God's activity in the present than in the future can still evoke hope. The very fact that so many songs that were said to bring people hope are about God's activity in the present may itself be an indication that *the experience of God's presence in the present moment of worship is in and of itself an experience of hope.* After all, if the ultimate reason for hope is not bodily resurrection or a renewed creation but the presence of God, then any foretaste of the future presence in the present is an experience of eschatological hope. To experience present

---

[2]Gordon D. Fee, *Paul, the Spirit, and the People of God* (Grand Rapids: Baker Academic, 1996), 53.
[3]Fee, *Paul, the Spirit, and the People of God*, 54.
[4]This is not the place for a much lengthier and more vigorous debate as to whether God is specially present when the congregation is at worship or whether believers are simply more aware of God's presence during times of corporate worship.

evidence of future realities, one need not sing about future resurrection or new creation; one need only to sing a welcome of God's presence here and now.

**The Spirit as God's powerful and empowering presence.** This leads to the second question. Phrased slightly differently in light of the response to the first question, we might ask: *Why does the experience of the Spirit as God's presence produce hope?* I propose that it is not simply because it is the experience of the future, eschatological, personal presence of God in the present, but also because it is the experience of God's *powerful and empowering* presence.

Here I want to place Snyder's theory of hope in conversation with Wright's exposition of Pauline eschatology. First recall from chapter three that Snyder understands hope from a cognitive perspective to be the result of both agency and pathway, the confluence of willpower and way power. When a person has the power and a plan, she will also, according to Snyder, have hope.

Next, remember that for Wright, Pauline eschatology is grounded in the faithfulness of God. God's faithfulness is seen in Christ's fulfilling and completing Israel's vocation; Jesus is the faithful Israelite on Israel's behalf, a different kind of Messiah. Jesus's representative faithfulness becomes a way for Israel to be saved and opens the way of salvation to the Gentiles. God's faithfulness is also seen in God's vindication of Jesus by raising him from the dead after his sacrificial death. For all who are in Christ, the basis of our future hope is God's past faithfulness. Because of God's faithfulness as revealed in the life, death, and resurrection of Jesus the Messiah, Christians have a sure and certain hope of their own future bodily resurrection and for the cosmos to be redeemed. To put it in Snyder's terms, all the agency of Christian hope is God's. God has the power, and God is faithful to act in power on behalf of his people.

I propose that in the act of worship, Christians are reenacting not just the drama of salvation, which reminds them of God's faithfulness in Christ; they are also enacting or reenacting the *transfer of agency* upward to God. In proclaiming that all the honor, glory, and power is God's, they are reminding themselves that salvation belongs to the Lord. Just as Moses at the Red Sea called on Israel to stand and see the salvation of the Lord, and just as the heavenly scenes of worship in the book of Revelation ascribe power and redemption to God (Rev 4–5; 15–16; 19), so in congregational worship, the church reminds itself that the agency—the power to save and to redeem—is the Lord's. This transfer of agency to God releases it from bearing the burden of solving its own problems.

I would go on to argue, then, that agency for the Christian becomes more important than pathway because once one transfers agency to God, one need not worry about how God will bring about change. This would place me in agreement with the critics of Snyder's theory of hope for naming *both* agency and pathway as necessary components of hope. Time and time again in my interviews and focus-group conversations, it became evident that for these worshipers, if they knew who was in charge, they did not need to know how things would resolve. If God is faithful, and if Christian hope rests on the faithfulness of God, and if worship is the transfer of agency upward to God, then hope begins to abound as Christians remember God's power in worship. Moreover, there are times in corporate worship when the Christians I interviewed saw signs of the Holy Spirit at work, reinforcing their trust in God's power.

That Christians trust God's agency more than their own has often led to concerns that Christians will become passive. This is what is sometimes meant by the phrase "too heavenly minded for earthly good." No doubt, historical examples could be cited to validate such concerns. Yet among some members in my focus group—particularly those in the Pentecostal-charismatic church—trust in God's power did not preclude or eliminate their own power. In fact, for many of them, the faithfulness and power of God resulted in a kind of returning of agency back to the believer. There was a sense—particularly for Pentecostal-charismatics—that the divine power was available to them. They could pray in Jesus' name and with Jesus' authority. They described praying with others, including church leaders and friends, about the various challenges they were facing. The members of the Presbyterian focus group demonstrated, in some sense, a greater peace or acceptance of things since God was sovereign. But the Pentecostal-charismatics had a kind of restlessness, an unwillingness to accept sickness or a bad doctor's report or other challenges as simply being the end.[5]

---

[5]These are simple observations, and it will require much more rigorous and focused research to determine whether these patterns play out along similar denominational lines in different contexts or simply appeared to be the case with the two churches in my fieldwork. I offer this here as the beginnings of what may be someone else's research question, not a fixed conclusion of mine.

The tendency of Pentecostal-charismatics to struggle against situations that they believe to be contrary to the will of God is rooted in a conviction that there is a spiritual battle and that believers are not passive bystanders in the battle. Such a worldview, of course, is not limited to Pentecostal-charismatics; it is, arguably, the way Paul saw the world and thus the way he wrote to the Ephesians. Spiritual gifts, in particular, are a manifestation of what Gordon Fee, among others, has described as God's empowering presence. In addition to the spiritual gifts texts such as 1 Corinthians 12; 14, this belief in the Spirit as God's empowering presence can also be seen in New Testament texts such as Philippians 4:13; 1 Corinthians 15:10; and Ephesians 3:16. Thus the Spirit is not simply God's powerful presence; he is also God's *empowering presence*.[6] Believing the first part of that phrase is enough to produce the act of hope. Believing both will produce the kind of hope that acts.

**The Spirit as God's incarnational or sacramental presence.** One final question remains for our theological reflection: *In what way is the Spirit present?* Or, perhaps another way to put this is, *How do we experience the presence of the Holy Spirit?* At Pathway, the Pentecostal-charismatic church, the experience of hope came through their emotions. At River Valley, the Presbyterian church, the experience of hope seemed to primarily take place through cognitive means such as the sermon and relationships with one another. I referred earlier to the phenomenon of experiencing hope through relationships as being incarnational, where God's hope was becoming flesh to them through one another.

Whenever someone claims to be experiencing something supernatural but the phenomena has alternative explanations that are what may be called natural, the supernatural is dismissed in favor of natural causes. If a person says that he experienced the joy of the Lord, for example, during a congregational worship time, but it can demonstrated that the science of group dynamics and music in certain key signatures and at certain tempos produces chemicals that are associated with feelings of well-being, then we are inclined to dismiss the idea that God was bringing a person joy and say that he was simply experiencing what the room and the music and the atmosphere was designed to produce. In fact, the research cited in the previous chapter from

---

[6]This is, indeed, the title of one of Gordon Fee's books on the Holy Spirit.

Wellman, Corcoran, and Stockly-Meyerdirk may be used in that way. What worshipers in megachurches call the Spirit, sociologist Randall Collins calls emotional energy rising through the feedback loop that Nelson has mapped in emotional worship services; but even that emotional energy may be chemically named as oxytocin (as Wellman et al. suggest).[7] In the face of such explanations, the supernatural seems to demystified by science.

A big part of the problem here is the term *supernatural*. It implies a working beyond and above nature. Such a term relies on a view of reality that is split into two levels: the natural realm, where humans are, and the supernatural level, where God is. But this, of course, is not how the Scriptures portray reality. The prophet Isaiah recorded the angels of heaven saying that the earth itself is full of God's glory (Is 6:3). The whole earth is the Lord's, the psalmist sings (Ps 24:1). Why should God not act *within* it? God is not an intruder or an imposter that he needs to "break in"; he is the Creator and Redeemer, the world's true and rightful Lord. He works from within the world he has made.

Later Christian theologians found different ways of expressing something similar when they grappled with what was going on with the bread and the cup at the Eucharist. While I argued at the beginning of this book that comparing contemporary worship singing to the Eucharist is not helpful, sacramental theology itself is a useful way of understanding how the Holy Spirit could inhabit and work with things that have material properties, such as musical and visual arts. This kind of sacramental theology is not a highly developed way of showing how things become something other than themselves, but rather a way of showing how God returns matter to its creational design.[8] What I am proposing here is that God communicates hope in the midst of congregational worship in a *sacramental* way; he uses the medium of music and gathered people and relationships to do his work of lifting our spirits.

Alternatively, it could also be said that the Holy Spirit operates in an *incarnational* way, that the Spirit works in and through our humanity. The trick with using the latter terminology it that for some the word *incarnation* is only

---

[7]James K. Wellman Jr., Katie E. Corcoran, and Kate Stockly-Meyerdirk, "'God Is Like a Drug . . .': Explaining Interaction Ritual Chains in American Mega-churches," *Eastern Sociological Society* 29, no. 3 (2014): 668.

[8]This is what Orthodox theologian Alexander Schmemann says about the blessing of the elements in his book on sacramental theology, *For the Life of the World*. Alexander Schmemann, *For the Life of the World* (Crestwood, NY: St. Vladimir's Seminary Press, 2004).

rightly used when referring to the second person of the Trinity. Yet because the mode of the Spirit's operation occurs through created realities such as the cognitive, the emotional, the physical, and the relational, it may be useful to call this a kind of incarnational presence with a lowercase *i* rather than to merely call it a sacramental presence.

Each term, while imperfect and inadequate, covers distinct though over-lapping elements. *Sacramental* helps draw our attention to the way the Spirit works within matter; *incarnational* highlights the way the Spirit works within the human. Both terms draw on the ancient reference to the Spirit as the Creator Spirit, or as the Creed confesses, the "Lord, the Giver of Life."[9]

I want to draw out at least one clear conclusion from all this, even if our terminology is imprecise. If the Spirit works through materiality and our physicality, then there is no need to place so-called therapeutic hope in oppo-sition to eschatological hope. This is true for two more reasons, beyond the theological ones I have just briefly presented. First, hope, though oriented toward the future, is experienced in the present. Second, the models of hope discussed in chapter three are only separated as concepts for the sake of academic analysis. The actual experience of hope, based on my interviews and focus-group conversations, is not either cognitive or affective, an emotion or a virtue; hope is all these at once. I am arguing here that a robust theology of the Spirit as the Creator Spirit allows us to see each dimension of hope as a mode of operation for the Holy Spirit. It is the Spirit who allows for the transfer of agency and pathway to God and empowers our own sense of agency; it is the Spirit who lifts our emotions by altering our perception; it is the Spirit who forms virtue—the fruit of the Spirit—in the Christian; and it is the Spirit whose presence is at work in us in the phenomenology of hope.

## SUMMARY

We began this chapter by identifying three key questions that emerged from setting the analysis of songs of hope beside the analysis of the experience of hope in worship services. The questions were:

1. How can the experience of hope be consistent when the encoded hope is so theologically weak?

---

[9]See the eighth-century hymn "*Veni Creator Spiritus*" and the third article of the Nicene Creed.

2. Why does the experience of God's presence produce hope?

3. In what ways is the Spirit present and active in congregational worship?

My approach has been to turn to a theology of the Spirit to deal with these questions. I have proposed here a recognition of the Holy Spirit as God's *eschatological presence*, as God's *powerful* and *empowering presence*, and as God's *sacramental* and *incarnational presence* in the church. Such a theology of the Spirit helps to give an account for an experience of hope that is consistent, resilient, and available through variant means. As Paul prayed in Romans 15:13, "May the God of hope fill you with all joy and peace in believing, so that by the power of the Holy Spirit you may abound in hope."

# 10

# CARRIERS OF HOPE

**WHERE DOES ALL THIS LEAVE US?** It is possible for someone to conclude from all that I have said that one ought to just trust the Holy Spirit to work in our context, whatever it is, and not obsess too much about the songs that we sing? It may seem as if I have led this book to the point of showing that though contemporary evangelical songs of hope are not theologically robust, the evangelical experience of hope somehow remains consistent, variant, and resilient because of the Holy Spirit's presence in the church, and thus worship leaders and songwriters, pastors and preachers, are off the hook. Reader, please know, such a conclusion is the furthest thing from my mind and heart.

To be sure, I *do* hope that the tension I have shown between the text (song lyrics) and performance (congregational singing) of the ritual of contemporary worship will slow down the critics of contemporary worship. Highlighting certain words or phrases or idioms that are cliché or imprecise may make for an oft-clicked blog, but it does not hold ground as a well-formed argument. Furthermore, the introduction into the conversation of sociological dynamics such as emotional energy, interactive ritual chains, and feedback loops in emotional religious services ought to help us begin to name the complexity of the congregational worship service. One cannot simply construct a neat paradigm of what worship ought to be, from Scripture and church history, and then proceed to list all the deficiencies of a contemporary worship service by its elements. A worship service is more than its elements; the experience in a congregation cannot be purely programmed by its parts. Our formation in worship cannot be predicted by simply having the "right" liturgy. There is a wildness to worship that cannot be tamed.

Too often critics of contemporary worship have dismissed the popularity or even the ubiquity of contemporary worship songs by calling them shallow.

My argument here is not that these songs are meaningless and empty. Yes, I have concluded that the songs we think of as songs of hope lack a robustness in their eschatological vision, but they are not self-obsessed or devoid of theology. They are full of imagery about God and his work, and in many cases they employ the very imagery used in the Scriptures. But these lyrics and images are obscured to the critic because of the heavy emotional quality of their presentation. I have tried to demonstrate that whether the emotion is high energy or low energy in layperson's terms, both the Pentecostal-charismatic and Presbyterian services produced what sociologist Randall Collins called emotional energy (see chap. eight). Emotion is not the issue. And if one wants to argue that it is, one should reflect more deeply on the theological claim underneath such an objection. Aesthetics, visual and aural, have always been a consideration—even though a problematic one—in evoking the affections toward Christ. We certainly would not want to suggest that the sacred does not mix with the earthy. As I argued in the previous chapter, the Holy Spirit inhabits the material and the physical; this is a claim that lies at the very heart of sacramental theology.

Yet, to cut off the other end of what I am *not* saying, none of this means that all forms are equal or that the content of our songs, sermons, and services does not matter. On the contrary, my hope is that this book has persuaded you to take more seriously that theological quality of all three. The dynamics of congregational experience, even when energized and animated by the work of the Holy Spirit, cannot paper over the deficiencies of our words. Words matter—much more so for people who believe in a God who speaks. Christians are people of the Book. Just as we do not sin more that grace may abound more, so we ought not use the kindness and condescension of God to breathe on our imperfect songs and sermons as a license to be sloppy.

With those two pitfalls of misunderstanding now named and preempted, we must turn to proactive action. This final chapter will provide three recommendations for church leaders that emerge from my own perspective within my ministerial context. I am limiting these to church leaders because preachers, worship leaders, and songwriters have the ability to change what Rappaport calls the encoded canonical messages, which in the church context are songs and sermons, and to affect what Rappaport calls the indexical messages, which would be the act of choosing which songs to sing in a service and with what frequency. Both the text and performance of the ritual can be created and curated by church leaders, by which I mean specifically preachers, pastors, songwriters, and worship leaders.

## SERMONS

The first recommendation is not related to the musical portion of the service but occupies the largest segment of cognitive messaging: the sermon. While the research in this monograph has only referenced sermons as a way of placing the operant theology of songs and worshipers in the context of the espoused theology of their churches, in a much smaller earlier study I did on funeral sermons I found virtually no reference to bodily resurrection and a restored creation. The sermons were about heaven as a respite from the troubles of this world. This is significant because if there were to be a place for preaching about eschatological hope, one would expect it to be at a funeral. The argument might be, as some preachers in my interviews in that study indicated, that in moments of grief, people need comfort, not theology. Yet this only affirms the pattern I have discovered here of preferring the therapeutic over the theological.

When eschatological hope surfaces in regular sermons given at weekend services, it is usually, as was the case at Pathway, the result of a special series. In other words, eschatology is only marginally relevant to the Christian life. Even then, eschatology is not about hope but about the end times. If my fieldwork at Pathway is indicative of how Pentecostal-charismatic churches, even megachurches, think and talk about the end times, then Christian hope is, to use the typology outlined in chapter six, *evacuation*. The goal of learning about the end times is simply to identify the signs and to interpret current events in light of alleged biblical prophecy. All this is meant to serve to strengthen the Christian's ability to endure until the end. Eschatology in this context ends at the return of Christ. Nothing further is said or taught about bodily resurrection or new creation. It is solely about our arrival in a different place, ostensibly heaven. Furthermore, when the direction of arrival is reversed—when the focus is not on the believer's entrance to heaven but heaven's arrival on earth—it is not usually talked about in an eschatological sense but rather as a way of understanding the miraculous.[1]

---

[1] See Bill Johnson, *When Heaven Invades Earth* (Shippensburg, PA: Destiny Image, 2003).

What looms in the background of many sermons that reference the end
or the afterlife, however, is the threat of final judgment with the accompanying hope of heaven and fear of hell. Apocalypticism, with its vivid imagery of
the end of the world and its resulting urgency for a decision to be made about
Jesus, has long nourished evangelical fervor. In fact, some have argued that
the impending end of the world, often depicted as a sinking ship, and the
corollary view of salvation through Jesus Christ, shown as a lifeboat out of
the wreckage, are at the very heart of modern American evangelicalism.[2]
Thus it is not the case the evangelical preaching is devoid of an eschatological
vision; it is that it draws from an impoverished vision and therefore offers an
anemic hope.

But it need not be this way. For preachers like the pastor at River Valley
who know and are able to articulate creedal Christian hope, they need to take
the risk to preach on it more and to allow that to form the metaframe or
invisible narrative structure behind all their gospel proclamation. One church
leader I interviewed in my funeral-sermon study said that he does not talk
about bodily resurrection because that is not related to the questions people
are asking. While this may be a pastorally wise decision in the midst of grief,
in the long run, pastors must be willing to preach on topics that are not what
people think they need.

I know from my own pastoral experience that preaching the grand narrative of salvation that includes the dramatic ending of resurrection and new
creation takes work. I was probably too clunky in the early going, trying to
say too much, or trying to correct smaller, reductionist views head-on. But
over time, I began to see the fruit. Grieving congregants would tell me that
the hope of bodily resurrection and new creation began to carry them through
their darkest hours. Somehow the idea of heaven as some far-off future had
little power to anchor their soul in sorrow. They needed to know that God
understood their grief, that God agreed that *this should not be.* The hope of
resurrection is an affirmation of the goodness of creation. It allows the grieving to say, "What I've lost—this person, this relationship, this lifetime of
love—is good and holy and beautiful." We are not meant to cast it aside in

---

[2]See Matthew Avery Sutton, *American Apocalypse: A History of Modern Evangelicalism* (Cambridge,
MA: Belknap, 2014).

favor of an ambiguous eternity. We are to "look for the resurrection of the dead and the life of the world to come." The world to come will be not simply a return to how things were in Eden but the completion and perfection of creation. Pastorally, this is the grounds for telling people that everything good and beautiful that they have known in this world will be completed and perfected in the world to come. Whatever things will be like *there*, it will be *more*, not less, than the best we have known *here*. Preacher, we can preach that good news.

When the end of the story is unclear or largely irrelevant, it is difficult to make sense of the moments leading up to it. When eschatology is reduced to end times—esoteric timelines and prophecy charts—we lose a vision of the end of the story and with it the ability to give people meaning and hope *now*. Similarly, when the end of the story is a cosmic reward or punishment, moralism becomes the most logical way of living in the present. As N. T. Wright quips,

> We have Platonized our eschatology (substituting "souls going to heaven" for the promised new creation) and have therefore moralized our anthropology (substituting a qualifying examination of moral performance for the biblical notion of the human vocation), with the result that we have paganized our soteriology, our understanding of "salvation" (substituting the idea of "God killing Jesus to satisfy his wrath" for the genuinely biblical notions we are about to explore).[3]

Perhaps there is a way to reverse engineer this in order to evaluate our implicit eschatology: if our preaching is primarily moralistic, maybe it is because our eschatology is Platonistic. Get the end of the story wrong, and the middle becomes muddled too.

## SONGS

Second, songwriters have to take more risks with content and creativity. To begin with, they must risk breaking with form. With CCLI's tracking of the use of songs and its creation of charts that rank them, there now exists an unofficial template for writing popular worship songs. Because ritual involves an adherence to form, as we saw with Rappaport, it is difficult to try to write songs that depart from the convention. In fact, my brief look at the imagery of the

---

[3]N. T. Wright, *The Day the Revolution Began* (New York: HarperCollins, 2016), 147.

songs that people said brought hope showed considerable overlap in metaphors and themes. Other research has also demonstrated the tendency to get stuck on a narrow band of themes, sometimes within particular movements.[4]

For many songwriters, theology is used as a *fence*. Anecdotally, from songwriting sessions I have been in, theology usually came up as the writing was in process. It was a sudden interjection—"Wait, is this OK to say? We're fine theologically, right?" Theology is a guardrail, a fence to keep us in bounds. That, of course, is indeed one of the functions of theology. It is certainly how many of the creeds were formulated. Nevertheless, songwriters can begin to use historical theology and well-worn prayer books and hymnals not simply as a fence but as a *doorway* into new themes. Imagine exploring a new house, a vacation rental or a friend's cabin. Every door opens up a room you have not seen before, a new place with new views. Historical theology found in creeds and confessions and prayer books can do this. Think of a project based on St. Augustine's *Confessions*, or one that sets the collects from the Book of Common Prayer to music. Rather than simply using theology as a fence to guard against heresy, theology found in these historic artefacts can help contemporary worship songwriters expand their range of thematic content.

Yet there is a complexity to this solution because even if writers are writing songs with creedal Christian hope encoded in them, there is no guarantee that these songs will find their way to churches or on recording projects. There are several independent writers or artists on small labels who are in fact mining old prayers and confessions and creeds for inspiration. Many of the songs that are emerging from these endeavors are artistically beautiful and innovative as well. Yet though they have a loyal following, it is still a comparatively small following. The Christian music industrial complex, as it were, of publishing companies, record labels, artist managers, tour promoters, radio programmers, and more, makes it difficult for new artists and songs to break in.

---

[4]Lester Ruth's collaboration with Vineyard worship leaders Andy Park and Cindy Rethmeier is one example of this on the theme of intimacy, as is Kate Bowler and Wen Reagan's work on the victory themes at Hillsong. But more work could be done on various movements such as Sovereign Grace, Passion, and more. See Andy Park, Lester Ruth, and Cindy Rethmeier, *Worshipping with the Anaheim Vineyard: The Emergence of Contemporary Worship* (Grand Rapids: Eerdmans, 2016); Kate Bowler and Wen Reagan, "Bigger, Better, Louder: The Prosperity Gospel's Impact on Contemporary Christian Worship," *Religion and American Culture: A Journal of Interpretation* 24, no. 2 (2014): 186-230.

This might be even more difficult if the song is a break from the current form. Perhaps the most successful contemporary Christian music song related to Christian hope is "I Can Only Imagine," a song about an otherworldly heaven. If this song represents the norm for the ritual, a new song with considerable thematic variance from it would have an uphill climb to the top of the charts.

The ideal candidates for breaking new ground are those with existing capital, such as the support of a large fan base, the commitment of a label, and the resources of a large church. Thankfully, there are many examples of this. One of the notable examples is Hillsong's "This I Believe." Written, as the story goes, as a response to a plea from the Anglican archbishop in Australia, the song takes the major themes of the Apostles' Creed and sets it to a soaring melody complete with an anthemic chorus. Critics who want to quibble about certain lines being out of order ought to bite their tongue; the global popularity of the song should hearten those who have wanted to see more theological substances in contemporary worship songs. Hillsong has other songs about the believer's resurrection: the final stanza in the songs "So Will I," "Beneath the Waters (I Will Rise)," and "O Praise the Name (Anastasis)" are other obvious examples. But Hillsong is not the only one. Songs from other influential artists that explicitly point to the believer's future bodily resurrection are becoming more common. To give just a few examples, there is "I Will Rise" from Chris Tomlin, "Our Living Hope" from Phil Wickham and Brian Johnson, and "Ain't No Grave" from Molly Skaggs (Bethel). Close to home and holding a special place in my heart are songs from Integrity Music songwriter and artist Jon Egan. Songs from his solo project include themes of inaugurated eschatology and creedal hope, as seen in lines such as "You broke the curse of our sin, the life of heaven begins," and "this [the resurrection of Jesus] changes everything." My favorite may be the chorus of a song called, "Be Strong" where worshipers remind their souls, "Be strong, be not afraid, for the Lord is soon on His way, He will breakthrough, He'll tear through the night."

Even if a song is not climbing the charts or spreading around the world, it can shape the vision of a local congregation. This should be the aim of every local church worship leader—to write songs for her own congregation that capture not only what the Spirit is saying and doing in a particular season but what the church has been singing and praying throughout the centuries. Work on the craft of songwriting. We cannot settle for catchy melodies with facile words, nor rich lyrics with clunky melodies. Write well because it glorifies God and edifies the church.

## SERVICE SHAPE

The final proposal here is more modest, returning the focus to the local church. Pastors and worship leaders can design an intentional gospel-storied shape to services. This places less stress on the songs and the sermon, the two weightiest portions of an evangelical worship service. If the service contained other elements that provided a narrative shape, it could mitigate the lack of narrative within individual songs. After all, no matter how hard a worship leader or songwriter may work, it is not likely that every song in a service will represent the past, present, and future of salvation history. But if there are elements within a service, such as references to the liturgical season, confessions of a creed, or prayers from a historic prayer book, an overarching narrative shape may be imparted.

This was, in fact, the intent of the Saturday evening Word and Table service at River Valley. Both the pastor and the worship pastor were able to articulate a clear vision for this, with formation as the goal of their design. Based on the responses from my focus group there, however, one may be tempted to conclude that such intentional designing of the worship service has no effect on the operant theology of congregants. However, I would suggest that such conclusions are not possible from the limited scale and scope of my study. It remains plausible that, with better preaching, richer songs, and a gospel-storied shape to the service, over the long haul the operant theology of hope within individual worshipers could come to resemble creedal Christian hope.

Speaking from my context as a pastor, changes to the shape of the service were ones we made in our congregation. At one of our evening services, we began to introduce weekly Communion. The Eucharist carries eschatological meaning. It is "the meal at which the messiah feeds his people as a sign of the feasting in the coming kingdom."[5] As a form of Christ's coming to his church,

---

[5]Geoffrey Wainwright, *Eucharist and Eschatology* (Akron, OH: OSL Publications, 2002), 117.

the Eucharist is, symbolically, a projection of Christ's future coming.[6] We often encourage our church as we receive Communion that at the Lord's Table we *remember* Christ's death, we *encounter* the presence of the risen Christ through the Holy Spirit, and we *anticipate* the return of Christ and the great feast to come. As we began receiving weekly Communion over a decade ago—in our nondenominational, evangelical, charismatic church—it became a keystone habit that reshaped existing practices, eliminated some practices, and led to the introduction of other practices. We then began to pray a prayer of confession—first out of Psalm 51, then out of the Book of Common Prayer. We started saying the Nicene Creed together. Then we began marking the seasons of the church calendar or Christian year, slowly introducing the collect prayers for the weeks of Advent and Lent. After a few years of doing this in our evening service, New Life Church began doing weekly Communion at the main morning services. Then we made the Nicene Creed our church's statement of faith. Now, in all our English-language congregations, the Lord's Table is the centerpiece and high point of every worship service. When we preach through various books of the Bible, we aim to keep the overarching grand narrative before the people. Our worship leaders and songwriters know how to ground people in a hope that is ultimate and unshakeable.

Furthermore, we began to learn from the logic of the liturgy even if we were not using the language of the liturgy. Sometimes we get fixated on praying specific prayers from the prayer book or observing the exact ordo. But we forget that when the English Reformer Thomas Cranmer was writing and curating the Book of Common Prayer, one of his goals was participation of the people. Today, prayers in Shakespearean English may only serve to reinforce class divides or to appeal to our aspirations of high-culture aesthetics, or they may simply carry too much baggage from a painful religious past. The goal is not to copy and paste the language; it is to learn from the logic. Historic practices of Christian worship had a certain shape to their services, often described as the fourfold shape of gathering, Word, Table, and sending. There is a way to trace this same shape in our services so as to invite people into the grand narrative. In a postmodern world, where everything is reduced to the moment and being present in it, the church can offer the wonder of being

---

[6]Wainwright, *Eucharist and Eschatology*, 115.

part of a drama already in progress. More than that, it is a drama with a good beginning—a good God who made a good world on purpose and with pleasure—and a glorious ending: bodily resurrection and new creation, the restoration and renewal of all things. Corporate worship can trace the contours of that story simply by being attentive to it.

Pay attention to sermons, songs, and service shape. We can look closely at our practices and think deeply about the theology that is embedded in them. We can reflect on the implications and consequences, intended or otherwise. In a way, this book ends in the way it began: by inviting all of us to become practical theologians. None of this guarantees a well-formed faith or even a robust vision of hope. But it can give the Holy Spirit more colors to paint with as he works in our midst to reveal Christ and the hope we have in him.

# CONCLUSION

THIS IS FAR FROM THE LAST WORD on the subject of hope in worship or the final note of the song. For researchers, there is much more work to be done in the study of congregational worship, and particularly in the field of practical theology. Because congregational worship is a weekly occurrence for most Christians, and because contemporary worship music is the style that is sweeping the globe with no signs of slowing, much more focused theological reflection is needed. Even within the study of the particular angle I used—hope in contemporary worship—there are many avenues for further exploration. Further work is needed to demonstrate whether the themes and trends I discovered appear again in other contexts. Do other congregations demonstrate a resilient hope? Do other worship services provide the impetus for the experience of hope? Additionally, broader work remains regarding contemporary worship songs. I have analyzed only a small selection of songs, songs that people said brought them hope. But to gain a clearer picture of whether these songs represent wider trends within the greater corpus of contemporary worship songs, a larger database of songs would need to be studied, at the very least for their verb and pronoun content in way that is similar to my analysis. Nevertheless, my hope is that this research will contribute to the literature by not adding simply a descriptive or prescriptive perspective. Rather, by engaging in theological ethnography and by narrowing the analysis to the theology of hope as it is both encoded in contemporary worship songs and experienced in contemporary worship services in two particular congregations, this can be an encouragement for further study in the field.

For pastors, worship leaders, songwriters, and ministry leaders in various contexts, I know that your faithful work, often done in hidden places and in unspectacular ways, is how the kingdom arrives on earth as it is in heaven. Every meeting over coffee, every moment in a hospital room, every worship service, and every living room gathering become holy moments and sacred spaces because of your attentiveness to the Holy Spirit. My prayer is that this book has further inspired you to bear witness in clear, compelling, and consistent ways to the glorious hope we have in Christ. Give the people of God a song of hope. To put a twist on the line attributed to St. Francis of Assisi about evangelism, I say: *Lead worship always; use music if necessary.*

Above all, for you, dear reader, wherever you find yourself today, I pray that the hope of resurrection and the life of the world to come will be your anchor in the storm. May you will lift up your head and fix your eyes on Jesus Christ the crucified, risen, reigning, and returning king. May the Holy Spirit strengthen your heart and inspire you with a song. Our hope is steadfast because our God is faithful. We know this because Jesus Christ is risen from the dead.

# BIBLIOGRAPHY

Abernethy, Alexis D., and Charlotte vanOyen Witvliet. "A Study of Transformation in Worship: Psychological, Cultural, and Psychophysiological Perspectives." In *Worship That Changes Lives: Multidisciplinary and Congregational Perspectives on Spiritual Transformation*, edited by Alexis D. Abernethy, 197-216. Grand Rapids: Baker Academic, 2008.

Adnams, Gordon. "'Really Worshipping' Not 'Just Singing.'" In *Christian Congregational Music: Performance, Identity and Experience*, edited by Monique Ingalls, Carolyn Landau, and Tom Wagner, 185-200. Surrey, UK: Ashgate, 2013.

Aldrige, Alan. *Religion in the Contemporary World*. Cambridge, UK: Polity, 2007.

Astley, Jeff. *Ordinary Theology: Looking, Listening, and Learning in Theology*. Surrey, UK: Ashgate, 2003.

Ballard, Paul, and John Pritchard. *Practical Theology in Action: Christian Thinking in the Service of Church and Society*. 2nd ed. London: SPCK, 1996.

Bauckham, Richard, ed. *God Will Be All In All: The Eschatology of Jürgen Moltmann*. Minneapolis: Augsburg Fortress, 2001.

———. *The Theology of Jürgen Moltmann*. Edinburgh: T&T Clark, 1995.

Bebbington, David W. *Evangelicalism in Modern Britain: A History from the 1730s to the 1980s*. Electronic ed. Abingdon, UK: Taylor & Francis Group, 1989.

Begbie, Jeremy. "Faithful Feelings: Music and Emotion in Worship." In *Resonant Witness: Conversations Between Music and Theology*, edited by Jeremy S. Begbie and Steven R. Guthrie, 323-54. Grand Rapids: Eerdmans, 2011.

Bowler, Kate. *Blessed: A History of the American Prosperity Gospel*. New York: Oxford University Press, 2013.

Bowler, Kate, and Wen Reagan. "Bigger, Better, Louder: The Prosperity Gospel's Impact on Contemporary Christian Worship." *Religion and American Culture: A Journal of Interpretation* 24, no. 2 (2014): 186-230.

Brower, Kent E. "'Let the Reader Understand': Temple and Eschatology in Mark." In *The Reader Must Understand: Eschatology in Bible and Theology*, edited by Kent E. Brower and Mark W. Elliott, 119-44. Downers Grove, IL: InterVarsity Press, 1997.

Buber, Martin. *I And Thou: A New Translation with a Prologue "I and You" and Notes*. Translated by Walter Kaufmann. New York: Simon & Schuster, 1996.

Bynum, Carolyn Walker. *The Resurrection of the Body in Western Christianity, 200–1336*. New York: Columbia University Press, 1995.

Cameron, Helen, Deborah Bhatti, Catherin Duce, James Sweeney, and Clare Watkins. *Talking About God in Practice: Theological Action Research and Practical Theology*. London: SCM Press, 2010.

Collins, Randall. *Interaction Ritual Chains*. Princeton, NJ: Princeton University Press, 2004.

Cone, James. *The Spirituals and the Blues*. 2nd ed. Maryknoll, NY: Orbis Books, 1992.

Daley, Brian E. *The Hope of the Early Church: A Handbook of Patristic Eschatology*. 2nd ed. Grand Rapids: Baker Academic, 2010.

Davies, Charlotte Aull. *Reflexive Ethnography: A Guide to Researching Selves and Others*. 2nd ed. New York: Routledge, 2008.

Dawn, Marva. *Reaching Out Without Dumbing Down: A Theology of Worship for This Urgent Time*. Grand Rapids: Eerdmans, 1995.

"Ecstasy and Exodus: Charismatic Christianity Thrives Among People on the Move." *The Economist*, January 23, 2016. www.economist.com/news/international/21688880-charismatic-christianity -thrives-among-people-move-ecstasy-and-exodus.

Ekman, Paul. *Emotions Revealed*. 2nd ed. New York: St. Martin's, 2003.

Fee, Gordon D. *Paul, the Spirit, and the People of God*. Grand Rapids: Baker Academic, 1996.

Gilbert, Daniel T., and Timothy D. Wilson. "Prospection: Experiencing the Future." *Science* 317, no. 5843 (2007): 1351-54.

Graham, Elaine. "Practical Theology as Transforming Practice." In *The Blackwell Reader in Pastoral and Practical Theology*, edited by James Woodward and Stephen Pattison, 104-17. Oxford: Blackwell, 2000.

Groeschel, Craig. *How Churches and Leaders Can Get It and Keep It*. Grand Rapids: Zondervan, 2008.

Guest, Mathew. *Evangelical Identity and Contemporary Culture: A Congregational Study in Innovation*. Milton Keynes, UK: Paternoster, 2007.

Hall, Christopher A. *Learning Theology with the Church Fathers*. Downers Grove, IL: InterVarsity Press, 2002.

Hochschild, Arlie Russell. *The Managed Heart: Commercialization of Human Feeling*. 2nd ed. Berkeley: University of California Press, 2003.

Hood, Ralph. *Handbook of Religious Experience*. Birmingham, AL: Religious Education Press, 1995.

Hybels, Lynne and Bill Hybels. *Rediscovering Church*. Grand Rapids: Zondervan, 1995.

Ingalls, Monique. *The Spirit of Praise: Music and Worship in Global Pentecostal-Charismatic Christianity*. Kindle ed. University Park: Pennsylvania State University Press, 2015.

Johnson, Bill. *When Heaven Invades Earth*. Shippensburg, PA: Destiny Image, 2003.

Johnson, Luke Timothy. *The Creed: What Christians Believe and Why It Matters*. New York: Image, 2003.

Keller, Timothy. *Prayer: Experiencing Awe and Intimacy with God*. New York: Dutton, 2014.

Lartey, Emmanuel. "Practical Theology as a Theological Form." In *The Blackwell Reader in Pastoral and Practical Theology*, edited by James Woodward and Stephen Pattison, 128-34. Oxford: Blackwell, 2000.

Lim, Swee Hong, and Lester Ruth. *Lovin' On Jesus: A Concise History of Contemporary Worship*. Nashville: Abingdon, 2017.

Manen, Max van. *Phenomenology of Practice: Meaning-Giving Methods in Phenomenological Research and Writing*. Edited by Janice Morse. Kindle ed. Walnut Creek, CA: Left Coast, 2014.

McGavran, Donald A. *Understanding Church Growth*. 3rd ed. Edited by C. Peter Wagner. Grand Rapids: Eerdmans, 1990.

McFayden, Alistair. *The Call to Personhood: A Christian Theory of the Individual in Social Relationships*. Cambridge, UK: Cambridge University Press, 1990.

McGowan, Andrew B. *Ancient Christian Worship*. Grand Rapids: Baker Academic, 2014.

Middleton, J. Richard. *A New Heaven and a New Earth: Reclaiming Biblical Eschatology*. Grand Rapids: Baker Academic, 2014.

Miller, Donald E., and Tetsunao Yamamori. *Global Pentecostalism: The New Face of Christian Social Engagement*. Berkeley: University of California Press, 2007.

Moltmann, Jürgen. *The Coming of God*. Translated by Margaret Kohl. Minneapolis: Augsburg Fortress, 1996.

———. *Theology of Hope*. Translated by James W. Leitch. Minneapolis: Augsburg Fortress, 1993.

Morewedge, Carey K., Daniel T. Gilbert, and Timothy D. Wilson. "The Least Likely of Times: How Remembering the Past Biases Forecasts of the Future." *Psychological Science* 16, no. 8 (2005): 626-30.

Morgenthaler, Sally. *Worship Evangelism*. Grand Rapids: Zondervan, 1995.

National Association of Evangelicals. "What Is an Evangelical?" www.nae.net/what-is-an-evangelical/. Accessed July 22, 2017.

Nelson, Timothy J. "Sacrifice of Praise: Emotion and Collective Participation in an African-American Worship Service." *Sociology of Religion* 57, no. 4 (1996): 379-96.

Osmer, Richard R. *Practical Theology: An Introduction*. Grand Rapids: Eerdmans, 2008.

Packiam, Glenn. "On 'Practical Theology' and My Experience at Durham." *Mystery of Faith* (blog), March 24, 2018. https://mysteryoffaithblog.com/2018/03/24/why-practical-theology-matters-and-a-bit-about-my-experience-at-durham/.

Park, Andy, Lester Ruth, and Cindy Rethmeier. *Worshipping with the Anaheim Vineyard: The Emergence of Contemporary Worship*. Grand Rapids: Eerdmans, 2016.

Phillips, Elizabeth. "Charting the 'Ethnographic Turn': Theologians and the Study of Christian Congregations." In *Perspectives on Ecclesiology and Ethnography*, edited by Pete Ward, 95-106. Grand Rapids: Eerdmans, 2012.

Rappaport, Roy A. "The Obvious Aspects of Ritual." In *Ecology, Meaning, and Religion*, 173-221. Berkeley, CA: North Atlantic Books, 1979.

——. *Ritual and Religion in the Making of Humanity*. Cambridge, UK: Cambridge University Press, 1999.

Rathe, Alan. *Evangelicals, Worship, and Participation: Taking a Twenty-First Century Reading*. Burlington, VT: Ashgate, 2014.

Roberts, Robert C. *Spiritual Emotions: A Psychology of Christian Virtues*. Grand Rapids: Eerdmans, 2007.

Ross, Melanie C. *Evangelical Versus Liturgical? Defying a Dichotomy*. Grand Rapids: Eerdmans, 2014.

Ruth, Lester. "Some Similarities and Differences Between Historic Evangelical Hymns and Contemporary Worship Songs." *Artistic Theologian* 3 (2015): 69-86.

Schmemann, Alexander. *For the Life of the World*. Crestwood, NY : St. Vladimir's Seminary Press, 2004.

Smith, Gary Scott. *Heaven in the American Imagination*. New York: Oxford University Press, 2011.

Smith, James K. A. *Desiring the Kingdom: Worship, Worldview, and Cultural Formation*. Grand Rapids: Baker Academic, 2009.

——. "Determined Hope: A Phenomenology of Christian Expectation." In *The Future of Hope*, edited by Miroslav Volf and William Katerberg, 200-227. Grand Rapids: Eerdmans, 2004.

——. *How (Not) to Be Secular*. Grand Rapids: Eerdmans, 2014).

——. *You Are What You Love: The Spiritual Power of Habit*. Grand Rapids: Brazos, 2016.

Snyder, C. R. "Adult Hope Scale." 2017. https://ppc.sas.upenn.edu/resources/questionnaires-researchers/adult-hope-scale.

——. "Hope Theory: Rainbows in the Mind." *Psychological Inquiry* 13, no. 4 (2001): 249-75.

Stark, Rodney. *What Americans Really Believe*. Waco, TX: Baylor University Press, 2008.

Stobbart, Andrew J. "Towards a Model of Christian Hope: Developing Snyder's Hope Theory for Christian Ministry." *Theology and Ministry* 1, no. 7 (2012): 1-17.

Strait, Brad. "What Is a Christian Mystic?" 2015. https://bradstrait.com/what-is-a-christian-mystic/.

Stringer, Martin D. *On the Perception of Worship*. Birmingham, UK: University of Birmingham Press, 1999.

——. *A Sociological History of Christian Worship*. Cambridge, UK: Cambridge University Press, 2005.

Sutton, Matthew Avery. *American Apocalypse: A History of Modern Evangelicalism*. Cambridge, MA: Belknap, 2014.

Tarnas, Richard. *The Passion of the Western Mind: Understanding the Ideas That Have Shaped Our World View*. New York: Ballantine Books, 1993.

Taylor, Charles. *A Secular Age*. Cambridge, MA: Belknap, 2007.

Vanhoozer, Kevin J., and Owen Strachan. *The Pastor as Public Theologian*. Grand Rapids: Baker Academic, 2015.

Wainwright, Geoffrey. *Eucharist and Eschatology*. Akron, OH: OSL Publications, 2002.

Ward, Pete. *Liquid Ecclesiology: The Gospel and the Church*. Leiden, Netherlands: Brill, 2017.

——. *Participation and Mediation: A Practical Theology for the Liquid Church*. London: SCM Press, 2008.

——. *Perspectives in Ecclesiology and Ethnography*. Grand Rapids: Eerdmans, 2012.

——. *Selling Worship: How What We Sing Has Changed the Church*. Exeter, UK: Paternoster, 2005.

Watkins, Clare, with Deborah Bhatti, Helen Cameron, Catherine Duce, and James Sweeney. "Practical Ecclesiology: What Counts as Theology in Studying the Church?" In *Perspectives on Ecclesiology and Ethnography*, edited by Pete Ward, 167-81. Grand Rapids: Eerdmans, 2012.

Wellman, James K., Jr., Katie E. Corcoran, and Kate Stockly-Meyerdirk. "'God Is Like a Drug . . .': Explaining Interaction Ritual Chains in American Megachurches." *Eastern Sociological Society* 29, no. 3 (2014): 650-72.

Westerholm, Matthew. "The Hour Is Coming and Is Now Here: The Doctrine of Inaugurated Eschatology in Contemporary Evangelical Worship Music." PhD diss., Southern Baptist Theological Seminary, 2016.

Wilkinson, David. *Christian Eschatology and the Physical Universe*. London: T&T Clark, 2010.

Wilson, Timothy D., and Daniel T. Gilbert. "Explaining Away: A Model of Affective Adaptation." *Perspectives on Psychological Science* 3, no. 5 (2008): 370-86.

Wollschleger, Jason. "Interaction Ritual Chains and Religious Participation." *Sociological Forum* 27, no. 4 (2012): 896-912.

Wright, N. T. *The Day the Revolution Began*. New York: HarperCollins, 2016.

———. *History and Eschatology: Jesus and the Promise of Natural Theology*. Waco, TX: Baylor University Press, 2019.

———. *Paul and the Faithfulness of God*. Vol. 2. Minneapolis: Augsburg Fortress, 2013.

———. *The Resurrection of the Son of God*. Minneapolis: Fortress, 2003.

———. "Revelation and Christian Hope: Political Implications of the Revelation to John." Episode 15 of *The N. T. Wright Podcast*. September 4, 2013. https://itunes.apple.com/us/podcast/revelation -christian-hope/id447840163.

———. *Surprised by Hope: Rethinking Heaven, the Resurrection, and the Mission of the Church*. New York: HarperCollins, 2008.

# SCRIPTURE INDEX

 DYNAMICS OF CHRISTIAN WORSHIP

Worship of the triune God stands at the heart of the Christian life, so understanding the many dynamics of Christian worship—including prayer, reading the Bible, preaching, baptism, the Lord's Supper, music, visual art, architecture, and more—is both a perennial and crucial issue for the church. With that in mind, the Dynamics of Christian Worship (DCW) series seeks to enable Christians to grow in their understanding of the many aspects of Christian worship. By harvesting the fruits of biblical, theological, historical, practical, and liturgical scholarship and by drawing from a wide range of worshiping contexts and denominational backgrounds, the DCW series seeks to deepen both the theology and practice of Christian worship for the life of the church.

## TITLES INCLUDE

+ John Rempel, *Recapturing an Enchanted World: Ritual and Sacrament in the Free Church Tradition*

+ Glenn Packiam, *Worship and the World to Come: Exploring Christian Hope in Contemporary Worship*

+ Esther Crookshank, *Christ Our Song: Psalms, Hymns, and Spiritual Songs in the History of Worship from the Early Church to Watts* (forthcoming)

## ADVISORY BOARD

Constance Cherry, Indiana Wesleyan University
Carlos Colón, Baylor University
James Hart, Robert E. Webber Institute for Worship Studies
Todd Johnson, Fuller Theological Seminary
Trygve Johnson, Hope College
Eric Mathis, Samford University
Glenn Packiam, New Life Downtown Church, Colorado Springs, CO
Emmett G. Price III, Gordon-Conwell Theological Seminary
Melanie Ross, Yale Institute of Sacred Music
Lester Ruth, Duke Divinity School
John Witvliet, Calvin Institute of Christian Worship